A Compendium
of Lacanian Terms

A Compendium of Lacanian Terms

Edited by

Huguette Glowinski, Zita M. Marks
and Sara Murphy

FREE ASSOCIATION BOOKS / LONDON / NEW YORK

First published 2001 in Great Britain by
Free Association Books
57 Warren Street, London W1T 5NR

www.fa-b.com

ISBN 1 85343 539 2 hbk; 1 85343 538 4 pbk

A CIP catalogue record for this book is available from the British Library.

10	09	08	07	06	05	04	03	02	01
10	9	8	7	6	5	4	3	2	1

Designed, typeset and produced for Free Association Books by
Chase Publishing Services, Fortescue, Sidmouth EX10 9QG
Printed in the European Union by TJ International, Padstow, England

Contents

Additional Terms

Preface

The work on the development of this compendium began at the end of a four-year programme studying the texts of Freud and Lacan with the Australian Centre for Psychoanalysis in Melbourne (formerly known as the Centre for Psychoanalytic Research). At the time we believed that a reference work of Lacanian ideas similar to that of Laplanche and Pontalis' (1973) *The Language of Psychoanalysis*, or Hinshelwood's (1991) *Dictionary of Kleinian Thought*, would be extremely useful, particularly for the English-speaking student of Lacan.

We hoped that such a volume would provide students with an entry into Lacanian discourse and, through the presentation of the chronological development of his ideas, provide a guide or broader framework in which to better understand his concepts.

We also believed that clinicians, theoreticians and scholars applying psychoanalytic insights to fields as diverse as film, art criticism and feminist theory, would appreciate a reference work illuminating his difficult, at times inaccessible, almost always obscure, yet perennially seductive work.

Several years have passed, and despite the foreboding of some, the support of many and the acknowledgement that one cannot capture the signifier and anchor it for perpetuity, we present our Lacanian compendium. Of course, now following the passage of time – the time to see, to reflect, and to act – many other very accessible works have been published that have ensured a steady dissemination of Lacanian discourse within the academy and the clinic.

This is a good and necessary development, with our compendium seen as yet another contribution to keep the signifiers shifting, adding to the richness of interpretation in the field, and maintaining the necessary openness of discourse without detracting from its complexity. The breadth, diversity and viability of Lacan's work are evident in its differential application throughout the world, ranging from literary criticism and the study of popular culture to academia and clinical practice: a new reference work can be seen as reflecting the movement of the Lacanian field.

In the light of our attempt to maintain a plurality of meaning, the compendium has gathered entries from the local (Australian) academic and clinical community, and from a number of European scholars, drawing primarily, though not exclusively, from the works of Lacan that have been translated into English.

We requested from our contributors work that reflected their own academic and clinical interests, and particularly that represented important, at times pivotal, concepts in Lacanian discourse, although it needs to be said that much of Lacan remains unpublished, indeed untranslated.

The compendium therefore contains only a selection of concepts, though these are believed to reflect the unique nature of Lacanian thinking. It also reflects a diversity of style, with French-speaking contributors having access to material as yet unavailable to their English-language colleagues. The entries too, are variable in length, which should not be interpreted as a corollary to the significance of the concept. Finally they elucidate the relationship between Lacan's ideas and other contemporary strands of thought.

Each entry therefore outlines the conceptualization of the idea, locating it within Lacanian discourse, its evolution in the development of his ideas and its interrelatedness with other concepts. To ensure a wider understanding of the aetiology, evolution and use of the concept, it has been cross-referenced to other concepts in the collection, and an additional list of terms useful for a more extended enquiry has been generated. The user of the compendium will also be provided with a reference list at the end of each entry.

The format of this compendium follows the traditional structure of a dictionary in that the entries are presented in alphabetical order. Some terms that are incorporated within larger items have been listed separately, with a reference to the article in which they occur. Where terms can be appropriately translated into English, this has been done; however, where a meaningful and suitable translation has not been possible, the French spelling has been used.

Throughout the enterprise, we have been aware that any attempt to understand and write about Lacan's work should avoid a dogmatizing of the text and a desire to achieve certitude of interpretation. Lacan's work is a teaching, and teaching should make a demand of the student who weaves the word into experience and experience into the word. We hope this compendium may help guide a closer reading of his work.

Acknowledgements

We would like to express our sincere thanks for the editorial encouragement, advice and patience we have received from Free Association Books. From our initial discussions to the final moments of the preparation of the compendium we have had their valuable professional guidance and very warm support. We have appreciated their management and collegiate style, particularly as represented most recently by David Stonestreet.

One of our fellow graduates from the Centre, Paul Grainger-Smith, provided input and resources at many of our early meetings. We thank James Anderson for his editorial input and Jane S. Marks for her enthusiastic and dedicated commitment to editorial refinement. We are also indebted to Dominique Hecq and Oliver Feltham for their work in translating some of the articles from the French and to Deanna Blakeley for her help with typing and layout.

Many colleagues, particularly Leonardo Rodriguez and Russell Grigg, have contributed to this work, and we are very grateful to them. We also appreciate the input and guidance of John McKay and the support of Louis Glowinski. We are deeply indebted to our contributors for their patience in the publication of this volume and for their fine work that has indeed attained an impressive level of excellence. We also thank the Australian Catholic University for an initial grant, and Deakin University for administrative support. Finally we acknowledge the students of Lacan who may find this volume useful.

Huguette Glowinski
Zita M. Marks
Sara Murphy
Melbourne, 2001

Contributors

Sidi Askofare is a psychoanalyst, doctor of psychology, coordinator of courses in clinical psychology and psychopathology at the University of Toulouse le Mirail, member of the Institute of Clinical Research of the same university, and a member of the International Forums of the Lacanian Field.

Nathalie Charraud trained in mathematics and psychoanalysis, is a practising psychoanalyst in Rennes and Paris, and lectures in psychoanalysis (Freudian and Lacanian) in the department of psychology at the University of Rennes. Her work on Georg Cantor, the father of the theory of sets, has enabled her to link the discourse of psychoanalytic theory to that of mathematics. The meeting of these two disciplines continues. The volume on the colloquia presented at Cerisy in September 1999 is currently being developed. Her work is a continual engagement with the mathème. Her principal publications are *Infini et Inconscient, essai sur Georg Cantor,* Anthropos-Economica, 1994 and *Lacan and Mathematics,* Anthropos-Economica, 1997. Her most recent articles are 'Cantor with Lacan', *La Cause freudienne* nos 39 and 40, and 'La Chose mathematique', *La Cause freudienne* no. 44.

Huguette Glowinski is a clinical psychologist who lectures at Deakin University, Melbourne, where she coordinates a postgraduate Diploma of Psychology, lectures in the Clinical Masters and Doctoral programmes, and is involved in cross-faculty teaching in the Master of Psychoanalytic studies. She is a member of the Australian Centre for Psychoanalysis. Her interests include the psychoanalytic study of organized religion and mental health.

Russell Grigg lectures in philosophy and psychoanalytic studies at Deakin University in Melbourne. He is a member of the *École de la Cause freudienne* and the Lacan Circle of Melbourne. He has translated Lacan's *Seminar III: The Psychoses* and *Seminar XVII: The Other Side of Psychoanalysis*. He is currently writing on Lacan's later seminars and also editing a collection of the early papers on female sexuality.

Dominique Hecq is a research fellow in psychoanalytic studies at Deakin University. She has a PhD in literature and a background in French and German, with an MA in translation. She has published in the field of literary studies and has had her own books of stories and poetry published. *The Book of Elise,* a novel, has just been released. Her short play, *One Eye Too Many,* has been translated into several languages.

Robert King is Senior Lecturer in the Department of Psychiatry at the University of Queensland, Australia, where he coordinates post-graduate coursework programmes, including a Masters programme in psychotherapy. He trained in psychoanalysis with the Melbourne Centre for Psychoanalytic Research (subsequently the Australian Centre for Psychoanalysis). His doctoral study was an investigation of the psychoanalytic understanding of psychosis and its relevance to clinical practice. His research interests extend from psychoanalysis to public mental health and he has published and presented extensively.

Michel Lapeyre is a psychoanalyst, doctor of Letters and Behavioural Sciences, coordinator of courses in clinical psychology and psychopathology at the University of Toulouse le Mirail, member of the Institute of Clinical Research at the same university, and a member of the International Forums of the Lacanian Field.

Carmela Levy-Stokes is a psychoanalyst in private practice. She worked for many years in psychiatric and psychotherapeutic clinics with adults and children. She is a member of the Australian Centre for Psychoanalysis and teaches with the Institute for Training of the Australian Centre for Psychoanalysis.

Katrien Libbrecht is Professor of Psychology at the Free University of Brussels and a consulting psychoanalytic psychotherapist at the Psychiatrische Centra Sleidinge, Belgium. She is a member of the Gezelschap voor Psyhcoanalyse en Psychotherapie, a studygroup of the European School for Psychoanalysis. She is the author of *Hysterical Psychosis: A Historical Survey* (1995).

Zita Marks is a psychologist who lectures in the Department of Psychology at the Australian Catholic University, where she is involved in teaching both undergraduate and postgraduate courses.

She completed a training programme with the Australian Centre for Psychoanalysis in Melbourne and is a member of the Centre. Her interests include the application of psychoanalytic theory to cross-cultural issues, the nature of religious experience, and the pre-Oedipal child and its relationship to the mother. She is a member of the Lacan Circle of Melbourne.

Sara Murphy is a clinical psychologist whose clinical practice as a psychoanalyst includes consultancy to the Children's Court in Victoria. She also teaches Clinical Practice at Victoria University. Her interests include the application of psychoanalytic concepts to cinema and popular culture as well as clinical work.

Leonardo Rodriguez is a psychoanalyst, a member of the Australian Centre for Psychoanalysis and the Melbourne Forum of the Lacanian Field, and a Senior Lecturer at the Department of Psychological Medicine, Monash University. He coordinates the Institute for Training of the Australian Centre for Psychoanalysis and is the current editor of *Analysis*. He is the author of numerous articles on psychoanalysis that have been published in English, French, Spanish and Portuguese, and of *Psychoanalysis with Children* (London: Free Association Books, 1999).

Silvia Rodriguez is a psychoanalyst, a founding member of the Australian Centre for Psychoanalysis and a member of the Forums of the Lacanian Field. She teaches psychoanalysis at the Institute for Training, Australian Centre for Psychoanalysis and at the Department of Psychological Medicine, Monash University. She has published articles on psychoanalytic theory and practice in Australia and overseas.

Marie-Jean Sauret is a psychoanalyst, doctor of Letters and Behavioural Sciences, doctor of psychology, professor of clinical psychology and psychopathology, director of the Institute of Clinical Research, and a member of the International Forums of the Lacanian Field.

Susana Tillet initially trained in Argentina and is an analyst with the Lacan Circle of Melbourne. Currently she practises and teaches in Melbourne and is the author of numerous publications on psychoanalysis. She is a member of the Lacan Circle of Melbourne.

Lacan Dossier

This brief overview of Jacques Lacan highlights the significant features of his teaching, and his major contributions to psychoanalysis that spanned almost fifty years.

Lacan was born into a middle-class family in 1901. The first of three children, he attended a prestigious Jesuit school and was an outstanding student. After he completed medical studies he trained in psychiatry during the years 1927–31 at Hopital St Anne, and Hopital Henri-Rouselle in Paris, and at the Burgholzi in Zürich. In 1932 Lacan presented his thesis *De la psychose paranoiaque dans ses rapports avec la personalité.*

He started his career in psychoanalysis through the International Psychoanalytic Association (IPA). In 1933, he commenced his analysis with Rudolph Loewenstein who, together with Heinz Hartmann, later established the School of Ego Psychology in the USA. In 1934 he became a member of the Société Psychanalytique de Paris (SPP).

Much of Lacan's work was presented in seminar form, establishing an oral tradition of teaching and dialogue, which has required an almost theological exegesis of his texts by his followers. He began a series of weekly seminars in 1951 in Paris, which were attended by leading intellectuals of his time. His early seminars focused on a return to Freud, insisting on a rereading and revaluing of Freud's writings. Before World War II, Lacan's major theoretical preoccupation was with the mirror stage and its accompanying notions of the ego, alienation, the imaginary and the Other. After World War II until 1960, language became a dominant theme in Lacan's thinking. His seminars focused less on Freud's texts and more on the elaboration of his own concepts, such as the barred subject, object a, and his four discourses. The 1970s saw a focus on more abstract concepts of topology, knots and mathèmes, demonstrating his theoretical evolution from the imaginary register and the specular relation, to the symbolic with its emphasis on the Name-of-the-Father, to the register of the real.

Amidst some controversy in 1964, Lacan split from the IPA to establish his own school, the École Freudienne de Paris (Freudian School of Paris). In the last twenty years of his life, Lacan's work was disseminated to a broader public. His ideas had a profound effect on the intellectual movements of the time; the influence of his ideas can be found in disciplines as widely divergent as political science, cultural theory, feminist studies, critical social theory and psychoanalytic theory and practice.

During this most theoretically fertile period of his life, he maintained a busy private practice, marked by his own idiosyncratic style (again not without controversy – for example, the well-known short analytic session as opposed to the traditional fifty-minute session).

He continued his teaching and his practice until his death in 1981.

The dissension within the psychoanalytic community continued after Lacan's death. He bequeathed to his son-in-law, Jacques-Alain Miller, the task of disseminating the vast body of his work into the field of psychoanalysis. With few texts readily accessible to a broad international audience, there remains much room for interpretation. The inaccessibility of his work is due partly to the difficulty of his writing style, a disjunction with his actual oral presentations, the complexity and unfamiliarity of his conceptual forms, and the small number of translated works. Nevertheless, his ideas are slowly and systematically penetrating diverse fields in the French-speaking and non-French speaking worlds. Since his death, the spirit of his work has offered an enlivening influence on the thinking of analysts and non-analysts alike.

Ultimately, one must formulate for oneself the essence of Lacan's ideas.

Agalma

By the early 1960s Lacan's seminars had begun to range beyond his earlier elaborations of the fundamental notions of psychoanalytic theory and technique, to explore with more fervour literary and philosophical texts. Seminar VII on *Ethics*, for example, includes much discussion about Aristotle and Kant, while the seminar of the following year, devoted to transference, focuses specifically on Plato's *Symposium*, and it is here that we find the first use of the term *agalma*.

Lacan states very early in this seminar that it will not be easy to give an account of *The Symposium*, a monumental and enigmatic text, yet it will be a necessary and illuminating detour to introduce an inquiry into the structure of love.

Love, he says, has been discussed for centuries, but analysts who make use of it have made no attempt to add to the term, a term of profound interest for the tradition of psychoanalysis.

Lacan considered *The Symposium* as a series of analytic sessions, which culminate in the discourse of Alcibiades presenting Socrates as the exemplar of Eros. Lacan turns to this discourse to talk about love, the question of the place of desire, and what happened in the first analytic transference, the dealing of which is the fundamental function of analysis, and the question of which is the guiding theme of Seminar VIII.

The Symposium has often been claimed to be one of the master-pieces of classical literature from which emerges a complex philosophy of love. Lacan acknowledges this and asserts that it can be seen as a model for analytic dialogue.

Socrates' position can be identified with that of the analyst and Alcibiades' with that of the analysand, who desires. Transference occurs between Socrates, who **knows**, he is the Master of Eros, and Alcibiades, who lacks. Therefore we see the basis and the meaning of the analytical relationship exemplified by Alcibiades who, through Socrates, discovers he desires. Lacan insists, in a discussion of psychoanalytic technique, that it is necessary in the analysis 'to isolate oneself with an other in order to teach him what he is lacking and, by the nature of transference, he will learn what he is lacking insofar as he loves: I am not here for his Good, but for him to love me, and for me to disappoint him' (cited in Marini, 1992, p. 180).

Alcibiades lacks; he is consumed by an intense infatuation for Socrates who does not. His eulogy is not to love, unlike the other discourses delivered at the supper party, but to Socrates, whom he declares bears a strong resemblance to Silenus-like statuettes that are hollow inside, yet contain little figures of gods. Silenus, mythologically, was the tutor of Dionysus, god of wine, portrayed as always drunk but believed to tell the truth even if it was told in riddles: *in vino veritas*.

In form too, Alcibiades says, Socrates resembles Marysas the satyr, who charms and fascinates, and who found the abandoned flute of Athene, the instrument that required only a breath to play beautiful music. Is this an allegory of Socrates who portrayed himself as the midwife of people's ideas, as he is portrayed in *The Symposium*, or is it a representation of the dialectic in discourse? (Anderson, 1993, pp. 104–8).

Was this Plato's intended meaning? Or importantly, was it Lacan's understanding too? He said that *The Symposium* should not be read as one reads *France-Soir*; its effects are surprising, truth is a function of speech, and language is the condition of the unconscious.

Thus, Socrates, the eros of Alcibiades, possesses a hidden treasure, the pleasing gift for the gods, the precious object, the jewel, or what Lacan says is important, what is inside. Alcibiades desires, because he believes Socrates possesses the *agalma*, the privileged and hidden object of desire, and desire is not a subject.

It is this concept that Lacan develops in Seminar VIII. The Lacanian formula that embodies the *agalma* is what we understand as *object petit a*, the object cause of desire, but in the seminar titled *Transference* Lacan introduces it as the partial object, and it exists as an object of desire, but determined within a larger relationship of love. Within this topology Lacan proceeds to argue that even if the subject does not know it, in the analytic situation the small *a*, the agalma, functions in the Other; this is a legitimate effect of transference that sees the analyst as the upholder of *object a*.

But the big O is not an absolute other, it is what Lacan calls a perpetually vanishing Other. By this very fact it puts us in a perpetually vanishing position. Therefore, the object, an overvalued one, notwithstanding one that was lost at the time of the constitution of the subject, functions by making us something other than a subject submitted to the infinite slipping of the signifier, something that revalorizes the signifier of the impossible.

We desire a position that is beyond the word that may be unique to us. Lacan says this is the true point at which he can designate the dignity of the subject, and it is here that we see the measure in which *object a* takes on the essential value of the fundamental fantasy. It is also in how the subject identifies with this fantasy that the dimension of desire takes its metonymic pathway.

Socrates, Lacan says, is only the envelope of desire, the semblant of *object a*, to whom the *Che vuoi* (What do you want?) is addressed. Socrates, who proclaims that the only knowledge he has is knowledge of love, provides the first embodiment of the position of the analyst because he refuses the position of the loved/desired object.

Socrates refuses Alcibiades' declaration and in so doing refuses to mask his lack. He insists that he acknowledge his desire by showing Agathon as the true object of his love. Socrates brought to light the manifestation of Alcibiades' desire – the project of analysis. Lacan mentions that the principle of this is to see that the subject is introduced as worthy of interest, of love, as *eromenos*. This he called the manifest effect, the latent he saw as linked to the subject's **unknowing**, an unknowing of desire except that it is already in the Other. The subject is constituted then as *erastes*, fulfilling Lacan's understanding of the phenomenon of love by the substitution of the *erastes* for the *eromenos*, the effects of which one can see in transference love from the beginnings of analysis where the subject seeks knowledge, the truth, the dialectic of desire – the *agalma*.

In Seminar X, *Anxiety*, Lacan was to develop further the function of *object a* as the cause of desire. However, its initial elaboration started from the *agalma* as a part object in Seminar VIII (1960–61), although there were references in Seminar VI, *Desire and its interpretation* in 1958. In *Subversion of the subject and dialectic of desire*, Lacan includes the *agalma* – the inestimable treasure – in the *object a*, the treasure that Alcibiades would like Socrates to cede to him, avowing his desire (Lacan, 1977).

In the *Proposition* of 1967 he alludes to the *agalma* as an algorithm 'of desire in the agencies of the subject'. Again, in *The Four Fundamental Concepts of Psycho-Analysis,* Lacan refers to the *agalma* as something, he knows not what, that Alcibiades asks of Socrates. Socrates' reply is what Lacan describes as the first adumbration of the technique of the mapping of the transference, *'look to your soul, look to your desire, look to your onions'* (1988, p. 255).

See also: **object a, real**
Other terms: *Che vuoi*, drive, fantasy, transference love

References

Anderson, D.E. (1993) *The Masks of Dionysos*. Albany: State University of New York Press.

Lacan, J. (1977) *Écrits: A Selection* (trans. A. Sheridan). New York: W.W. Norton.

Lacan, J. (1981) *The Four Fundamental Concepts of Psycho-Analysis* (ed. J.-A. Miller, trans. A. Sheridan). New York: W.W. Norton.

Lacan, J. (1992) [1959–60] *Seminar VII: The Ethics of Psychoanalysis* (trans D. Porter). New York: W.W. Norton.

Marini, M. (1992) *Jacques Lacan: The French Context* (trans. A. Tomiche). New Jersey: Rutgers University Press.

Plato (1951) *The Symposium* (trans. W. Hamilton). Harmondsworth: Penguin Books.

Zita M. Marks

Aggressivity

Lacan outlines his views on aggression or aggressivity in chapter 2 of *Écrits*, presenting his thoughts as a series of theses. For Lacan, unlike Melanie Klein, aggressivity does not stem from the death drive, nor, unlike Fairbairn, from frustrated desire. In line with Freud, Lacan sees aggression as part of the life instinct, opposing the death drive. At both the individual and species levels, aggressivity is seen as part of the struggle for survival and domination. Indeed, in times of war, society makes use of the individual's propensity for aggression. It is only the need for cultural subordination within a community that necessitates the sublimation of aggression. Lacan poses the question of the connection between aggression and the death drive, concluding that only when aggressivity is a response to frustration is it a desire for death (Lacan, 1977, p. 42).

A central point in this essay is the relation Lacan draws, following Freud (1957), between aggressivity and narcissistic identification, narcissistic identification being the infant's ambivalent identification with his/her mirror image. Lacan's central thesis is that aggressivity is the correlative tendency of narcissistic identification that determines the formal structure of the ego (not Freud's perception-consciousness system but Lacan's system of misperception and alienating images). It is an integral part of the subject's experience of another like him-/herself, the visual image being a determining factor in the person's relations with others.

This thesis throws up at least two ways of conceiving the sources of primitive aggressivity. The first is essentially a paranoiac structure of the ego and results when the ego encounters another subject like himself and there awakens in him a desire for the object of the other's desire. Prior to this moment, the infant experiences himself as undifferentiated from his counterpart, so that there is no internal conflict or ambivalence. In this conception then, aggressivity originates in the threat posed by the other in the triangular relationship of self (ego)–other–thing (object), in which the subject desires what the other desires. This is the basis of rivalry or jealousy. To put it

5

another way, as the person comes to identify with others, he/she begins to take on their desires, producing aggressive rivalry between the person and the other for the object desired by the other. Paranoiac alienation dates from the deflection of the specular I which links the I to social situations and necessitates taking into account the mediation of the desire of the other (Lacan, 1977, p. 45).

Muller and Richardson (1982, p. 49) present a second way of conceiving the origins of primitive aggressivity. They infer from Lacan's claim that aggressivity has its source in narcissistic modes of identification that give the ego (*moi*) its identity. This narcissistic passion converts into primitive aggressivity when the fragile unity of the ego is threatened. In this, Lacan would concur with Klein, but Muller and Richardson are careful to present their ideas as hypotheses, since Lacan's text does not fully clarify the matter of the origins of aggressivity. They further suggest that, in Lacan's scheme, the aggressive imago of the fragmented body is the inversion of the Gestalt of the unified ego. Fear of the imago of fragmentation arouses aggression. This idea is closely related to Klein's critical, punitive, primitive super-ego. Internal bad objects and the fear of fragmentation lay the groundwork for aggressivity. The realization of the gap between lived experience of the minimally competent and fragmented body on the one hand, and narcissistic identification with the unity of the visual image during the mirror stage on the other, produces disturbing feelings which are displaced as aggressive tendencies towards others. In other words, the discrepancy between fragmented bodily experiences and the unified imaginary identity produces primordial paranoia in the *moi*.

Thus, both the relation to the other and the alienation from actual experience present possible sources of aggressivity. Lacan distinguishes these possible sources of aggression from aggressive intention and its effective manifestation in consciousness and in discourse with an other. The experience of aggressivity is in the form of intended aggression (i.e., the pressure of intention to act aggressively) and an image of corporeal dislocation. Its effect is destructive to others, though not generally manifest as open violence. Here, aggressivity is presented as a pressure or impulsion that interrupts overt behaviour, breaking through in unguarded moments with disruptive effects. The aggressive drives are represented through certain images – for example, castration, mutilation, devouring (i.e., imagos of the fragmented body) – corresponding to bodily experience prior to the alienating identification with a unitary image in the mirror. From this point of view, the ego (narcissistically conceived and embedded in misconceptions) is the cause of aggression.

Chronologically, Lacan's concepts of the mirror stage and aggressivity converge in 1948–49, implying a common development of ideas around the notion of narcissistic identification and the distorting effects of the mirror image on the development of the ego. In both papers, the concept of an illusory unity or imaginary 'whole' ego is central, together with the threat of an image of bodily disintegration.

In chapter 2 of *Écrits* (1977), Lacan writes specifically about aggression within the psychoanalytic context. Here, the analyst's impassive posture elicits the analysand's aggressivity, the effect of which is the creation of psychic imagos invoking fragmentation of the body. The psychoanalytic session allows aggressive intention to emerge in the negative transference, when archaic imagos are de-repressed or reactualized, thereby creating a controlled paranoia. The *moi*, as demonstrated in the ego's resistance to treatment, can be seen to be aggressive in its operations (i.e., opposition, negation, deception) as part of its attempt to maintain an illusion of unity, an illusion originally founded (according to Freud) in the ego's relation to its ideal. Without the moderating effect of interpretation, the mirror image which the impassive analyst would otherwise reflect back to the analysand would cause unbearable anxiety.

Thus Lacan links aggression to paranoia and to narcissism, a connection that Freud also made in his paper on narcissism. The secondary Oedipal identification is more pacifying, the link to cultural norms providing security or containment. It is the genital libido that subordinates the individual to the species, forcing the individual to transcend and sublimate his/her narcissistic primitive aggressivity in an internalized move towards cultural subordination.

See also: **body, gaze, imaginary, mirror stage**

References

Freud, S. (1957) [1914] 'On narcissism: An introduction' (vol. 14, pp. 67–102) *Standard Edition, Complete Psychological Works*: London: Hogarth Press and Institute of Psycho-Analysis.

Lacan, J. (1977) *Écrits: A Selection* (trans. Alan Sheridan). London: Routledge.

Muller, J. P. and Richardson, W. J. (1982) *Lacan and Language: A Reader's Guide to* Écrits. London: Karnac Books.

Huguette Glowinski

Alienation and Separation

Lacan introduces the terms alienation and separation in his *The Four Fundamental Concepts of Psycho-Analysis* as two complementary operations necessary for the constitution of the subject. In this work, alienation is linked to division, to the splitting of the subject, the split referring here to the choice between meaning (produced by the signifier) and being.

By choosing meaning, the being of the subject disappears, a phenomenon Lacan calls *aphanisis*; by choosing being, the subject falls into non-meaning. He thus ties the disappearance of being to the signifier that exists in the field of the Other, thereby portraying alienation as a function of an exterior field.

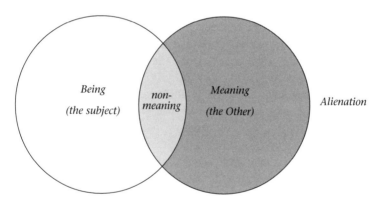

Figure 1 Alienation
Source: Lacan (1981), *The Four Fundamental Concepts of Psycho-Analysis*, p. 211.

Lacan's conceptualization of the being of the subject in this model seems to relate to innate biological or sensate functioning, whereas meaning is tied to the other, to something outside the self. The disappearance of the subject as the signifier assumes dominance, or, to put it another way, the eclipse of being by the signifier, is the price we pay for meaning.

On the other hand, the choice of being deprives the subject of meaning or sense, which is presumably an unbearable state, since the subject seeks meaning in everything. Whatever the choice may be, the consequence involves the loss of part of the other alternative. The subject is alienated forever, through the signifier, from his/her sensate self and yet the possibility of achieving sense is also beyond his/her grasp.

Lacan uses the term alienation variously throughout his work: in the context of the subject's relationship to him-/herself, to the Other and to language. In the first meaning, which is elaborated in *Écrits* (chapter 1), the subject becomes aware of an external referent of meaning, a unified specular image which provides both a necessary sense of wholeness and also a sense of alienation, a break with the sensate or biological being. At this imaginary level, the subject looks to an illusory image of him-/herself as a unified being but loses forever, or is alienated from, his/her essential biological experience of being.

Our image gives us a (necessary) illusion of unity, while at the same time casting our sense of ourselves to an outside reference point (the mirror, the Other). The subject identifies both with his/her specular image (other), and with the lack in the Other. This image is a distortion, a defence, and yet it is our reality; it casts the subject in both imaginary and symbolic terms.

In the second meaning (developed in *The Four Fundamental Concepts of Psycho-Analysis* as noted above), that which relates the subject to an other, Lacan moves from the imaginary to the symbolic register, as the reference point for the subject's sense of meaning is located in an external agent. This version of alienation is linked to symbolic castration; Lacan moves from the specular phenomenon to the domain of language.

Due to the fact that we are speaking beings, the subject is split in its entry into the symbolic order. The signifier illuminates the subject's division from him-/herself, that is, the separation between thinking and being, between conscious experience and biological or sensate states. Thus Lacan grants to alienation a fundamental causal role in the formation of the subject, and to the signifier he grants the role of instigator of alienation. The moment of alienation occurs when unconscious meaning is created, but, at that point, the subject is deprived of being. (Laurent (1995) notes that the introduction of the concepts of alienation and separation as the two operations constituting the subject, is a break from Lacan's previous emphasis on metonymy and metaphor as constituting the work of the unconscious.)

In the third meaning, which is closely related to the second, the focus is on the importance of language in positioning the subject within the signifying chain. Alienation here implies that language divorces the subject inevitably and forever from an internal sense of agency and makes him/her a (fragmented) subject of linguistic determination.

The common thread running through these accounts is that the concept of alienation implies that a subject cannot be defined in terms of his consciousness of self, but only through the other. It is a way of describing the relationship of subject and other as well as the formation of a specular image of oneself which operates in the imaginary register, but borders also on the symbolic (how the Other and language define the subject). We cannot trust our knowledge of ourselves but must refer to an external criterion for knowledge. The subject defines him-/herself in the signifying chain and in terms of his/her *jouissance* (as related to the Other). Thus the subject receives his/her definition in a field that is exterior to him/her; he/she is radically dependent on the signifier.

Alienation then, on the imaginary level, constitutes the me or *moi*; at the symbolic level, alienation condemns the subject to a division between being and sense (sense is in the Other, produced by the signifier). There is a disjunction between thinking and being, which the subject wishes to ignore (in the imaginary), ensuring a sense of continuity of his/her being.

In a question at the end of chapter 16 in *The Four Fundamental Concepts of Psycho-Analysis*, Miller poses an interesting distinction between the alienation of a subject whose definition exists in a field that is exterior to him/her and, the alienation which produces a loss of a 'consciousness-of-self' (1981, p. 215).

This question, which Lacan does not address, seems to point to the distinction between alienation as a split between intuitive self-awareness and a rational distance from oneself (the self as observer) on the one hand, and alienation as an internal subjectivity/external signifier split on the other. In any case it can be said that the subject must interiorize and make personally meaningful the external field, but in the process loses direct access to organismic or intuitive self-awareness.

It could be argued that Lacan offers no account of psychic interiority. For him personal meaning is tied to something outside and other. In describing alienation he emphasizes the meaning/being dichotomy, and the inevitability of a split within the subject; a perception of inconsistency in his/her being.

Separation

Separation, also introduced in *The Four Fundamental Concepts of Psycho-Analysis*, is the second necessary operation for the bringing into being of the subject. Whereas alienation concerns a division within the subject and the opposition of being and meaning, separation is tied to a lack, particularly to the recognition of lack in the Other. It is an intersubjective phenomenon.

Separation, based as it is in Freud's concept of splitting of the ego, is actually a splitting of the phallic object. It constitutes the recognition of a gap in the Other and in the subject, an acknowledgement of a limit to sense and to absolute knowledge.

The subject finds in the other's desire what he/she is as subject of the unconscious and is actualized through the Other's lack or loss. The subject apprehends a lack in the Other, something the Other wants. The subject locates his/her own lack at the point of lack perceived in the Other. The first object the subject proposes as the lost object or lack is him-/herself – can he/she lose me? – the fantasy of one's death or disappearance (the subject producing the lack in the Other following the course of the death drive).

The child seeks out the space in the (m)other where he/she is lacking, in order to be the object of her desire. Two lacks are superimposed, creating a link between the desire of the subject and the desire of the Other. Intersubjectivity is marked by deprivation and lack, recognition of desire, and not by affective or intersubjective feeling.

See also: **jouissance**, **desire**
Other terms: aphanisis, lack, *moi*, other

References

Lacan, J. (1977) *Écrits: A Selection* (trans. A. Sheridan) 'The mirror stage as formative of the function of the I'. Chapter 1. New York: W.W. Norton.

Lacan, J. (1981) *Four Fundamental Concepts of Psycho-Analysis* (trans. A. Sheridan). ch. 16. New York: W.W. Norton.

Laurent, E. (1995) 'Alienation and separation'. In R. Feldstein, B. Fink and M. Jaanus, *Reading Seminar XI*. New York: New York University Press.

Huguette Glowinski

Anamorphosis

Anamorphosis is the name of a form of 'optics' (which later came to be called perspective) that is used to create an image of an object that appears in its correct proportions only by looking at it from an off-centre angle.

Its basis rests on the incontrovertible fact that we cannot see around corners. Looking requires the travelling of straight light rays from the object to the retina. Hence we see the object from only one aspect; we have to guess what it may look like from another aspect. Lacan refers in particular to two pioneers of the technique. The first of these was Dürer, whose famous woodcut of 1525 actually depicts an experiment with string representing the passage of light from object to retina. Lacan points out that Dürer demonstrated how vision works to create flat, two-dimensional images.

The other important reference made by Lacan was to the 1533 Hans Holbein painting, *The Ambassadors*. The actual technique was used by Holbein (rather than demonstrating how it is done as in the Dürer woodcut) to depict the skull that is suspended, seemingly in mid-flight across the foreground of the composition. It is not immediately recognizable. It must be looked at from an angle to see its form.

Historically, these names are important in that they show what was happening in the intellectual, artistic and social context that was to allow Descartes' *cogito ergo sum* to erupt into the philosophical canon about a century later.

Lacan thought enough about this aspect of creating an image to devote a whole chapter on it to his section about the gaze in *The Four Fundamental Concepts of Psycho-Analysis*.

The question of the construction of the image – as opposed to the mapping of space which is not only the prerogative of the sighted person – is very much part of Lacan's theorizing on the imaginary. The imaginary register is the site of the ego, the sense of self-consciousness and of self-image. The construction of the image and the distortion it is prey to with a mere shifting of the gaze, exemplifies one of the illusory features of the imaginary register, forever marked by *méconnaissance*.

See also: **imaginary, the gaze**

Reference

Lacan, J. (1981) [1973] 'Of the gaze as *object petit a'* in *The Four Fundamental Concepts of Psycho-Analysis*. New York: W.W. Norton.

Sara Murphy

Aphasia

From the viewpoint of the neurosciences, aphasia may be defined as a disturbance in language processing or production arising from neurological causes. Modern linguistics has identified ten types of neurologically-based aphasias arising from impairment to the language centres in the brain (Broca's or Wernicke's area) and/or their connecting pathways via the auditory or motor cortex (see, for example, chapter 11 of Caplan, 1987).

Lacan acknowledges his debt to linguistics, in particular, the two pioneers of modern linguistics, Saussure and Jakobson. Aphasia in the context of Lacanian psychoanalysis refers to the forms that relate to the two coordinates of language first identified by the linguists, but which have become central to Lacan's theory of language and to the practice of analysis. The two coordinates are the vertical and horizontal axes along which discourse flows. Lacan expressed it in the following way in 'The agency of the letter':

> There is, in effect, no signifying chain that does not have, as if attached to the punctuation of its units, a whole articulation of relevant contexts suspended vertically, as it were, from that point. (*Écrits*, 1977, p. 154)

The first type of aphasia, then, is that associated with the vertical axis, or the axis of similarity or of *selection*. Subjects with this type of disorder may be able to maintain a degree of fluency, but they do not hear that what they are saying is not making sense.

It is a disorder of the symbolic or metaphoric function while the propositional function of language is retained. Associations slide along the horizontal axis, hence subjects are able to make metonymic associations ('cup'–'saucer'), but lose the capacity for substitution ('cup'–'drinking vessel').

The second type of aphasia is that associated with the horizontal axis, or the axis of contiguity. With this type of disorder, subjects experience a breakdown in the propositional or metonymic function of language while the metaphoric function is maintained. They lose fluency and grope around for words they want to use. Breakdown may be total, making it hard to find words, or to move from one word to the next, or it may be partial, resulting in telegraphic speech and abundant use of homonyms (words that sound the same but have different meanings, e.g.: sale–sail; current–currant; muscle–mussel). While contiguity is lost or impaired, however, metaphoric associations are available and subjects can find substitute associations for words.

There are numerous references throughout Lacan's work to the two axes of language and the necessity, in the analytic discourse, for there to be an ear to the two. Some of the best known occurred in his lectures and essays that took place during the 1950s, up to 1960. Examples are: the report to the Rome Congress of 1953, 'The function and field of speech and language in psychoanalysis': Seminar III on the Psychoses, 'Introduction to the question of the psychoses', delivered in 1955–56; the 1957 essay, 'The agency of the letter in the unconscious, or reason since Freud', and the paper delivered at the conference '*La Dialectique*' in 1960 entitled 'The subversion of the subject and the dialectic of desire in the Freudian unconscious'.

In Seminar III Lacan offers a mild criticism of Saussure's notion of the linear (i.e., unidirectional) flow of language: 'it is not quite exact to say that it is a simple line, it is more probably a set of several lines, a stave' (p. 54). By 1957, however, in 'The agency of the letter', he came to ascribe the formulation of the algorithm S/s to Saussure: '... although it is not found in exactly this form in any of the numerous schemas, which nonetheless express it ...' (*Écrits*, p. 149).

In the same essay, he also pays tribute to Jakobson, in particular to his seminal text, 'The fundamentals of language', which had only recently been published (1956), and which seems to have been the subject of frequent discussion between Lacan and Jakobson (see notes 6 and 20 following the chapter in *Écrits*). Tribute to the two linguists can be found again in 'The subversion of the subject'. By this time (1960) the notion of the two axes of language was well incorporated into Lacan's theorizing on the subject.

See also: **metaphor, metonymy**

References

Caplan, D. (1987) *Neurolinguistics and Linguistic Aphasiology*. Melbourne: Cambridge University Press.

Jakobson, R. (1971) [1956] *Fundamentals of Language*. The Hague: Mouton Gravenhage.

Lacan, J. (1977) [1966] *Écrits: A Selection* (trans. A. Sheridan). London: Tavistock.

Lacan, J. (1993) *Seminar III: Introduction to the Question of the Psychoses* (trans. R. Grigg). New York: W.W. Norton.

Saussure, F. de (1966) [1915] *Course in General Linguistics* (eds C. Bally, A. Sechehye, A. Riedlinger; trans. W. Baskin). New York: McGraw-Hill.

Sara Murphy

Autism and Childhood Psychosis

Specific references to autism and the psychoses of childhood in Lacan's written works and seminars are scarce. Yet his theses on the structure of psychosis (see foreclosure; psychosis), have enlightened the clinical approach to those conditions and generated a wealth of research, theoretical developments and debate among psychoanalysts of the Lacanian orientation who work with children.

The topic is, however, of relevance for the theory and practice of all Lacanian analysts, as the psychoanalytic field is one, and interest in particular clinical or conceptual problems should not be understood as being the domain of only 'specialized' forms of psychoanalysis. Whether autistic, psychotic or neurotic, it is as a subject that the child (or the adult, for that matter) enters the psychoanalytic experience.

In Lacanian psychoanalysis, the child works in this experience as a subject in his/her own right and in the full sense of the term; this is so despite the fact that the psychotic or autistic subject is outside discourse (*hors discours*) and cannot therefore be considered to be a 'subject of the unconscious' constituted by the operations of alienation and separation. It is still the aim of the psychoanalytic experience that the psychotic or autistic subject establish a 'workable' link with discourse.

Within Lacan's works, the main references that have inspired the psychoanalysts who work with psychotic and autistic children (leaving aside for the moment the distinction between the two terms) are:

- The doctoral thesis on paranoia (1932).
- The article on the family published in the *Encyclopédie française* (1938).
- The commentaries on the cases of Dick (treated by Melanie Klein; Klein 1930) and Robert (treated by Rosine Lefort; Lefort and Lefort 1988). Both are part of the 1953–54 seminar, or Seminar I.

- The seminar on the psychoses of 1955–56.
- The now 'classical' 1959 paper on the treatment of psychosis included in the English-language selection of the *Écrits* (1977).
- The intervention at the conference on childhood psychosis organized by Maud Mannoni (1968).
- The note on the child addressed to Jenny Aubry (1969).
- The revision of the concept of the Name-of-the-Father and the function of the symptom developed in the seminars of 1974–75 (*R.S.I.*) and 1975–76 (*Le Sinthome*).
- The 1975 Geneva lecture on the symptom.

Diagnosis

The first question that faces the practitioners in the field, both of practical and conceptual significance, is that of diagnosis which, from a Lacanian perspective is necessarily structural.

In his seminar on the psychoses, Lacan speaks of 'the structure of the psychotic phenomenon': the observable phenomena are moments of the structure, rather than epiphenomena.

From a clinical perspective, 'observable' phenomena are not perceived unless the clinician's conceptual mapping is prepared to admit them; and this requires structural hypotheses.

In the Lacanian orientation, childhood and adult psychoses are identical from the viewpoint of their structure; this position contrasts with the view adopted by the authors of current psychiatric classifications. In making of psychosis a developmental disorder, what the psychiatric orientation represented by the *DSM-IV* causes is, in the first place, to consider the psychotic phenomenon as a deficit, rather than a production; and secondly, to define the deficits of the patient in terms of developmental norms external to the structure of the subject as such.

Diagnosis is thus established on the basis of what the subject has not achieved developmentally and his/her deviation from norms which combine medical and educational criteria, adaptation to conventional social demands being the central point of reference. This is a questionable criterion for clinical phenomenology, since the emphasis is placed on what is absent and not on what is phenomenologically observable, which is a production.

Lacan always insisted on the notion of the psychotic phenomenon as a production, a view taken already by Freud since the beginnings of psychoanalysis and the best example of which is Freud's analysis of President Schreber's psychotic productions.

A clinic of production, as opposed to a clinic of the deficit, necessarily requires a structural approach and a positive explanation for clinical phenomena which, in turn, is indispensable for any therapeutic intervention. A clinic of the deficit is content with verifying the presence of malfunction or disorder, and not interested in the order which exists, since psychosis is one of the possible organizations of the speaking being, including the cases in which the subject does not actually speak (catatonia, autistic mutism). Even in such cases the subject is subjected to language and, for instance, the absence of verbal productions is interpreted by those around the subject as a refusal to speak, rather than as an absolute inability to speak.

The following are the diagnostic categories generally accepted in the Freudian field, although there is no unanimity as to exact definitions:

1. Paranoia, whose existence as one of the psychoses of childhood is maintained, contrary to the opinion of non-psychoanalytic psychiatry. *Les structures de la psychose*, by Rosine and Robert Lefort (1988), contains a full account of the treatment of Robert, the Wolf Child, and a detailed comparison of Robert's and President Schreber's clinical presentations, which has led the authors to assert the structural identity of both cases. Paranoiac psychosis manifests clinically through delusional formations and hallucinations which are the spontaneous attempts at recovery on the part of the patient, an attempt to reconstruct a world that has collapsed and where it has become impossible to live.

2. Schizophrenia, which manifests itself through fragmentary delusional formations and hallucinations; incoherence of speech and thought; blunted or bizarre affective responses and catatonic behaviour, all of which represent the subject's attempts to deal with a collapse of the representation of the body, or inability to construct that representation in a relation with the small other, $i(o)$, the body thus becoming a place almost impossible to inhabit.

3. Melancholia, which has not received much attention but which appears during childhood, characterized by delusional feelings of worthlessness, insomnia or hypersomnia, poor appetite, failure to thrive, suicidal ideation and actions, and apathy (which may be interrupted by manic episodes). These phenomena represent an identification with the real lack in the Other, that is, the absence of the desire of the Other which remains as an unsymbolized nothingness, the locus of the suicidal identification. There remains an open question whether melancholia can be considered as a structure in its own right, or whether it is a variant of paranoia – and, in some cases, perhaps, of schizophrenia.

4. Autism, for which Leo Kanner's (1973) original description of 1943 remains valid, characterized by inability to relate socially, aloneness, the failure to assume an anticipatory posture, the profound disturbance of language, the presence of excellent rote memory in many cases, echolalia and delayed echolalia, literalness and the mechanical repetition of pronouns, with onset within the first thirty months after birth. Such clinical features suggest an absence of the Other as the locus of the representation of both the world and the body. There is no unanimity as to the specificity of autism: whether it constitutes a structure in its own right, separate from the psychoses; or whether it is a variation and the earliest clinical version of schizophrenia. Current research by Lacanians who work with autistic and psychotic children deals with this question and the related issue of the evolution of the autistic subject, that is, what becomes of the autistic child when he/she enters adulthood.

Conceptual foundations for diagnosis

A minimum of four terms is needed to map and describe any clinical phenomenon:

S_1, the master signifier, or signifier of the subject (although originated in the field of the Other);

S_2, the signifier of the Other, or signifying chain less the S_1;

$\$$, the subject, necessarily divided, an effect of the signifying chain: that which is represented by a signifier for another signifier; and *a*, the object cause of desire, which represents the function of *plus-de-jouir* (surplus enjoyment) and a localization of *jouissance*.

These are the four constitutive terms of what Lacan called discourse, or social bond, that defines the position of the subject even before he utters any statement. Each of the four discourses posited by Lacan represents a particular combination of these four terms, which occupy places that are invariant:

$$\frac{\text{agent}}{\text{truth}} \quad \rightarrow \quad \frac{\text{other}}{\text{production}}$$

In this sense of the term, discourse, Lacan says that the psychotic is outside discourse (*hors discours*); but the psychotic is not outside language. In addition – and this is particularly relevant to a discussion of the psychoses and autism – any diagnostic account must consider the vicissitudes of the specular relation, for which three more terms, that are not directly represented in the matheme of the discourse, are necessary: i(o), the image of the specular other, or small other; i'(o), the ego; and I, the ego-ideal. The Schema L of Lacan, as presented in his seminar on the psychoses, is the basis of subsequent elaborations on these terms:

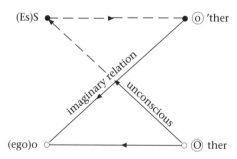

Figure 2: Schema L
Source: Lacan (1993), Book III, p. 14.

The imaginary axis is improperly constituted in psychosis, and virtually absent in the case of autism. While the symbolic order is the support of the imaginary, there is no proper access to the symbolic without the intermediation of the imaginary. The subject's encounter with a 'bare' signifier without an imaginary cover (a signifier reduced to being something real) has the uncanny, enigmatic effect that the psychotic subject typically reports.

The subject is constituted as such through the two operations of alienation and separation. The concept of alienation refers not so much to the fact that the subject is already determined in the field of the Other, even before his birth, through his name, position in the kinship system and the family, the family myths and the whole symbolic universe that precedes him, but rather to his determination by the binary structure of the signifier. A signifier represents the subject, but for another signifier:

$$\frac{S_1}{\$} \quad \rightarrow \quad S_2$$

The operation of alienation constitutes the subject as subject of language. The operation of separation is necessary for the constitution of the subject as subject of discourse:

$$\frac{S_1}{\$} \quad \rightarrow \quad \frac{S_2}{a}$$

The object a effects the separation (hence its designation as a 'separator' or 'separating object'). As Colette Soler has argued, the separation in question does not separate the subject from the object, but from the signifying chain – from the Other, in so far as the Other represents the signifying chain (Soler, 1990, pp. 9–24):

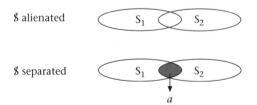

$\$$ alienated

$\$$ separated

The object falls from the other

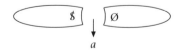

Figure 3: The object falls from the Other
Source: Soler (1990), pp. 9–24.

In the neuroses, the subject wants to occupy the place of the object of the Other's desire: to be the object a or to have it, which is what the structure of fantasy represents: $\$ \diamond a$. The relation between subject and object is one of impossibility, since this object is a lost one – not because it has been actually lost, but lost as an effect of the structure. The image of the other, i(o) acts as an a, that is, it functions as a separator from the Other of the mirror. Thus, the inscription of the loss of the object a in the symbolic register requires the experience of the mirror and the constitution of the imaginary register.

In the psychoses and autism, the function of separation does not take place, which means that the subject remains un-separated from the signifying chain (or the Other as the locus of the signifying chain). The object a is not constituted, and therefore there is no subject of the unconscious – which is equivalent to saying that there is foreclosure of the Name-of-the-Father, since this is the signifier that introduces a lack or hole in the primordial Other, the mother. In psychosis, the unsymbolized lost object emerges as an object 'in excess' (*objet en plus*), which the subject desperately tries to get rid of.

The concept of holophrase was introduced by Lacan to designate a variety of clinical effects of the lack of separation between S_1 and S_2 (Lacan, 1964, pp. 237–8; Stevens, 1987). The holophrase is a word that expresses the meaning of a whole sentence or several sentences, and is a normal phenomenon at the beginnings of the development of speech; for example, 'wet', for 'my pants are wet', or 'truck', for 'I want to play with the truck'.

Without an interval between S_1 and S_2, the object a does not fall from the field of the Other. The psychotic's experience of perplexity at facing the enigma posed by the signifier for him could be explained as an effect of this soldering of S_1 and S_2: since the signifier does not refer to another signifier, it appears as devoid of signification.

Captured in the holophrase, the subject in psychosis and autism cannot be a subject of discourse, even if he is still inscribed in language. Discourse requires two discrete positions: subject and Other. That is why in psychosis the function of the shifters (also called deictics, or *embrayeurs*) is disturbed.

Shifters are those expressions whose referent can only be determined with respect to the interlocutors in an act of enunciation, such as the pronouns of the first and second persons, 'here', 'yesterday', 'at this time', etc.

Emile Benveniste has shown that deictics constitute an irruption of discourse within language, since their meaning, although depending on language, can only be defined with reference to their use (Benveniste, 1971, chapter 5; Ducrot and Todorov, 1979, pp. 252–3). Autism shows an extreme position of fusion of the subject in the holophrase S_1S_2, manifested as absence of the function of the deictic, which is tantamount to saying: absence of the subject of the enunciation.

Different modalities of the failure of the operation of separation

The modality of the failure in separation can be used as a criterion for differential diagnosis. Without the separating object, the subject is exposed to a direct, unmediated and therefore enslaving and terrifying relation with the Other. All spontaneous attempts at recovery in the psychoses and autism, delusional or otherwise, tend to establish a distance in relation to the Other. The absence of the object a means that *jouissance* is not localized and permanently threatens with invading the subject: for the psychotic, sexual activity is actually or at least potentially traumatic. In psychosis, as *jouissance* is literally the Other's *jouissance*, it invades the subject and becomes a compulsory and compulsive torment for him.

In paranoia and schizophrenia, the Other occupies the position of an absolute Other, and the subject, recognizing a lack in the Other but an unsymbolized one, attempts to complete the Other, since the Other's lack is unbearable, experienced as the destruction of the Other. This completion is achieved by the subject becoming the object of the Other's *jouissance*, the plaything of the Other. The case of Schreber is, in this sense, and once more, paradigmatic. Robert, the Wolf Child, treated by Rosine Lefort in the early 1950s, shows a mode of relationship with the Other identical to Schreber's (Lefort and Lefort 1990).

In paranoia, the delusional production is an attempt to stabilize the disarray of the world produced by the invasion of the Other's *jouissance*, whereas in schizophrenia the location of the disarray is the subject's body, that is to say, the imaginary representation of the body. In paranoia, the subject is at the mercy of the Other's engulfment. In schizophrenia, the subject is at the mercy of the Other's fragmentation as experienced in the body itself.

In autism, on the other hand, the Other is absolute but does not present a separable object, an object that could be extracted from the Other. Rosine and Robert Lefort are of the view that the autistic child tries desperately to produce a separable object in the Other, and therefore his position *vis-à-vis* the Other is the opposite of that of the paranoiac: instead of trying to complete and unify the Other (as in paranoia), the autistic subject tries to divide or de-complete the Other, so that the object can be produced. This would explain the particular quality of the destructive behaviour of autistic children, which usually involves making holes, cutting and scratching, which the Leforts interpret as the attempts to obtain a real lack in the Other – real, and not symbolic, due to the failure of the symbolic instruments.

By attempting to create a lack, the autistic subject attempts to create desire in the Other, which is the condition for the emergence of the subject's own desire. In autism, the Leforts argue, the Other is reduced to an absence; the Other is present, but in the paradoxical form of an absence: the Other is murdered (Lefort and Lefort, 1992, 1994).

In melancholia there would be an identification of the subject with the lack in the Other as such: not the lack that creates desire, but the lack of lack – the identification with a pure emptiness, the absence of desire in the Other. This could also be understood as a particular moment in a paranoiac structure, characterized by a failure of the imaginarization of the a. The specificity of melancholia as a structure is thus open to further research.

The question of the specificity of autism

Is autism a separate structure, different from psychosis, although structurally produced by the foreclosure of the Name-of-the-Father, or is it a variation and the earliest form of schizophrenia? Both positions have supporters in the Freudian field.

Another question, related to the first, on which there is no consensus, and which has generated research and animated discussions, is that of the existence of a 'progression' of autism (at least in some cases) towards a paranoiac-like position. Rosine and Robert Lefort are in favour of separating autism from the psychoses, for the reasons outlined above, which stress the differences in the ways the autistic subject and the psychotic subject relate with the Other.

The Leforts emphasize observable clinical differences between the two categories, and other authors have pointed out clinical features in autism that could be used to stress the distinction with respect to the psychoses.

Colette Soler has pointed out four features of autism which have been generally accepted in the clinic.

1. A persecution emanating from the Other, especially through the voice and the gaze.
2. Consistent attempts at the annihilation of the Other (by not talking, looking at or doing anything with the Other).
3. The dimension of appeal from and to the Other is virtually or completely absent in the autistic subject: the autistic child does not demand, or his demands are minimal.
4. There appear in autistic children difficulties with separation – not in the Lacanian, but in the concrete sense of the term (Soler, 1990, pp. 16–18).

Are these traits, and others that can be enumerated, sufficient to justify the affirmation of a separate structure?

Pierre Bruno and others consider autism as a form of schizo-phrenia. They emphasize the failure of the imaginary register and the representation of the body in autism, and consider it to be structurally identical to what has been described in schizophrenia (Bruno *et al.*, 1992).

Bruno accepts that autism can be differentiated from paranoia, but not from schizophrenia. He refers to a remark made by Lacan in his Geneva lecture on the symptom, in which Lacan refers to 'something frozen' in the relation that both the schizophrenic and the autistic subject have with language (Lacan, 1975, p. 20).

Autism would be the earliest form of schizophrenia. As in schizo-phrenia, the operation of alienation becomes disturbed as a result of the failure of separation. The subject is inscribed in language, but is not addressed by the Other. The status of the speech of the schizophrenic and the autistic subjects would be:

$$\frac{\text{'It speaks about him' (signifier)}}{\text{'He apprehends himself there' (signified)}}$$

Pierre Bruno expresses it eloquently:

> What will become of him [the autistic or schizophrenic subject] if 'it speaks of him' without ever 'addressing to him', that is to say, without a demand being addressed to the subject, thus extracting the subject from the anonymity of language in order to transform him in a being of speech?
>
> In order to become an object of the maternal desire, a demand addressed to the subject himself is indispensable, not just a 'speaking about him' in the third person. (Bruno *et al.*, 1992, p. 293)

Colette Soler remarks that the autistic subject remains a pure signified of the Other; he does not enunciate: he is not a subject of the enunciation (Soler, 1990, p.18).

The question of the specificity of autism and its autonomy as a separate structure remains, therefore, an open one.

Strategy of the transference

Outside the Freudian field, the analysts who have experience in the treatment of autism (such as M. Mahler, F. Tustin, D. Meltzer) have considered that the analyst comes to occupy the place of the primordial Other, the mother, and therefore there is a tendency towards the incorporation of this Other in the delusions (in paranoia) as a persecutor, or towards its being absent, with sporadic persecutory irruptions (in autism). The identification of the analyst with a maternal position is not favoured by the Lacanian orientation.

By occupying the position of the semblant of the object *a*, which is the place of a lack, the analyst opens the possibility of becoming an object cause of desire for the patient. Consequently, the analyst's interventions tend to be minimal.

Especially in the case of autism, one must bear in mind that any initiative coming from the Other is experienced as invading and intrusive. Speech itself becomes persecutory, due to the failure in the transmutation of the real into the signifier: the signifier itself acquires the weight of the real. It is therefore better to wait until the patient initiates.

This, undoubtedly, requires patience in the analyst. Sooner or later, the patient takes the initiative. Psychotic and autistic children who are at the very limits of what constitutes analytic transference, nevertheless make progress in analysis.

Rosine Lefort is in favour of the analyst adopting a position of deliberate passivity: a secretary and an object for the child. In her view, the analyst should never say 'no' to a psychotic or autistic child, since that 'no' has the effect of making the child feel that s/he is being annihilated.

See also: **alienation, body, discourse, foreclosure, ideal ego, mirror stage, Name-of-the-Father, object a, phallus, psychosis, schema, separation**

References

American Psychiatric Association (1994) *Diagnostic and Statistical Manual of Mental Disorders, Fourth edition (DSM-IV)*. Washington, DC.

Benveniste, E. (1971) *Problems in General Linguistics*. Miami: University of Miami Press.

Bruno, P. *et al*. (1992) *L'autisme et la psychanalyse*. Toulouse: Presses Universitaires du Mirail.

Ducrot, O. and Todorov, T. (1979) *Encyclopedic Dictionary of the Sciences of Language*. Baltimore: Johns Hopkins University Press.

Freud, S. (1958) [1911] 'Psycho-analytic notes on an autobiographical account of a case of paranoia (Dementia paranoides)'. *Standard Edition of the Complete Psychological Works of Sigmund Freud*. Vol. 12. London: Hogarth Press.

Kanner, L. (1973) [1943] 'Autistic disturbances of affective contact', *Nervous child* 2: 217–50; republished in Kanner, L., *Childhood psychosis: initial studies and new insights*. Washington DC: Winston and Sons.

Klein, M. (1975) [1930] 'The importance of symbol-formation in the development of the ego', *The Writings of Melanie Klein* 1: 219–32. London: Hogarth Press and Institute of Psycho-Analysis.

Lacan, J. (1964) *The Four Fundamental Concepts of Psycho-Analysis* (trans. A. Sheridan). London: Tavistock.

Lacan, J. (1972) [1968] 'Discours de clôture des journées sur les psychoses chez l'enfant'. *Recherches*: Paris, republished in *Enfance aliénée*, coll. 10/18, Paris: UGE.

Lacan, J. (1975) *R.S.I., Séminaire XXII (1974–75), Ornicar?* Nos 2, 3, 4, 1975; No. 5, 1975–76 [Provisional transcription].

Lacan, J. (1975) [1932] *De la Psychose paranoïaque dans ses rapports avec la personalité.* Paris: Seuil.

Lacan, J. (1976) *Le Sinthome, Séminaire XXIII (1975–76), Ornicar?* Nos 6, 7, 8, 1976; Nos 9, 10, 11, 1977 [Provisional transcription].

Lacan, J. (1977) [1959] 'On a question preliminary to any possible treatment of psychosis', in *Écrits: A Selection* (trans. A. Sheridan). London: Tavistock.

Lacan, J. (1977) 'Ouverture de la section clinique', *Ornicar?* 9: 12–14.

Lacan, J. (1984) [1938] 'La famille', in *Encyclopédie française*, vols 8, 40 (3–16) and 42 (1–8). Paris: Monzie; republished as *Les complexes familiaux dans la formation de l'individu.* Paris: Navarin.

Lacan, J. (1988) *The Seminar, Book I, Freud's Papers on Technique, 1953–1954.* Cambridge: Cambridge University Press.

Lacan, J. (1989) [1975] 'Geneva lecture on the symptom', *Analysis* 1: 7–26. Melbourne: Centre for Psychoanalytic Research.

Lacan, J. (1990) [1969] 'Note on the child', *Analysis* 2: 7–8. Melbourne: Centre for Psychoanalytic Research.

Lacan, J. (1991) *Le Séminaire, Livre XVII, L'envers de la psychanalyse, 1969–1970.* Paris: Seuil.

Lacan, J. (1993) *The seminar of Jacques Lacan Book III The psychoses, 1955–1956,* (translated with notes by Russell Grigg). London: W.W. Norton.

Lacan, J. (1995) [1964] 'Position of the unconscious', in R. Feldstein, B. Fink and M. Jaanus, eds, *Reading Seminar XI*. Albany: State University of New York Press.

Lefort, R. and Lefort, R. (1988) *Les structures de la psychose: L'Enfant au loup et le président.* Paris: Seuil.

Lefort, R. and Lefort, R. (1990) [1983] 'The first three sessions of the treatment of the wolf child', *Analysis* 2: 9–19. Melbourne: Centre for Psychoanalytic Research.

Lefort, R. and Lefort, R. (1992) 'Autisme et psychose. Deux signifi-
ants: "partie" et "cassé"', in Bruno, P., *L'autisme et la psychanalyse*.
Toulouse: Presses Universitaires du Mirail.

Lefort, R. and Lefort, R. (1994) [1980] *Birth of the Other*. Urbana:
University of Illinois Press.

Soler, C. (1990) 'Hors discours: autisme et paranoia', *Les feuillets
psychanalytiques du Courtil* 2: 9–24, Leers Nord.

Stevens, A. (1987) 'L'holophrase', *Ornicar?* 42.

Leonardo S. Rodriguez

Body

Both Lacan and Freud contributed little to knowledge of the body as biological entity, or to the biological or physiological functioning of the human body. However, this does not mean that the body is absent in both Freud's and Lacan's writings and teachings. On the contrary, Freud's early texts on hysteria already show that Freud was interested in the hysteric's relation to the body and to the bodily parts, as presented in the hysterical conversion symptom.

The notion of the body, when it appears in Lacan's texts and teachings, is not that of the biological body, referring to the organic substratum and to the living organism. Lacan's contribution to this subject is, rather, situated on the level of the human body as psychic reality which is constructed and constituted, and which is a function of man's capacity to acknowledge his own mortality and of his being subject to death.

According to Lacan, the living organism is not sufficient to construct a body. A person is not born with a body as such, the body is not a pre-established reality. The reality of the body can rather be characterized as *hors corps*, because the body is alien to the subject and alienating of the subject. This general proposition can be considered as a guiding principle throughout Lacan's work. Strictly speaking, the notion of the body cannot be coined a Lacanian concept, but the regular references to the 'body' trace certain developments in Lacan's thinking on the constitution of the subject. In the course of this evolution, at least four different elements and/or aspects of man's relation to the body are elaborated: the image, the trait, the signifier and *jouissance*.

In Lacan's early texts, that is until the mid-1950s, the imaginary register predominates and the image's formative function for the subject is in the foreground. The major reference to this formative function of the image is the so-called mirror phase that manifests 'the affective dynamism by which the subject originally identifies himself with the visual Gestalt of his own body: in relation to the still very profound lack of coordination of his own motility, it represents an ideal unity, a salutary imago' (*Écrits*, Lacan, 1977).

This experience of identification with the image of the body goes beyond the experience of an infant that recognizes its image in a mirror as being its own. This experience is rather of anecdotal significance to the first structuring moment of the subject, being the identification with a visual Gestalt. The use of the term Gestalt stresses the element of unification, of identification with a total unity, bridging the gap of man's biological prematurity, the anatomical incompleteness of the newborn infant, characterized as a state of fragmentation.

In this respect, Lacan refers to animal ethology – the structure of the animal world – and to the notion of the Gestalt, but he foremost invokes Freud's elaboration of narcissism, structuring all of man's relations with the external world. Indeed, in Lacan's reading, the image of the body is the principle of every unity perceived in objects. This unity or totality is perceived from the outside and in an anticipated manner, meaning that it is external and thus alien to the subject, and that the ideal of total unity which testifies to the fundamental human dynamics of mastery, is in fact unattainable; it can be anticipated but never realized.

Thus the image or rather the Gestalt introduces some form of mastery, but this mastery is illusory. Moreover, the identification with the Gestalt installs a radical alienation: the subject has no direct access to the body; its only access is through the image of the (idealized) other; hence the notation i(a) – *image de l'autre*.

Lacan's reference to Freudian narcissism enables him to understand the relation between the structure of the animal world and that of the human world – the formative function of the image for humans – and links the assumption of the reflected image – the image of the body – to the development of the ego. More particularly, Lacan speaks of a symbolic matrix in which the I is precipitated in a primordial form, 'before it is objectified in the dialectic of identification with the other' (*Écrits*, 1977).

Within this context, the notion of the imago is often referred to by Lacan. The imagos, for instance the imago of one's own body and the imago of the fragmented body, can be characterized as original imaginary matrices.

From the mid-1950s onwards, Lacan shifts his attention from the function of the imaginary to the function of language and of the symbolic in the constitution of the subject. (For example, 'The function and field of speech and language in psychoanalysis', 1953; and 'The agency of the letter in the unconscious or reason since Freud', 1957, both published in *Écrits*, 1977). This shift, which is clearly influenced by the work of Claude Lévi-Strauss, reflects itself in Lacan's considerations on the body.

It would however be wrong to state that the function of the symbolic in the subject's relation to the body is only introduced at this later stage. Already in his earliest descriptions of the experience of the mirror stage – the mirror phase was continuously re-elaborated and revised – Lacan mentions the presence of a symbolic element.

By means of this third, symbolic party – the artificial or human support materialized in one of the parents holding the child – the child is able to recognize and assume the reflected image of his/her own body. This third party introduces the position and the role of the Other (of language) in the constitution of the subject. The Other's speech, or his/her gaze, points out to the child 'what it is'. This 'You are this' allows the child to recognize itself in the desire of the Other. The child hence reflects itself in the Other in such a way as to make itself an object of desire, a desirable object. Essential for the child to recognize itself in the Other and thus for the image of the body to be authenticated by the Other is the symbolic trait, I. This *trait unaire* is taken from the Other and represents for the child the Other's obscure desire. The introjection of this trait – I(A) – enables the subject to recognize itself as a unity in the desire of the Other, and marked by this trait the child becomes desirable for the Other. To put it differently, the unary trait makes it possible to recognize oneself as desirable for the Other.

In this sense, a trait that marks the body through inscription (a tattoo, for instance), eroticizes the body and turns the body into an erotic object.

In his Rome Report (1953) Lacan posits that language is the condition for the realization of the subject. Furthermore, he writes that 'speech is in fact a gift of language, and language is not immaterial. It is a subtle body, but body it is' (*Écrits*). Lacan will gradually develop the idea that language is the first body, is the first symbolic corpus. Every other corpus or body is considered secondary to this. In this sense, the symbolic, and more particularly the signifier, takes over the role of the imaginary, more precisely the imago or

Gestalt, in transforming the organism into a body. The signifier introduces the one – *le un* – and introduces the body in its spoken dimension.

It is important to add that Lacan does not consider the symbolic or language as a super-structure or as an abstraction, but rather as a reality which pre-exists the subject and determines the reality of the subject as a spoken reality.

In his 1970 article 'Radiophonie', Lacan speaks at length of the body as spoken reality. The symbolic is presented as the first corpus, making the organism a body, a support for the being. The first corpus produces the second by incorporating itself in it. This means that for Lacan language seizes the organism and affects it. The effects of this incorporation are the subject divided by language, and the spoken body, or else a subject disjointed from his body. In this sense the organism, which is considered here as a unity, is cut up by language as the body of the signifier(s).

From all this, the following points can be deduced:

- one has a body by grace of the signifier; the body would not exist if we were not able to speak (of) it
- the body appears as an outstanding place of inscription for the signifier, which, as we saw earlier, has an eroticizing effect
- the body does not belong to the subject; the body as spoken is attributed by the Other of language and is thus alien to the subject
- like the image or imago of one's own body, the spoken body is essentially *hors corps*.

A fourth element of development in Lacan's conceptualization of the body is also connected with the operation of the signifier, but concerns the notion of *jouissance*, as linked to the dimension of the real. The signifier affects the organism by introducing the body as a spoken body, but also affects the body's *jouissance*. The concepts of *jouissance*, *plus-de-jouir* and the localization of *jouissance* are developed in Séminaire XVII, *L'envers de la psychanalyse*, Séminaire XX, *Encore* and 'Radiophonie'. In 'Radiophonie', Lacan speaks of a certain *dépens* or cost; the living organism enters language at the cost of *jouissance*. In this sense, the signifier empties the body of *jouissance*, transforming the body into what Lacan calls a desert of *jouissance*. This means that *jouissance* can also be characterized as *hors corps*.

The rest of *jouissance* that is linked to the signifier and is marked by the signifier, is redistributed. More particularly, it is located on the anatomic rims of the body, the so-called erogenous zones, and their respective objects, which are also *hors corps*. This introduces the dimension of the object a and of *plus-de-jouir* – referring both to what is lost and what is gained of *jouissance*. The object a is materialized in the partial objects of the breast, the faeces, the voice and the gaze, which are 'parts of the body', cut from the body, through the operation of the signifier.

See also: **imaginary, jouissance, mirror stage, object a, symbolic.**

References

Lacan, J. (1970) 'Radiophonie', *Scilicet*, 2(3), pp. 55–98.

Lacan, J. (1975) [1972–73] Le Séminaire, Livre XX: *Encore* (ed. J. A. Miller). Paris: Seuil.

Lacan, J. (1977) [1949] 'The mirror stage as formative of the function of the I'. *Écrits: A Selection* (trans. A. Sheridan). London; Tavistock.

Lacan, J. (1991) [1969–70] Le Séminaire, Livre XVII, *L'envers de la psychanalyse*. Paris: Seuil.

Katrien Libbrecht

Borromean Knot

The Borromean knot, a figure developed and reformulated at different moments of theorizing, allows Lacan to conceptualize and illustrate that the registers the Imaginary, the Symbolic and the Real are linked, but interdependently so. That is, the registers are linked conceptually in such a way, that if one is interrupted, undone or collapses, all three are affected. The structure of the knot implies as well that the three terms are not hierarchically arranged, therefore one register does not assume a priority over the other, 'there is no privileged point and the chain is strictly homogenous' (Lacan, 1998, p. 130).

The Borromean knot can be seen as an instance of a topological structure, one of many that Lacan began to use in his theorizing which was to become increasingly influenced by formal logic and mathematical formalization.

His interest in a discourse between analytic theory and mathematics can be detected in relatively early work from the mid to late 1940s, through the 1950s where the elaboration of formulas and mathemes was becoming evident, to the conception of topological figures. The Borromean knot, framed in the early 1970s, but discussed first in Seminar XIX (... *Or Worse*) in 1972, is one such figure (see Marini, 1992). This is perhaps the one most invested with changing theoretical formulations and controversy, the latter concerning its dubious mathematical status, and its purported non-theorizability. Notwithstanding, the Borromean knot assumes its ultimate theoretical significance when, by way of a further and later refinement, a fourth knot is introduced, and conceptualized as the symptom, or *sinthome*.

However, these developments occurred not only within a broader shift in Lacan's thought (e.g., in the notion of the subject, and the shift from many of his terms from the symbolic to the real (Fink, 1995, p. 123)), but to his increasing commitment to the place of logic and mathematization in his discourse (Marini, 1992, p. 68). (Marini also refers the reader to the work by Nathalie Chaurraud for a more specific elaboration of Lacan's topological theorization.) The fact, however, that Lacan attempted to theoretically ground the subject, the unconscious, sexual difference and other psychoanalytic concepts mathematically and topologically, generated considerable debate and controversy before the introduction of the Borromean knot, the identity of which was introduced to him by a mathematician. (The Borromean knot represents the heraldic crest of the sixteenth-century Milanese Borromeo family, and consists of three interlinking circles that represent three alliances (Roudinesco, 1997, p. 363)). Nevertheless, his theoretical perseverance that saw the development of a new terminology, a new discourse based on symbolic logic and structural models – *mathèmes* and *topological models* – emerged as a discourse able to access the impossibility of language – the Real, rather than one necessarily meant to deal effectively with the question of whether or not psychoanalysis can be quantified. This theoretical recasting, albeit a 'theoretical experimentation with limits', as Roudinesco points out, opened up the way for a re-conceptualization of familiar theoretical notions, but precisely within a mathemic conceptualization (1997, p. 359). Indeed, the invocation of topological structures, Fink argues, gives us the possibility of seeing beyond the symbolic in ways that other discourses, notably philosophy, may not (1995, p. 123). Perhaps therefore, despite the controversy, Lacan's dedication to a mathemic formulation may be regarded as considerable theoretical moment and vindication; furthermore, Lacan did point out that all truth is mathematizable.

There have been other reasons cited for the establishment of new metaphors to ground theoretical discourses beyond the fact that algebraic formulations have substantial heuristic value. These relate to the acknowledgement that surfaces or threads can be linked, but if one is cut or loosened, the others experience a similar fate. Hence we confront a situation of some impossibility, of some uncertainty and contradiction. Perhaps we are even confronted with the conception of the uncanny – Freud's *Unheimlich* – the essence of which gives us a clue to the basic project of psychoanalysis in much the same way that topological structures may, precisely because they 'leave some sort of substance in abeyance' (Lacan, 1998, p. 128). Lacan's response to the question posed by Francois Wahl of whether or not topology is a method of discovery or of exposition, maps clearly his theoretical conviction (Wahl in

Lacan, 1981). 'It is the mapping of the topology proper to our experience as analysts, which may later be taken in a metaphysical
perspective' (Lacan, 1981, p. 90). His appeal to topology became
more evident as he became preoccupied with the Real (for a close
reading of this register refer to the entry Real), recognizing that new
ways of understanding it were possible through the use of topological models. His seminar of 1972–73, Seminar XX, *Encore* (Lacan,
1998) takes up the notion of the Borromean knot but he develops
it further, so that in Seminar XXII, *R.S.I.* (1974–75), it assumes a
central focus. In this seminar the Real is given theoretical primacy
and the Borromean knot provides an illustration of Lacan's attempt
to order mathematically the dimensions of the knot of human
experience – the Imaginary, the Symbolic and the Real. Each ring of
the knot, so called, represents one of these orders. In this seminar
Lacan insisted that the theory of the knots 'is still in its infancy';
however, he did assert that 'speaking beings are mis-situated
between two and three dimensions' (Marini, 1992, p. 242).
Topology was becoming more important as a way of dealing theoretically with the impossibility of the Real:

> The knot, the torus, the fibre, connections, compactness, all the
> forms through which space is a rift or an accumulation, are
> meant here to provide the analyst with what he lacks, that is, a
> support other than metaphorical, in order to sustain metonymy
> with it. (Lacan, cited in Marini, 1992, p. 243)

Seminar XXIII (1975–76), *Le Sinthome* – the seminar on James Joyce
– revises the figure of the Borromean knot; now it can be seen as a
four-term figure with the additional loop, the symptom, the 'heart'
of the figure tying all the rings together. Lacan identified this fourth
loop as that which prevents the other loops from unravelling,
which he claimed is what occurs with psychosis. In the case of
Joyce, writing was the *sinthome* that held together the Real, the
Symbolic and the Imaginary. It was used by Joyce to 'the point of
reaching his Real' (Lacan, cited in Marini, 1992, p. 244). This is the
presence of paternal deficiency, thus the theoretical query raised by
Nathalie Charraud in her entry Mathème is worth contemplating
in terms of the question of the real of the symptom being equivalent to the father.

A major property of the Borromean knot that identifies the core of Lacan's thought at this time could be the names of the Father under the forms of the Imaginary, the Symbolic and the Real, 'because it is these names that the knot fits' and without it everything falls apart (Marini, 1992, p. 75). So what is at stake for Lacan in the conceptualization of the Borromean knot is the attainment of mathematical formalization, 'mathematization alone reaches a real ... The real, I will say, is the mystery of the speaking body, the mystery of the unconscious' (1998, p. 131).

The Borromean knot Lacan argued 'is the best metaphor of the fact that we proceed only on the basis of the One' (Lacan, 1998, p. 128).

The Borromean knot, emblematic of a Milanese dynasty, but in its Lacanian formulation some centuries later, is more than a structural representation of three alliances. Its continuing theoretical elaboration saw that alliance reconceptualized by a fourth term. The fourth term, the *sinthome*, an aspect of the knot but beyond it, beyond the symbolic and beyond metaphor, is the support of the subject in his or her own way of relating to *jouissance*; this is Lacan's creation.

See also: **jouissance**, **mathème**, **real**, **symptom**

References

Fink, B. (1995) *The Lacanian Subject*. New Jersey: Princeton University Press.

Lacan, J. (1981) *The Four Fundamental Concepts of Psycho-Analysis* (ed. J.-A. Miller, trans. A. Sheridan). New York: W.W. Norton.

Lacan, J. (1998) [1975] *The Seminar, Book XX, Encore 1972–1973, On Feminine Sexuality, The Limits of Love and Knowledge* (ed. J.-A. Miller, trans. B. Fink). New York: W.W. Norton.

Marini, M. (1992) *Jacques Lacan: The French Context* (trans. A. Tomiche). New Jersey: Rutgers University Press.

Roudinesco, E. (1997) *Jacques Lacan* (trans. B. Bray). Cambridge: Polity Press.

Zita M. Marks

Castration

Castration is referred to throughout the work of Freud and Lacan. Although it undergoes certain referential changes, castration retains its place as a necessary element in the structuring of sexuality for the speaking being.

The notion of castration in Freud's work

In all of his discussions on sexuality, Freud emphasizes castration. What Freud learned from his clinical practice is that sexuality always involves a dimension of the impossibility of reaching total satisfaction. In order to achieve some satisfaction it is necessary to renounce total satisfaction and this renunciation is one of the references to castration, where castration is a condition for satisfaction.

Definition

Castration refers to the movement of separation installed by the Oedipal law between mother and infant and is thus a requirement of culture; it is the positive side of the prohibition of incest. Freud emphasizes that instinctual renunciation is necessary for all cultural achievement, associating it with the Oedipus complex and its resolution.

Freud (1951) first used the term castration complex in 1908 in reference to an infantile theory of sexuality adopted by children to explain the difference between the sexes. Freud emphasizes the phallocentrism of children, who, assuming the possession of a penis in all living creatures, attribute the lack of it to a castration. This very attribution of a lack is the result of a fantasy of a castration in relation to which the boy will experience castration anxiety and which will contribute to an experience of disillusionment in the girl.

Freud's argument in the case of the boy is that his wish to take his mother as his sexual partner is given up due to the threat from the father that he will lose his penis – that instrument of erotic sensations – if he carries out his wishes. The narcissistic investment in the penis leads the boy to a renunciation of the mother as his sexual partner, and to wait for a time when he can take another woman as his partner.

The actual effect of castration takes place for the boy following the perception of the female genitals and the acknowledgement that the organ in which he has invested such value, and which is so essential to his self-image, is not present on the body of the girl. At this structuring moment the boy remembers the threats made concerning his masturbatory habits which at an earlier moment had little effect.

This deferred action now comes into effect with the fear of castration, a powerful influence in all his subsequent development. Interestingly, the effects of castration can be experienced without it being carried out and expressly formulated. This indicates the Freudian thesis of the structuring function of the Oedipus complex.

The girl's castration complex is also started by the sight of the boy's genital. She notices the significance placed on it and resulting from this perception is a feeling of having been wronged. The subsequent 'envy for the penis' leaves a permanent trace on the girl's psyche, persisting in the unconscious. Freud argues that in the case of women the castration complex does not work so well. There is something problematic in woman's relation to castration and to the Oedipal law, due to the girl only partially being able to resolve her Oedipus complex. This is because she is not as vulnerable to the threat of losing a penis that she does not have. The girl's vulnerability shows itself in an anxiety related to the loss of love.

The castration complex is central for Freud. He argues that it is the necessary structural foundation from which a subject can take part in the world of sexual desire. It is only from a position of renunciation of the incestuous object that it is possible to go out into the world and seek a partner other than the incestuous one. The prohibition of the primordial object, the mother or whomever comes to her place, produces a lack which will orient a subject to look elsewhere. In this way desire is inaugurated.

The castration threat and the Oedipal law, which articulates a prohibition and a prescription, both give an orientation to the child. Without it, the child is stuck within a world of incestuous objects and a constant fear of actual loss.

In 1923 Freud (1951) introduced the primacy of the phallus. Although the boy and the girl initially share the same object – the mother and a 'masculine' or phallic sexuality – Freud argues an asymmetry between the sexes. The castration complex and the Oedipus complex work differently for the boy and the girl. The Oedipus complex in the boy illustrates the separating function of the law of the father and its conversion in the super-ego.

The function of the castration complex is to end the boy's Oedipus complex. For the girl, the castration complex inaugurates her into an Oedipus complex which will succumb to repression. She will transfer her love to the one who seems to have the phallus, the father or substitute. The girl will desire to have the phallus in the form of a baby along the lines of the symbolic equation that will make the phallus equal a baby.

In 1933 Freud elaborated three possible outcomes of the castration complex for women. The first is a total repudiation of sexuality, the second is the adopting of a masculine position and the repudiation of penis envy and the third solution is that of motherhood as a treatment of penis envy through the symbolic equation of penis equals child.

The asymmetrical situations of the boy and the girl were what Freud (1951) returned to when he wrote in 1937 of the limits of an analytic treatment. The man will forever fear castration and the woman will forever endure envy of the penis, the castration complex contributing to a basic rejection of femininity for both sexes.

As Freud increasingly placed the castration complex at the centre of his theoretical and clinical writings, there developed resistance in the analytic world, particularly in the debates of the 1920s and 1930s on female sexuality. For a number of analysts the castration complex did not have the major structuring role in the construction of sexual difference and they turned rather to biological and developmental theorization.

Freud's very last paper in 1938 referred to the castration complex and its effects on the very construction of the subject. It illustrates clinically that the ego, in a moment of encounter with the threat of a loss, undergoes a split which is insistently maintained. As a reaction to the castration complex a fetish is constructed, confirming that the object is lost and the subject is split (1951).

Castration in the work of Lacan

Early on in his writings, in the 1930s, Lacan viewed castration as a fantasy of the mutilation of the penis, linking it with a series of fantasies of bodily mutilations which begin with the image of the fragmented body.

It is in the 1950s that the function of castration is discussed in reference to the Name-of-the-Father and the paternal law which forbids the mother and the child the satisfaction of being the sole desire of each other. The paternal law installs the phallus as signifier of a lack which refers mother and child to the dimension of the symbolic. The mother does not have the phallus and therefore desires it elsewhere. Thus castration orients the child and the mother beyond each other.

In his seminar of 1956–57, Lacan (1994) delineates the difference between privation, frustration and castration in relation to the symbolic, imaginary and real. Lacan emphasizes that it is not possible to articulate anything about castration without this distinction. He claims that it is the confusion of castration with privation and frustration that has led a number of psychoanalysts to founder in their theoretical and clinical orientation. He singles out Ernest Jones who substitutes for castration his concept of aphanisis, disappearance of desire, as an example of an analyst unable to surmount the difficulties of managing the castration complex.

It is also in this seminar that Lacan elaborates the relation between castration and the phallus. Lacan attributes to Freud the introduction of the phallus as a third imaginary term between the mother and the child. The phallus thus has a major signifying role.

Freud insists that in the world of objects the function of the phallus is decisive. Here Lacan will use the term imaginary phallus which is not to be confounded with the real penis. The lack referred to in woman is not, after all, a real lack. In the Freudian thesis the woman counts the phallus among her lacking objects and this brings her child into an exact connection with her relation to the phallus, because a child can come to stand in for and calm her longing for the phallus.

Based on the premise that the object is lacking, Lacan points to three different ways in which it can lack:

1. In **frustration** the lack is imaginary and the subjective experience is that of a damage most typically attributed to the time of weaning and loss of the breast. While the lack is imaginary, the object, such as the breast, is real. Lacan is not referring here to any actual experience. The agent of the frustration is the mother, at the level of the symbolic.

2. **Privation** refers to a real lack due to the loss of a symbolic object, the phallus as signifier. It especially refers to the fact that the woman does not have a penis and the assumption of this fact is a constant in nearly all of the accounts of Freud's cases. The notion of privation implies the symbolization of the object in the Real, because in the Real nothing is missing. The absence of something in the Real can only be purely symbolic. To indicate that something is not there, requires a supposition that it is possible for it to be present. This introduces the elementary symbolic order into the Real. The agent of privation is the imaginary father.

3. **Castration** is the symbolic lack of an imaginary object. It is essentially tied to the symbolic order and to the central position given by the Oedipus complex. It refers to the symbolic debt in the register of the law. The clinic provides evidence that castration refers to the loss of the phallus as imaginary object. The agent of castration is the real father.

Agent	Object Lack	Object
Real father	Castration **Symbolic debt**	Imaginary (= phallus)
Symbolic mother	Frustration **Imaginary injury**	Real (= breast, penis)
Imaginary father	Privation **Real hole**	Symbolic (= phallus, child)

In 1958, Lacan refers to the unconscious castration complex as having the function of a knot in the structuring of symptoms and as 'the regulator of development' through 'installing in the subject an unconscious position without which he would be unable to identify with the ideal type of his sex, or to respond without grave risk to the needs of his partner in the sexual relation, or even to receive adequately the needs of the child thus procreated' (*Écrits*, 1977, p. 281).

It is in this 1958 paper that Lacan orients the questions which emerge from the clinic back to their origins in Freud. This reorientation of Lacan is due to the fact that by the 1950s many analysts had moved away from any reference to the castration complex, which was so central to the Freudian clinic.

However, from 1958 Lacan diverges from Freud and views castration as a function of the order of the signifier in its connection with the cultural law that imposes the sacrifice of *jouissance*, rather than as a purely psychical phenomenon referring to fantasy or fear. Here, castration refers to the universal effect of language, which by necessity requires a giving up of *jouissance*. This is due to the human being having to use the signifier in speech which can never match the thing exactly, thus necessitating a loss of the complete *jouissance* of the Other. This is the operation of symbolic castration. Language separates the subject from the immediate *jouissance* of the body of the Other.

Although we can say that Lacan diverges from Freud, and that he considers that Freud fails to make a distinction between imaginary and symbolic castration, he in fact never loses the reference to the relation of castration to the phallus. The sexuality of desire and *jouissance*, which is both cause and consequence of the Oedipus complex and the paternal metaphor, is the relationship between the phallus and castration, where the phallus is the signifier of castration, in the very act of saying 'no' and by virtue of the fact that the phallus can be used as a reference for the subject's desire following the structuring operation of symbolic castration.

It is in 1975 that Lacan (1998) breaks from the Oedipus complex as myth and develops a logification of sexual difference based on the different relationship of man and woman to the signifier. Here the phallic function refers to a castration brought about by the use of signifiers.

Where for Freud, the castrated one is the woman, for Lacan it is the man who is castrated, in so far as he is completely subjected to the signifier which says 'no' to complete satisfaction. The boy is totally subjected to the law and thus to symbolic castration. It is only at the imaginary level that he appears not to be castrated in his possession of a penis. The only exception to this rule that all men are castrated is that of the father of the primal horde. In its connection with the incest taboo, the effect of castration is to divide women into those who are accessible and those who are not.

The only one who has not succumbed to castration is Freud's mythical primal horde father who considers himself as being able to have access to all women including those to whom he is related. This uncastrated exception confirms the rule of castration following the logic that every rule requires at least one exception.

It is the woman who is not-all-castrated in that not all of her is subject to the phallic law. This not-all-castrated leaves the way open for a supplementary form of *jouissance*, feminine *jouissance*, which may be experienced in addition to the phallic form of *jouissance*. Lacan's argument is that although there is no woman who is not subject to the phallic law, and thus castrated, not all of her is subjected to it.

Clinical application

In his 1937 paper, Freud (1951) discusses the bedrock of castration around which the analytic work so often founders. The neurotic protests against castration, the sacrifice to be made, retaining the demand for the phallus, the major focus of the whole imaginary play in the analysis of a subject. For a woman, penis envy and the demand to the analyst to compensate for her lack is ever present. For a man, the difficulty in subjecting himself to another man remains a constant concern in terms of his castration anxiety.

Lacan follows Freud in pointing to the rejection of castration as the fundamental problem at stake in all the psychopathological structures.

In neurosis, where the mechanism of defence is repression, *Verdrangung*, awareness of castration and the lack in the Other is repressed.

What the neurotic does not want, and what he strenuously refuses to do right up until the end of his analysis, is to sacrifice his castration to the Other's jouissance, allowing it to serve the Other. (*Écrits*, p. 323)

It is beneath his or her ego that the neurotic covers the castration that he or she denies yet clings to. The structure of fantasy, $\$\lozenge a$, contains within it the imaginary function of castration. This hidden function has an effect on one or other of the terms of the unconscious fantasy, for the hysteric, the object, and for the obsessional, the subject.

Instead of seeing the lack in the Other and correlatively in him- or herself, a recognition that is part and parcel of symbolic castration, the hysteric maintains desire only in the form of lack of satisfaction and eludes him- or herself as object. The obsessional denies the desire in the Other and emphasizes the impossibility of him- or herself disappearing as subject. In both cases there is an incomplete symbolic castration with castration being attributed to the demands from the Other for his or her castration rather than what is essentially required from a speaking being.

In the structure of perversion, disavowal (*Verleugnung*) is the form of defence which passes through castration and disavows it. The prototype of perversion is the fetishist who uses the fetish object as a substitute for the penis of the mother. Freud, in his article of 1927, illustrated how the perverse subject both recognizes the lack in the mother and disavows it via the construction and use of the fetish (1951).

In the structure of psychosis, castration is foreclosed and lack is neither accepted nor borne. Freud called it *Verwerfung*, repudiation. The place of lack is lacking and castration returns in the real as happens, for instance, in the case of hallucination.

Lacan tried to theorize beyond the bedrock of castration with his ideas on the end of analysis. With his notion of the crossing of the fundamental fantasy, the analysand has the possibility of separating from object a and encountering the point where the fantasy becomes the drive, a point of recognizing his or her own castration.

See also: **desire, imaginary, *jouissance*, knot, Name-of-the-Father, phallus, real, separation, sexuation, symbolic**
Key words: fantasy, frustration, fundamental fantasy, Oedipus complex, privation

References

Freud, S. (1951) [1908] 'On the Sexual Theories of Children' (vol. 11, p. 207) *Standard Edition, Complete Psychological Works*. London: Hogarth Press and Institute of Psycho-Analysis.

Freud, S. (1951) [1912–13] *Totem and Taboo*, *S.E.* vol. 13, p. 1.

Freud, S. (1951) [1923] 'The Infantile Genital Organization', *S.E.* vol. 19, p. 141.

Freud, S. (1951) [1924] 'The Dissolution of the Oedipus Complex', *S.E.* vol. 19, p. 173.

Freud, S. (1951) [1925] 'Some Psychical Consequences of the Anatomical Distinction between the Sexes', *S.E.* vol. 19, p. 243.

Freud, S. (1951) [1927] 'Fetishism', *S.E.* vol. 21, p. 149.

Freud, S. (1951) [1930] *Civilization and its Discontents*, *S.E.* vol. 21, p. 59.

Freud, S. (1951) [1931] 'Female Sexuality', *S.E.* vol. 21, p. 223.

Freud, S. (1951) [1933] 'Femininity', *S.E.* vol. 22, p. 112.

Freud, S. (1951) [1937] 'Analysis Terminable and Interminable', *S.E.* vol. 23, p. 3.

Freud, S. (1951) [1938] 'Splitting of the Ego in the Process of Defence', *S.E.* vol. 23, p. 273.

Lacan, J. (1984) [1938] *Les complexes familiaux dans la formation de l'individu. Essai d'analyse d'une fonction en psychologie*. Paris: Navarin, 1984.

Lacan, J. (1994) [1956–57] *Le Séminaire. Livre IV. La relation d'objet, 1956–57* (ed. J.-A. Miller). Paris: Seuil.

Lacan, J. (1977) [1958] 'The signification of the phallus', in *Écrits: A Selection*. London: Tavistock, pp. 281–91.

Lacan, J. (1977) [1960] 'The subversion of the subject and the dialectic of desire in the Freudian unconscious', in *Écrits: A Selection*. London: Tavistock, pp. 292–325.

Lacan, J. (1973) [1964] *The Seminar. Book XI. The Four Fundamental Concepts of Psychoanalysis* (trans. A. Sheridan). London: Hogarth Press and Institute of Psycho-Analysis.

Lacan, J. (1998) [1975]. *On Feminine Sexuality, The Limits of Love and Knowledge* (trans. B. Fink). New York, London: W.W. Norton.

Carmela Levy-Stokes

The Cut

This term first appeared in one of Jacques Lacan's seminars: 'Le désir et son interprétation' (1958–59). At the time, Lacan used it in a broad sense, linking it with splitting and signifying division, then he gradually reduced it to its topological value. Thus, because of its structure and effects, the cut became homologous to the analytical interpretation.

Contrary to the notion of foreclosure, and like most Freudian concepts in German, the cut (*coupure*) is not a commonly used word in French. It is indeed a noun derived from the verb to cut (*couper*). However, it is obvious that the verb conjures up two significant registers in psychoanalysis: discourse and speech on the one hand (to cut somebody short, to cut the cackle) and the threat of castration on the other (to cut them off).

The notion of cut, as Lacan defines it further in his teachings, proceeds as much from these two connotations as from the topological definition of cut.

There are at least four steps in this Lacanian development of the cut.

1. In 'Le désir et son interprétation' (1958–59), the first step in Lacan's construction of the cut is nothing other than the discrete and discontinuous characteristic of signification in diachrony, namely, that which is expressed differently in the definition of the subject of the unconscious – for instance, what a signifier represents for another signifier $S/S \rightarrow S/S \rightarrow S/S$.

Following the logic of this enunciation, Lacan argues that the ultimate point in the cross-examination of the subject about his desire, is the point where the 'primary guarantors' are the 'absent signifiers' $S(A/)$. It is to the cut that something in the signifying chain answers, and for the subject. It is the object which supplements the impossible significance of the subject in the desire of the Other by virtue of its structure of cut – as cut in the drive. **S cut of a** is the simplest way to read this primary fantasy.

The first step occurs on two levels: (i) the cut of the subject by the object, and (ii) the signifying cut of the object. What should be stressed, though, is that the cut foregrounds the discontinuous and successive character of a vectorialized chain, that is, what the signifier enforces when incarnated in the voice. The cut is here reduced to the gaps in between signifiers, which determines the temporal articulation inherent in diachrony.

2. In a second step, Lacan displaces the cut from the in-between-signifiers to what we call the inter-signifying, in so far as he identifies the cut with the bar which separates the signified from the signifier in the Saussurean algorithm S/s. In addition, the link to the doctrine of interpretation becomes more explicit and decisive. In 'The subversion of the subject and dialectic of desire in the Freudian unconscious' (1960), Lacan says:

> Lest the hunt be in vain for us analysts, we must bring everything back to the function of the cut in discourse, the strongest being that which acts as a bar between the signifier and the signified. There the subject that interests us is surprised, since by binding himself in signification he is placed under the sign of the pre-conscious. By which we would arrive at the paradox of conceiving that the discourse in an analytic session is valuable only in so far as it stumbles or is interrupted: if the session itself were not instituted as a cut in a false discourse, or rather, to the extent that the discourse succeeds in emptying itself as speech, in being no more than Mallarmé's worn coinage that is passed from hand to hand 'in silence'. (*Écrits*, 1977, p. 299)

This bringing 'everything back to the function of the cut' points to a kind of universal theory of the cut underpinned by the definition of the drive as cut. In the same seminar, he says:

> It [the drive] is that which proceeds from demand when the subject disappears in it. It is obvious enough that demand also disappears, with the single exception that the cut remains, for this cut remains present in that which distinguishes the drive from the organic function it inhabits: namely, its grammatical artifice, so manifest in the reversions of its articulation to both source and object ... (*Écrits*, 1977, p. 314)

3. From his seminar on identification (1960–61) onwards, Lacan increasingly focuses on the articulation between his logic of the signifier and the topology of surfaces, an articulation made possible by notions of combinatory associations and signifying chain, on the one hand, and the conception of the unconscious as depthless place and space, on the other. The cut is the concept which enables a differential classifying of surfaces in this topology, notably the definition of gender, i.e. the maximum number of sealed cuts one could effect on such a surface without causing it to split up.

In the register of topology, cuts generate surfaces. It should be stressed, however, that for Lacan there is a strict equivalence between the two: cuts are surfaces. Nothing exemplifies better this Lacanian conception than the Möbius strip with its longitudinal cut and its surprising effect used to define this surface topologically. Indeed, the cut along the strip does not separate two pieces cut off from each other, it describes the outline of the inner eight, and subverts the structure of the strip. There is one single piece left: it is twice as long and comprises four semi-torsions, but it now has one back and one front. It is a two-sided surface with two sides similar to a standard strip. The essential characteristics of the Möbius strip have disappeared. The disappearance of the Möbian structure effected by the cut allows a shift from the Möbius strip to its cut (without physically destroying the topological object). On the basis of this topological experiment, Lacan establishes, in 1972 in 'L'Étourdit', the parallel between interpretation and cut as topological subversion of the subject.

4. With Séminaire XX, *Encore*, Lacan reintroduces the paradigm R, S, I in his argument and shifts from the topology of surfaces to the topology of knots. It is, among other things, Lacan's subversion of the traditional relationship between surfaces and cuts in topology that leads him to his theory of knots. If it is assumed that a knot consists of any intertwining of strings that needs to be cut in order to disappear, then a knot can be defined negatively through the need to be cut. Besides, the cut also topologically leads to the knot, provided there are cuts on the surfaces producing knots. Thus a median cut along a Möbius strip leaves the strip whole, but with four semi-torsions. When this strip is cut again, it splits into two pieces, yet two knotted pieces.

From *R.S.I.* up to his last seminar, 'La topologie et le temps', Lacan relentlessly explores the nodal topology which remains focused through the notion of cut and whose clinical and doctrinal implications we can now just fathom.

See also: **Borromean knot, castration, discourse, topology**
Other terms: demand, drive, interpretation, signifier

References

Lacan, J. (1958–59) Le Séminaire, Livre VI, 'Le Désir et son inter-prétation'. Unpublished.

Lacan, J. (1961–62) Le Séminaire, Livre IV, 'L'identification'. Unpublished.

Lacan, J. (1973) 'L'Étourdit', *Scilicet*. Paris: Seuil.

Lacan, J. (1977) [1966] 'Subversion of the subject and the dialectic of desire in the Freudian unconscious', *Écrits: A Selection* (trans. A. Sheridan). London: Tavistock.

Lacan, J. (1978/79) Le Séminaire, Livre XXVI, 'La topologie et le temps'. Unpublished.

Sadi Askofare, Christiane Alberti, Michel Lapeyre,
Marie-Jean Sauret (trans. D. Hecq)

Desire

The concept of desire is at the centre of Lacanian psychoanalysis as a theoretical, ethical and clinical point of reference. Theoretically, Lacan's elaboration of the concept is supported by, yet goes beyond, its Freudian origins. From the ethical perspective, Lacan has examined in an original way the relationship between desire and the law, and its implications for psychoanalytic praxis.

Clinically, the attention to the subject's desire is for Lacan a permanent requirement in psychoanalysis: the end of the analysis demands not only that the analysand knows about his/her desire, but also acts ethically in consonance with that knowledge. Lacan's elaboration of the concept culminates with his original contribution of another concept, which from his viewpoint informs the direction of the treatment and the formation of psychoanalysis – the desire of the analyst.

Freud's *Interpretation of Dreams* established the basis for the psychoanalytic conception of desire (including Lacan's own contributions), even if the Freudian *Wunsch* (translated as 'wish' in the *Standard Edition*) does not exactly coincide with Lacan's desire (Lacan, 1977 [1959], pp. 256–7).

By shifting the object of study from the imagery of the manifest content of the dream to its unconscious determinants in the dreaming subject, Freud unveiled the structure of both the dream and the subject. Beyond the preconscious wishes attached to a number of desirable objects that the dream-work utilizes, there lies the unconscious wish – indestructible, infantile in its origins, the product of repression, permanently insisting in reaching fulfilment through the dream and the other formations of the unconscious.

The indestructibility that Freud attributes to the unconscious wish is a property of its structural position: it is the necessary, not contingent, effect of a fundamental gap in the subject's psyche; the gap left by a lost satisfaction (cf. the seventh chapter of *The Interpretation of Dreams*; Freud, 1953, pp. 509–621).

Such a structural gap in the subject is of a sexual order; it corresponds ultimately to a loss of sexual *jouissance* due to the fact of the prohibition to which sexuality is subjected in the human being. This prohibition is a structural cultural necessity, not a contingency, and its subjective correlate is the Oedipus complex – which is a normative organization, rather than a more or less typical set of psychological manifestations.

The model of the unconscious wish elucidated by Freud in his monumental work on dreams remained his guide for the rest of his theoretical and clinical production; in particular, it continued to inform, until the end, Freud's clinical interventions – interpretations and constructions in analysis – and his rationale for them. This model is inseparable from the form of discourse that Freud created: the rule of free association, the subject's speech, reveals his/her desire and the essential gap that constitutes it.

Lacan's elaboration of the praxis (theory and practice) of desire extends over his half-century of work in psychoanalysis, and attempting to abbreviate it or replace the necessary reading with a summary would be imprudent and misleading. Therefore, we can only indicate some suggestions for further reading (in Lacan's works) and further lines of enquiry.

A first ingredient of the concept of desire in Lacan's work contains a Hegelian reference, according to which desire is bound to its being recognized – even if later on Lacan emphasized the difference between his and Hegel's positions (Lacan, 1977 [1959], pp. 292–325).

But the reference to Freud's analysis of desire as revealed in the dream is from the start highly significant. Lacan emphasized that the analysis of the dream is in fact an analysis of the dreamer, that is, a subject who tells the dream to an other (with whom the subject is engaged in a transference-relation). In 'The function and field of speech and language in psychoanalysis' (1953), Lacan writes:

> Nowhere does it appear more clearly that man's desire finds its meaning in the desire of the other, not so much because the other holds the key to the object desired, as because the first object of desire is to be recognized by the other. (Lacan, 1977 [1959], p. 58)

That the other holds the key to the object desired takes on added value later in Lacan's work. Yet that desire emerges in a relationship with the other which is dialectical, that is, which is embedded in discourse, is an essential property of human desire. Human desire is the desire of the Other (over and above the others who are concrete incarnations of the Other), not 'natural', endogenous appetites or tendencies that would push the subject in one direction or another irrespective of his/her relations with the Other; desire is always inscribed in and mediated by language (cf. *The Four Fundamental Concepts of Psycho-Analysis*, which is an essential reference in its entirety; Lacan, 1977).

Lacan's study of the dialectical nature of desire led to his distinction between desire, need and demand. The three terms describe lacks in the subject; yet it is indispensable to identify each of these lacks, and their interrelations. The satisfaction of vital needs is subject to demand, and makes the subject dependent on speech and language.

The least noisy appeal of the infant is already inscribed in language, as it is interpreted by the 'significant' others as speech, not as a mere cry. This primordial discursive circuit makes of the infant already a speaking being, a subject of speech, even at the stage in which he/she is still infant. This subordination to the Other through language marks the human forever. Lacan writes:

> The phenomenology that emerges from analytic experience is certainly of a kind to demonstrate in desire the paradoxical, deviant, erratic, eccentric, even scandalous character by which it is distinguished from need [...]
>
> Demand in itself bears on something other than the satisfactions it calls for. It is demand of a presence or of an absence – which is what is manifested in the primordial relation to the mother, pregnant with that Other to be situated short of the needs that it can satisfy.
>
> Demand constitutes the Other as already possessing the 'privilege' of satisfying needs, that is to say, the power of depriving them of that alone by which they are satisfied [...].
>
> In this way, demand annuls (*aufhebt*) the particularity of everything that can be granted by transmuting it into a proof of love, and the very satisfactions that it obtains for need are reduced (*sich erniedrigt*) to the level of being no more than the crushing of the demand for love.

Thus desire is neither the appetite for satisfaction, nor the demand for love, but the difference that results from the subtraction of the first from the second, the phenomenon of their splitting (*Spaltung*). (Lacan, 1977 [1959], pp. 286–7)

This residual status of desire constitutes its essence; at this point the question of the object of desire acquires crucial importance. Lacan considered his theory of this object to be his only original contribution to psychoanalysis.

Although an exaggeration in reality, Lacan's position is justified because with that theory he introduced in psychoanalysis a conception of the object that is genuinely revolutionary and that makes possible a rational critique of the notion of 'object relations' and its clinical applications.

For what Lacan emphasized was the illusory nature of any object that appears to fulfil desire, while the gap, the original splitting which is constitutive of the subject, is real; and it is in this gap that the object a, the object cause of desire, installs itself. (Lacan 1977; in particular, chapter 20).

Desire requires the support of the fantasy, which operates as its *mise en scène*, where the fading subject faces the lost object that causes his/her desire (Lacan 1977 [1959], p. 313). This fading of the subject in the fantastic scenario that supports his/her desire is what makes desire opaque to the subject him-/herself. Desire is a metonymy (p. 175) because the object that causes it, constituted as lost, makes it displace permanently, from object to object, as no one object can really satisfy it.

This permanent displacement of desire follows the logic of the unconscious; thus Lacan could say that desire is its interpretation, as it moves along the chain of unconscious signifiers, without ever being captured by any particular signifier (cf. Seminar VI, 'Desire and its Interpretation'; Lacan, 1958–59).

In the analytic experience, desire 'must be taken literally', as it is through the unveiling of the signifiers that support it (albeit never exhausting it) that its real cause can be circumscribed (Lacan, 1977 [1959], pp. 256–77).

Desire is the other side of the law: the contributions of psychoanalysis to ethical reflection and practice have started off by recognizing this principle (Lacan, 1990; 1992). Desire opposes a barrier to *jouissance* – the *jouissance* of the drive (always partial, not in relation to the body considered as a totality, but to the organic function to which it is attached and from which it detaches), and that of the super-ego (with its implacable command to enjoy; Lacan, 1977 [1959], p. 319).

Thus, desire appears to be on the side of life preservation, as it opposes the lethal dimension of *jouissance* (the partiality of the drive, which disregards the requirements of the living organism, and the demands of the superego – that 'senseless law' – which result in the self-destructive unconscious sense of guilt). But desire itself is not without a structural relation with death: death at the heart of the speaking being's lack-in-being (*manqué à l'être*); death in the mortifying effect of those objects of the world that entice desire, inducing its alienation, without ever satisfying any promise.

There is no Sovereign Good that would sustain the 'right' orientation of desire, or guarantee the subject's well-being. As a consequence, the ethics of psychoanalysis require that the analyst does not pretend to embody or to deliver any Sovereign Good; it rather prescribes for the analyst that 'the only thing of which one can be guilty is of having given ground relative to one's desire' (Lacan, 1992, p. 319).

The analyst's desire, 'a desire to obtain absolute difference', is the original Lacanian concept that defines the position of the analyst in analytic discourse, and represents a culmination of his elucidation of the function of desire in psychoanalysis (Lacan, 1977, p. 276; 1991).

This position is structural, constitutive of analytic discourse – not a psychological state of the analyst. It is his/her lack-in-being, rather than any 'positive' mode of being that orients the analyst's direction of the treatment (Lacan, 1977 [1959], p. 230). This means that the analyst cannot incarnate an ideal for the analysand, and that he/she occupies a position of *semblant* of the cause of desire (Lacan, 1991; 1998). Only in this way may the analyst's desire become the instrument of the analysand's access to his/her own desire.

See also: **jouissance**, **subject**

References

Freud, S. (1953) [1900a] *The Interpretation of Dreams. Standard Edition of the Complete Psychological Works of Sigmund Freud*, Vols 4 & 5. London: Hogarth Press.

Lacan, J. (1958–59) 'Le désir et son interpretation' (seven sessions, ed. by J.-A. Miller). *Ornicar?* 24 (1981):7–31; 25 (1982):13–36; 26/27 (1983):7–44. The final three sessions appeared as 'Desire and the Interpretation of Desire in Hamlet'. *Yale French Studies* 55/56 (1977):11–52. There are unedited transcripts of the whole seminar available in French and English.

Lacan, J. (1977) [1959] *Écrits: A Selection*. London: Tavistock.

Lacan, J. (1977) *The Four Fundamental Concepts of Psycho-Analysis*. London: Tavistock.

Lacan, J. (1990) 'Kant with Sade'. *October 51*. Cambridge, MA and London: MIT Press.

Lacan, J. (1991) *Le Séminaire, Livre XVII, L'envers de la psychanalyse, 1969–1970*. Paris: Seuil.

Lacan, J. (1992) *The Seminar, Book VII, The Ethics of Psychoanalysis, 1959–1960*. New York: W.W. Norton; London: Routledge.

Lacan, J. (1998) *The Seminar, Book XX, Encore, 1972–1973, On Feminine Sexuality: The Limits of Love and Knowledge*. New York: W.W. Norton.

Leonardo S. Rodriguez

Discourse

Lacan's term 'discourse' corresponds to Saussure's *'lien social'*, or social bond. Discourse constitutes the basis of social organization. It is a structure, a necessary structure, one that goes beyond the more or less occasional or episodic nature of speech. Lacan's concept of discourse implies the rejection of the view that there is a community of interest in which, like Adam Smith's invisible hand, the interests of the individuals coincide in such a way that it is in the interest of each that they come together to form a community.

The concept of discourse comes into particular prominence in Lacan's work with the introduction of the four discourses. These were first announced by Lacan in 1968–69 in his Seminar XVI, 'D'un Autre a l'autre'. However, it is during the seminar of the following year, *L'envers de la psychanalyse* (1969–70), that the theory of the four discourses is extensively elaborated and effectively becomes the theme of his seminar for that year. The theory was again further developed at length in 1972–73 in his seminar, *Encore*, and featured prominently in 'Radiophonie' in 1969 and in *Television* in 1973.

The four discourses are developed in a four-part mathème that consists of the following four places:

$$\frac{\text{agent}}{\text{truth}} \qquad \frac{\text{other}}{\text{product}}$$

The four places can be taken to be implied in any speech act. A speech act is directed at another, who may or may not be an individual person. Each speech act is uttered in a particular name or from a given place, which implies an agent, though the latter need not be identical with the person actually making the utterance. Truth is, as the Freudian theory of the lapsus and other parapraxes shows, typically latent truth that is always liable to manifest itself in discourse, interfering in the discourse itself. Finally, the product of a discourse can be taken to correspond to the fact that every speech act actually produces an effect.

Lacan maps the four terms

S_1 master signifier
S_2 knowledge
a surplus *jouissance*
$\$$ divided subject

onto the four places, taking what he calls 'the discourse of the master' as his starting point:

$$\frac{S_1}{\$} \rightarrow \frac{S_2}{a}$$

Discourse of the master

By a purely formal operation that consists of rotating the four terms and holding the places constant, Lacan generates three further discourses, which he calls the discourse of the hysteric, the discourse of the analyst and the discourse of the university.

$$\frac{S_1}{\$} \rightarrow \frac{S_2}{a} \qquad \frac{\$}{a} \rightarrow \frac{S_1}{S_2}$$

Discourse of the master   Discourse of the hysteric

$$\frac{a}{S_2} \rightarrow \frac{\$}{S_1} \qquad \frac{S_2}{S_1} \rightarrow \frac{a}{\$}$$

Discourse of the analyst   Discourse of the university

Lacan's four discourses

Prior to articulating the theory of the four discourses Lacan had appealed to the Saussurian concept of speech, which contrasts in Saussure's work with language, to account for a range of phenomena going from the general notion of intersubjectivity through to the efficacity of psychoanalytic practice. In a way that was typical of Lacan's approach, he combined this linguistic notion of speech with Hegel's master–slave dialectic, to articulate the thesis that speech creates a social bond that overcomes the erotic and aggressive ego-to-ego relationship characteristic of the imaginary. If we take intersubjectivity to be a relationship based upon the bond instituted by true speech, it can be viewed as overcoming the imaginary relationship between ego and other of the mirror stage. This structure finds expression in Schema L

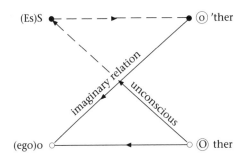

Figure 4: Schema L

The efficacity of psychoanalytic treatment is also at this time to be explained as the effect of speech. A neurotic symptom is an encoded message that has been excluded from the circuit of speech and can therefore only be communicated in a disguised form. It is speech in the form of free association that produces the transference. Within the transference the analyst becomes the addressee of the symptom's hidden message and, through interpretation, the analyst inserts the communication back into discourse. Operating solely by means of speech, analysis reconstructs the continuity of the subject's history through retroactively giving meaning to opaque elements of the subject's discourse.

This, at least, was Lacan's view throughout the Fifties, beginning with 'The field and function of speech and language in psychoanalysis' (1977). With the increasing emphasis upon the more purely formal level of language, construed as a pure network of signifiers located in the locus of the Other, the concept of speech plays an increasingly minor role in Lacan's teaching.

It is therefore of some interest to see, with the four discourses, the appearance of a conceptualization that has its roots in earlier views about the function of speech in psychoanalysis. This is not to say that nothing has changed; on the contrary, there are some striking innovations in the four discourses that reflect Lacan's subsequent theoretical and clinical preoccupations.

If the discourse of the master is the point of departure from the other three discourses, this is because it expresses not only the elementary structure of language but also its imperative nature. The eventual, explicit, appearance of this discourse in 1969 gives meaning retrospectively to many previous observations about language. This elementary structure is that the signifier represents the subject for another signifier:

$$\frac{S_1}{\$} \quad\rightarrow\quad S_2$$

The $\$$ here is the divided subject of the Freudian unconscious, whose division is the split in the subject brought about by language, by the signifier, and where this split takes the form of *Verdrängung*, or repression, in neurosis; *Verwerfung*, or foreclosure, in psychosis; or *Verleugnung*, or disavowal, in perversion.

S_1 is the master signifier, which represents the subject for another signifier, S_2. S_1 was introduced as an alternative formulation to $S(\cancel{A})$, the signifier of the lack in the Other. As the signifier for which all other signifiers represent a subject, its lack will be of momentous consequences. Its lack in the symbolic order Lacan calls foreclosure and psychosis is the consequence. This implies that $S(\cancel{A})$ can be identified with the Name-of-the-Father, whose lack or foreclosure is characterised by Lacan as the condition of psychosis.

At times Lacan also suggests a Freudian or Oedipal interpretation of this signifier, $S(\cancel{A})$. The big Other, 'A', is the signifier of the mother, or more precisely, the signifier of unlimited enjoyment, *jouissance*, of the mother's body; and the barring of the 'A' indicates the prohibition of unlimited access to and enjoyment of the mother. The father is typically the source or agent of this prohibition and his function as prohibitor is symbolised as $S(\cancel{A})$.

If the lack of $S(\cancel{A})$, the signifier that signifies the lack in the Other, is the foreclosure that produces psychosis, in the case of the neurotic $S(\cancel{A})$ is in the special position of being the signifier for which all other signifiers represent the subject. Bruce Fink (1991) writes this as

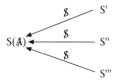

Figure 5: The Lacanian subject
Source: Fink (1991), *Analysis* 3, p. 25.

and points out that in the case of the neurotic the subject is invariably implied by every utterance he or she pronounces, implying a subjective position. In the four discourses then, the $S(\not{A})$ is correlated with S_1, the master signifier, where each of the signifiers S', S", S''', is an S_2.

In terms of the four discourses, in psychosis the master signifier, S_1, is missing from its place; this has the consequence that the S_2s do not locate the subject within discourse, but outside it. As a consequence we get the rather special relationship to language that typifies the position of the psychotic, with all the consequences that flow from this.

S_2 can be any other or all other signifiers. It is an alternative term for the big Other; the two are identical.

This formula for the primary structure of the signifier is complementary to the elementary cell of the graph in 'The subversion of the subject and the dialectic of desire', *Écrits*, p. 303.

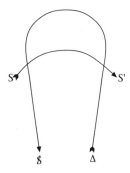

Figure 6: Elementary cell of the graph of desire
Source: Lacan (1977), *Écrits. A Selection*, p. 303.

In this elementary cell, introduced in the seminar on the formations of the unconscious in 1957–58, S_2 retroactively gives meaning
to S_1 and, at least in the formations of the unconscious, produces
that effect of surprise that accompanies the episodic and retroactive
coming into being of the subject of the unconscious.

While S_1 in the four discourses is clearly related to the Name-of-
the-Father, it would be incorrect to regard them as equivalent. For
one thing, S_1 is not restricted to any particular signifier but can
refer to any signifier – a name, a word, a phrase that is a puzzle or
an enigma through having been isolated from the rest of language
and hence through losing its connections with other signifiers.
Because of this isolation it is a nonsense and, as becomes apparent
in analysis, this signifier can be a proper name or any other word:
a disease, an illness, the letter 'W'.

Thus analysis is the process of unfreezing such signifiers through
re-establishing their links with other signifiers, thus also the importance of free association.

Linking one signifier with another will of course produce
meaning, sometimes new and sometimes surprising meaning. But
this production of meaning is a side effect, an epiphenomenon, of
what the process of analysis is about, which is to liberate, unfreeze
(Lacan uses the term 'dialectise' in *L'envers de la psychanalyse*), signifiers previously excluded from any dialectical process.

The discourse of the master defines the fundamental structure of
language. In this discourse the master, who occupies the place of S_1,
is there to be obeyed. The master's discourse is a discourse of imperatives, to be obeyed for no other reason than that they *are* the
master's imperatives. Do this! Do that! Not because you, or we all,
will be better off, not because it is to our advantage that you do so,
not for the general well-being, but simply because it is the master's
imperative. Obey, because! Just because! This is also the discourse of
the super-ego and the Kantian categorical imperative.

It would be wrong to think that we obey the master out of fear for
our own safety or well-being. We do not obey the law because it is in
our interest to do so, not even when it *is* in our interest to do so. One
obeys the law for the sake of obeying the law – and, moreover, one
derives a secret satisfaction from doing so. There is no ultimate justification for the law; it is a brute fact, irrational and arbitrary. It is
because of this law, which we all erect in our own hearts, whose

advantages for ourselves and society are dubious, that it is possible to claim a foundational and universal place for the master's discourse.

Following Hegel, if the master, S_1 in the place of the agent, commands; the slave, S_2 in the place of the other, obeys. This is also the place of knowledge, *savoir*. In the discourse of the master, as in Hegel's master–slave dialectic, it is the slave who possesses the knowledge. Being put to work by the master, the slave acquires the knowledge of how things work, the instrumental knowledge necessary to be able to obey the imperatives of the master, to satisfy the master's desire.

Knowledge, on the other hand, is irrelevant to the master who requires only that things work; indeed, the possession of such knowledge is even an indication that the master is not quite the absolute master – the true master barely lifts a finger.

The $ in the master's discourse indicates that there is a hidden truth, namely the subject's division. There are a number of ways of understanding this point about the divided subject – one is, of course, that the hidden truth is that the master is also, as a being of language, a divided and thus castrated subject. Another is that the master does not know his own desire, whereas the slave knows the master's desire only too well, since he/she is subject to its every whim.

Surplus enjoyment, production and loss indicate that in classical capitalism the exploitation of the worker by the capitalist produces surplus value. The capitalist puts the worker to work and remunerates him at a certain level, and the difference between the remuneration and the value to the capitalist of the work done is the surplus value. In Seminar XVI surplus value and surplus enjoyment are equated.

In terms of the super-ego this surplus enjoyment in the place of the product is the enjoyment that, with respect to the super-ego, the subject derives simply and solely from his or her submission to the law. This idea, a paradoxical one, that from the very act of submitting to the law and thereby forsaking some source of pleasure (note that 'forsaking' is much closer to Freud's '*Versagung*' than 'frustration' by which it is translated in the *Standard Edition*) one derives satisfaction and enjoyment, lies at the heart of Lacan's concept of *jouissance* and its link with the Freudian notion of (primary) masochism.

One may be tempted to think that there is a chronological progression from one discourse to the next, given that each is derived from the previous one by a ninety degree revolution in the terms occupying the places. However, this does not appear to be so.

On the other hand, one should not think that these are four timeless, eternal, structures dictated by the structure of the signifier. The emergence of the discourse of the university can be located reasonably precisely in the thirteenth century; and of course the discourse of the analyst is a relatively recent phenomenon also. However, one should not make a particular discourse a property of the profession, as it were. Not everything uttered by an analyst belongs to the discourse of the analyst; a hysteric can speak the discourse of the university. We should remember too that Lacan puts Socrates, in *The Symposium*, in the place of the analyst.

Note that this last remark points to an ambiguity in the notion of discourse. Sometimes it refers to an institution; sometimes it refers to the place of the subject; sometimes, perhaps, to both. Indeed, not all the discourses are equivalent in this respect; compare, for example, the discourse of the hysteric and the discourse of the university.

Finally, on this point, Lacan suggests that the same discourse may vary in quite important ways over time. For instance, in *L'envers de la psychanalyse* he is inclined to position the modern form of the discourse of the master under the discourse of the university. The reason for this is the role that bureaucracy plays in the modern capitalist state: S_2, knowledge, as the all-knowing dimension of modern bureaucracy, is in the 'dominant' position of the agent. Thus, bureaucratic capitalism has the structure of the discourse of the university.

However, it is equally true, at least according to Lacan, that the university discourse was historically a product of the discourse of the master. With respect to the master's discourse, the university discourse has historically played a dependent role of legitimating the discourse of the master and rationalizing the master's will.

How does it happen that the role of the university is to justify the master's discourse? The first point to make in this connection is that in the university discourse the dominant position of the agent is occupied by S_2, knowledge, instead of (as in the master's discourse) by the master signifier. That is to say that instead of the blind authority of S_1 emanating from the dominant place, the university discourse subjects everything to the need to be justified, rationalized, explained. Within the university discourse everything has an explanation; nothing is immune to the requirement that there be found some ultimate justification and explanation.

The second point is that historically the university discourse, in meeting this requirement, has effectively reversed the role of legitimating and rationalizing the social, political and scientific practices that have grown up around it. Lacan is inclined to the view that philosophical understanding or knowledge, whether absolute or not, is always obtained after the fact. For instance, historically, the philosophical theories of liberalism and individualism were developed after, or contemporary with, the appearance of laissez-faire capitalism – their overwhelming success has made them the basis of the legitimation of the capitalist societies in which we live. We might say, then, that the 'hidden truth' of the university discourse is that it is effectively a cover for the blind authority of the master's discourse.

The requirement that everything have an explanation and/or justification excludes the barred subject – that is, the subject of the university discourse is a knowing, conscious subject and thus excludes the divided subject. Furthermore, one should not forget the importance of the anonymity of academic and scientific knowledge. While, in a sense, the name of the game in the academy is 'to make a name for oneself', the knowledge produced is desubjectified and made into objective knowledge.

In discussing the Greeks, Lacan argues that philosophy has filled the function of depriving the slave of his or her knowledge and making it the possession of the master – this is the consequence, if I understand him correctly, of converting practical knowledge, technique, *savoir* as *savoir faire*, which is the knowledge of the slave, into the theoretical knowledge, the pure knowledge, of the master.

It is probably for this reason that Lacan sees a close link between the university discourse and science. Scientific knowledge, first, is used in the service of rationalizing and justifying the discourse of the master; secondly, it effectively alienates the slave of his technique by appropriating it and helping to convert it into scientific knowledge. The history of science has been a movement away from craft, where the locus of the knowledge is the individual craftsman, towards technology, where the knowledge resides in large-scale, impersonal institutions and social structures.

Finally, it should be added that Lacan subsequently located science with the discourse of the hysteric. Knowledge justifies authority and justifies the position of the academic in the discourse of the university, whereas knowledge is utilitarian for the master and eroticized for the hysteric. The real driving force behind the hysteric's discourse is the impossible, the Real; the same goes for pure science, for quantified science. Gödel's incompleteness theorem is, for Lacan, an important demonstration of the fact that a science can create its own internal point of impossibility, its own aporia, its own function of the real. And in so far as science is motivated by the impossible, it has a certain relationship to the discourse of the hysteric.

See also: **imaginary**, *jouissance*, **real**, **subject**, **symbolic**

References

Fink, B. (1991) 'The Lacanian Subject'. *Analysis* 3: 25.

Lacan, J. Le Séminaire de Jacques Lacan. Livre XVI. 'D'un Autre a l'autre'. 1968–1969. Unpublished.

Lacan, J. (1970) 'Radiophonie'. *Scilicet* 2/3: 55–99.

Lacan, J. (1973) *Télévision*. Paris: Seuil. [*Television: A challenge to the psychoanalytic establishment* (ed. Joan Copjec, trans. Denis Hollier, Rosalind Krauss and Annette Michelson). New York: W.W. Norton, 1990.]

Lacan, J. (1977) 'The field and function of speech and language in psychoanalysis'. *Écrits: A Selection*. London: Tavistock.

Lacan, J. (1991) *Le Séminaire de Jacques Lacan. Livre XVII. L'envers de la psychanalyse. 1969–1970*. Paris: Seuil.

Lacan, J. (1998) *The Seminar of Jacques Lacan. Book XX. Encore. 1972–1973*. New York: W.W. Norton.

Russell Grigg

Foreclosure

The notion of foreclosure is essential to any understanding of psychosis in a Lacanian framework. Lacan has suggested a paradigm for distinguishing between psychosis and neurosis, which entails a conceptual shift from Freud's.

Freud's suggestion that the neurotic represses the psychical contents destined to become unconscious, while the psychotic represses the real world, seems to imply that all repression is pathogenic. Lacan disputes this, arguing that primal repression is, through the establishment of the Name-of-the-Father, essential to the subject's insertion in the symbolic order, which is precisely what the psychotic is unable to achieve. Lacan therefore suggests that the term 'repression' be kept for neurosis as opposed to 'foreclosure', which designates the exclusion of the phallic signifier and the failure of primal repression.

While repression can be conceived as a bracketing of an experience that is structured, and which is likely to return to consciousness, foreclosure radically crosses out what it rejects because the psychotic has neither access to symbolization, nor to the judgement required for this experience to be inscribed in the symbolic. Thus, foreclosure designates a process of 'symbolic abolition', which precedes any possibility of repression. This, of course, has disastrous consequences for the subject's relations with language and with his or her own body.

What causes the failure of primal repression in the psychotic and places the psyche under the rule of foreclosure is determined by what Lacan calls an 'accident in the symbolic register and of what is accomplished in it, namely the foreclosure of the Name-of-the-Father in the place of the Other and in the failure of the paternal metaphor' (Lacan, 1977, p. 215). The establishment of the Name-of-the-Father is indeed of primary importance in the structuring of the unconscious through the installation of the phallus as symbolic signifier: since the Name-of-the-Father substitutes metaphorically for the desire of the Mother, the paternal metaphor defines castration as symbolic and the subject therefore adopts a particular position with regard to sexual differentiation. Lacan describes how the foreclosure of the signifier in psychosis produces two holes in the Other in the places where the Name-of-the-Father and the phallus should be, respectively (p. 201). With the foreclosure of the Name-of-the-Father and the absence of the representation of the subject, the relation between the imaginary, symbolic and real Orders is out of kilter. When psychosis is triggered off, psychotic symptoms are produced, being imaginary attempts to patch the two holes in the symbolic.

Lacan borrowed the term 'foreclosure' (cancellation or repudiation, from a French grammar by Damourette and Pichon) to convey the exclusion of a signifier in psychosis, although the concept itself can be traced back to Freud's earliest work. Consequently, an understanding of the evolution of the term 'foreclosure' is inconceivable without a return to Freud.

'Foreclosure' roughly corresponds to the German *Verwerfung* (repudiation) used by Freud in his case study of the wolf-man, where he opposes it to *Verdrangung* (repression) in the context of the logic of fantasy. Lacan points out that Freud uses the term to dismiss something as if it did not exist, which is quite different from repression. This is an indication that Freud's work bears the mark of his awareness and recognition of the differences between the three psychopathological categories. His unrelenting search for appropriate terms to pin down differing mechanisms of fantasy is in fact a testimony to this: the term *Verleugnung* (disavowal), for instance, is emphasized in his 1923 paper ('The infantile genital organisation', in *SE 19*) to describe a phenomenon more radical than *Verwerfung* (repudiation); only in his 1927 paper ('Fetishism', in *SE 21*), however, is it opposed to *Verwergung*. Yet, even through Freud stresses the importance of fantasy as a structuring formation for psycho-sexual development, nowhere in his work does he trace the structural and clinical vicissitudes of fantasy-formations pertaining to the three major psychopathological structures. Lacan's contribution in this field, then, is probably best understood in terms of the gaps in Freud's work.

It is possible to discern four important conceptual stages in Freud's writings on psychosis and its 'world of fantasy' as well as the vicissitudes of terms pertaining to their relations.

The period of Freud's correspondence with Fliess and of his two studies on what he called the 'neuro-psychoses of defence' ('The neuro-psychoses of defence', in *SE 3*, 1894) sees an exploration of the origins and structuring role of fantasy, particularly in hysteria, though there is an appreciation of differences between fantasy in neurosis and psychosis.

It is, however, the Schreber case that enables Freud to differentiate fantasy in neurosis from delusion in psychosis through a meticulous study of the mechanisms at work in paranoia. Schreber's fantasies make it possible for Freud to say that while the psychotic's libido is detached from the external world, it is redirected onto the ego, that the failure of repression has consequences that are typical of psychosis, and that the psychotic's ultimate attempt at recovery, which is an attempt to restore libidinal investments in objects, corresponds to the formation of symptoms in the neurotic.

With the 'wolf-man' case described in 'From the history of an infantile neurosis' (1918 [1914]), Freud proposes the notion of a repudiation of castration which he contrasts to repression twice in the same paper. He also points out that there is, in the wolf-man's case, no judgment regarding castration; it is as though one of the contrary currents of the psyche rejected castration. Though the wolf-man case is not a specific case of psychosis, he did, however, experience a psychotic episode at the time of his analysis with Ruth Mack Brunswick who detected symptoms of paranoia.

Freud's major statement concerning the differences between neurosis and psychosis occurs in the aftermath of the discovery of the primacy of the phallus (1923) when castration assumes theoretical dominance. The term *Verleugnung* (disavowal) is introduced at this time in an attempt to understand better what differentiates psychosis from perversion. The two 1924 studies, 'Neurosis and psychosis' and 'The loss of reality in neurosis and psychosis' are central here. In 'Neurosis and psychosis', Freud described neurosis as a conflict between id and ego, and psychosis as one between id and the external world, while maintaining the view that what distinguishes the two is that in neurosis libidinal investment is made in objects in fantasy whereas it is withdrawn into the ego in psychosis. The psychotic's delusions then function as a patch over the original rift in the ego's relation to the external world. 'The loss of reality in neurosis and psychosis' adds conceptual precision to the former study. Both neurosis and psychosis entail a loss of reality. In neurosis a piece of reality is avoided by flight, whereas in psychosis it is completely restructured. In other words, the neurotic ignores a piece of reality and replaces it with some structurally related fantasy, while the psychotic disavows it and replaces it with something completely new and external to it. Of particular import is the fact that 'disavowal' is now used specifically as denial of castration. With 'Fetishism' (1927), Freud hints at the structural significance of disavowal through linking it with what he calls *Ichspaltung* (splitting of the ego). In his 1938 paper 'Splitting of the ego in the process of defence', he finally distinguishes between *Verleugnung* in psychosis as opposed to its use in fetishism.

Lacan's contributions on psychosis and on the logic of fantasy in psychosis (see his 1955–56 seminar on psychosis in particular, but also the 1960s seminars) are striking for their conceptual precision; one example is his revision of Freud's notion of *Verwerfung* (repudiation) and the introduction of the term 'foreclosure'.

On the basis of his re-reading of the 'wolf-man' and the Schreber cases and of his reappraisal of Freud's notion of *Verneinung* (negation), as prompted by J. Hyppolite's work (1956), Lacan redefines Freud's *Verwerfung* as a 'symbolic abolition' occurring at the outset of psychic life. There is a primary structuring moment of the subject in which he identifies with the constitutive moment of expulsion of the real correlated to a process of *Bejahung* (affirmation). Whilst the primary *Bejahung* means that the subject takes things in (which involves a positive judgment of attributes) and enters the symbolic order, a non-*Bejahung*, which is thus opposed to it, precludes any symbolization and constitutes what is rejected. Consequently, repression can no longer be seen as a defence mechanism, but rather takes on a constitutive or structuring significance. Furthermore, the gap between what Freud meant by repression and repudiation widens considerably. At this stage of his reflection, Lacan rethinks the opposition between the two concepts in terms of structural difference. This is also evident in his writings on the wolf-man. It is in his seminar 'On psychosis', which focuses on Judge Schreber's case, that it all seems to fall into place for Lacan. Foreclosure is exchanged for Freud's *Verwerfung*, defined as a process of exclusion of a primary signifier, marked by the foreclosure of the Name-of-the-Father. Here is the origin of the Lacanian formula for psychosis as a hole, a lack at the level of the signifier.

For Lacan then, foreclosure is the very mechanism that distinguishes psychosis from neurosis. It is determined by the failure of the fundamental symbolic operation at the structural moment of the installation of the Name-of-the-Father and hence by the failure to enter into the symbolic. However, it should be stressed that there is no particular timing for psychosis to be triggered off.

See also: **Name-of-the-Father, psychosis, phallus, symbolic**
Other terms: disavowal, neurosis

References

Freud, S. (1951) [1884] 'The neuropsychoses of defence'. Vol. 3 In: *Standard Edition of the Complete Psychological works of Sigmund Freud*. London: Hogarth Press.

Freud, S. (1918) [1914] 'From the History of Infantile Neurosis', *SE 17*.

Freud, S. [1923] 'The infantile genital organization'. *SE 19*.

Freud, S. [1924] 'Neurosis and psychosis'. *SE 19*. 'The loss of reality in neurosis and psychosis'. *SE 19*.

Freud, S. [1927] 'Fetishism'. *SE 21*.

Freud, S. [1938] 'Splitting of the ego in the process of defence'. *SE 23*.

Lacan, J. (1981) [1955–56] *Le Séminaire, livre III, les Psychoses*. Paris: Seuil.

Lacan, J. (1977) *Écrits: A Selection* (trans. A. Sheridan). London: Tavistock.

Dominique Hecq

Formulas

Even before introducing the notion of mathème, Lacan tried to formalize his discourse in various ways. Indeed, he condensed his discourse into schemas and graphs as in *Écrits*, for instance. Examples are: schema L for the dialectic of intersubjectivity; the optical pattern of the upside-down vase; schema R for psychosis; the Z-like schemas for Sadean desire; and, of course, the graph for desire.

Formulas, however, cannot be represented by schemas. Like algebraic formulas, Lacan's formulas are transcriptions, but unlike algebraic formulas whose outcomes are equations, Lacan's formulas lead to much more complex assertions. We intend to focus here on the more famous and widely used formulas, that is, the formulas for metaphor and metonymy.

Metaphor and metonymy

In 'The agency of the letter in the unconscious or reason since Freud' (*Écrits*, 1977, pp. 146–78), Lacan shows how Freud's *The Interpretation of Dreams* exactly anticipated Saussure's definition of the signifier. Furthermore, the mechanisms of condensation and displacement inherent in the primary process correspond to what Jakobson describes, on the basis of his work on two main types of aphasia, as relations of similarity or contiguity between signifiers.

Aphasics have difficulties of one sort or another, depending on the nature of the anatomical lesions affecting their brains. Obviously, this common structure is then no different from the structure of signifiers, with signification made possible by crossing the Saussurean line signalling the unbridgeable gap between signifier and signified. Lacan uses the algorithm S/s to transcribe this structure.

There is no fixed equivalence between the signifying chain and the flow of the signified. Through the interplay of rhetorical tropes though, signification can emerge. The signified is thus a function of the signifier; the formula is: $f(S)$ $1/s$. Since one signifier constantly refers back to another one, this is a metonymic process. The resistance of signification remains. Lacan therefore places the sign parenthetically to stress that the bar is maintained in metonymy, which he writes (*Écrits*, 1977, p. 164):

$$f(S \ldots S') \cong S(-)s$$

Thus, in metonymy one signifier replaces another in a relation of contiguity (e.g., the part for the whole). Metaphor occurs when one signifier is substituted for another which is metonymically connected to it in the signifying chain. This substitution creates an *effet de signification* or meaning, whereby the line of the Saussurean algorithm is crossed. It is transcribed:

$$f\left(\frac{S'}{S}\right) \cong S(+)s$$

At the end of the text Lacan signals that desire is a metonymy and that the symptom is a metaphor. Now, Lacan's text on psychosis in *Écrits* introduces another formula to transcribe metaphor which enables him to explain more clearly the paternal metaphor as the substitution of the Name-of-the-Father for the desire of the mother.

Here the formula for metaphor is:

$$\frac{S}{\not{S}'} \cdot \frac{\not{S}'}{x} \rightarrow S\left(\frac{I}{s}\right)$$

This transcription shows that the signifier S is substituted for the signifier S' whose signified was the unknown x, hence creating meaning. According to this paradigm, the transcription for the paternal metaphor is (*Écrits*, p. 200):

$$\frac{\text{Name-of-the-Father}}{\text{Desire of the Mother}} \cdot \frac{\text{Desire of the Mother}}{\text{Signified to the subject}} \rightarrow$$

$$\text{Name-of-the-Father} \left(\frac{O}{\text{Phallus}}\right)$$

The substitution of the Name-of-the-Father for the desire of the mother introduces the phallic signification in the Other.

See also: **aphasia, discourse, mathème, schema, sexuation**

References

Freud, S. (1986) [1900/01] *The Interpretation of Dreams* (Parts 1–2) (vols 4–5). *Standard Edition, Complete Psychological Works:* London: Hogarth Press and Institute of Psycho-Analysis.

Lacan, J. (1977) [1966] *Écrits: A Selection* (trans. A. Sheridan). London: Tavistock.

Nathalie Charraud (trans. Dominique Hecq)

The Gaze

To define the gaze we need go no further than the words of Lacan himself. His series of lectures in the English edition of *The Four Fundamental Concepts of Psycho-Analysis*, published in French in 1973 but not available to English readers until 1978, begins with a preamble, then leads up to the definition: 'In our relation to things, insofar as this relation is constituted by the way of vision, and ordered in the figures of representation, something slips, passes, is transmitted, from stage to stage and is always eluded in it – that is what we call the gaze' (p. 73). The definition contains within it reference to aspects central to Lacan's notion of the gaze; vision, representation and that elusive thing behind both vision and representation that slips forever from our grasp – object a.

The gaze is also distinguished from the conscious act of looking. Looking, as a conscious act, like other acts of consciousness, is seen as marked with the deceptiveness of *méconnaissance*. The gaze, however, surrounds us from from all sides even before we are born. Nonetheless, the gaze is always connected to the look.

Lacan refers several times in the series to 'the split' in the gaze. In the first section he talks of the split referred to by Freud between perception and consciousness, the split that touches the Real and is the site of repetition. The notion of the gaze as 'object a' is the culmination of a concept that had been in the making, some scholars would say, from as early as 'The Object Relation' (1956–57), building and elaborating through 'Desire and its Interpretation' (1958–59), 'Transference' (1960–61) and 'Anxiety' (1962–63).

While the series of lectures on the gaze read, in translation, like a work of poetry, they do not flinch from conveying to the reader the grief of human reality that has object a inextricably bound up with notions of **lack**, derived from the experience of primordial separation, 'induced by the very approach of the real' and thereby confronting the subject with the fathomless anxiety of castration.

From the moment the gaze appears, says Lacan, the subject tries to adapt himself to it. 'He becomes that point of vanishing being with which the subject confuses his own failure.' However, 'The subject manages to symbolize his own vanishing in the illusion of the consciousness of *seeing oneself see oneself'* (1978, p. 74, Lacan's own italics).

Here the notions of the Other and of desire are referred to. The gaze is about other people, but it is not that the gazee is the object of the gazer, reduced to annihilation, which would confuse attributes of the gaze with the look. The gaze, Lacan says, integrates the domain of vision into the field of desire. The split that is there, always, between the gaze and the look is what undoes the look, in a sense.

The voyeur, supposedly in command of his own subjectivity, is caught out in the act of looking, perhaps reduced to shame, perhaps not – that is beside the point – rather, he is caught as a subject 'sustaining himself in the function of desire'. In that moment, the moment of the *tuche*, the subject is confronted with his own signifying dependence.

Lacan talked at length of aspects of representation in the lectures. Through a consideration of representation, say painting (he was particularly fond of the work of Cezanne, for example, where the colours are juxtaposed and with spaces between the colours occupying as significant a part of the discourse of the painting as the colours themselves), Lacan leads us to the place of desire in the gaze, and to its corollary in representation. Vision is different from the mapping of space (which is not only the prerogative of sighted persons) in that it is the source of the 'look'. Nonetheless, it is also central to the 'gaze', to the aspects of desire and of the field of scopic drive that the gaze gives birth to. The momentary feeling of unbalance when we chance to see something by accident, perhaps as a result of a brushing glance as we turn away, is the gaze at work.

To illustrate this, Lacan refers to the Hans Holbein painting, *The Ambassadors* in which there is a skull in the foreground. The skull is represented by the use of 'anamorphosis', that is, it is painted in such a way as to be only recognizable when looked at from a certain angle. For the gaze, this is one example of the entrapping power of the picture.

But vision, as an attribute, is itself illusory. It is totally dependent on light. 'The essence of the relation between *appearance* and *being* ... is in the point of light', Lacan says in the lecture on 'The Line and Light' (p. 94). He spends some time illustrating the nature of this relation with the use of two intersecting triangles so that the apex of each comes to rest on the base of the other.

At the point of intersection is the 'screen'. The screen, then, becomes the mediation between the gaze and the picture. The screen, moreover, is the locus of the 'stain' which, in turn, is the focal point of desire. Anthony Quinet (1995) points out that a better translation to English of the stain is 'the spot', having the signifying link with 'spotlight'. In the spotlight, the subject is flooded with light, is in the overwhelming gaze of the Other.

The ambivalence of that situation is never more acutely felt than when the spotlight follows the subject, so there is no escape – it becomes a kind of torture. But equally, the subject can be completely annihilated by a shift of the spotlight, reduced to nothing, out of gaze – out of the spotlight. 'And if I am anything in the picture, it is always in the form of the screen, which I earlier called the stain, the spot' (1978, p. 97). Later Lacan refers to the gaze as coming from outside, making the subject a 'picture' in the gaze of the Other. 'I am looked at, that is to say, I am a picture ... I am *photo-graphed*' (Lacan's italics; p. 106).

There are other aspects of the picture that are noteworthy. One is the presence of the gaze in the picture for both painter and viewer. Not that the painter wishes to be looked at, Lacan says, like the actor; the painter offers something 'beyond' the picture, something for the gaze to be appeased by – something 'given up', something 'yielded to'. This is a most poignant aspect of the work of the picture, and explains the calming effect of viewing a work of art. He agrees with Freud that it is sublimation that is involved in artistic creation, but it is not just the painter who experiences sublimation.

Something else can also be conjured up by the gaze, something very different from the calming properties of the picture, and that is the evil eye of envy – the sort of envy that is aroused by witnessing another's satisfaction, even if the object in question is no longer desired by the envious eye (such as experienced by St Augustine as he witnessed his little brother at his mother's breast). The painting, inviting our gaze, invites us to an act of 'renunciation of desire', even if momentarily.

There are other social functions of the work of art. The object a emerges in the fiscal arena – paintings are objects par excellence that become the cause of desire. The social function of the icon in the work of pleasing the deity is another example. The icon as well as being under the gaze of the viewer, is under the gaze of he/she whom it represents – God, say. That is, the artist is conscious of his/her creation as an act that will also arouse the desire of God.

Lacan also takes great pleasure in pointing out the social significance of battle scenes as subjects of painting. 'The people' come to view these, he says, and what do 'the people' see? 'They see the gaze of those persons who, when the audience are not there, deliberate in this hall. Beyond the picture, it is their gaze that is there.' In other words, the gaze of the Other is 'always behind' the picture, in the big spectacle that draws the crowd.

See also: **anamorphosis, castration, desire, object a, separation**
Other terms: envy, lack, *méconnaissance*, primordial separation, representation, screen, stain, *tuche*

References

Lacan, J. (1978) [1973] 'Of the gaze as object petit a', *The Four Fundamental Concepts of Psycho-Analysis* (pp. 67–119). New York: W.W. Norton.

Quinet, A. (1995) 'The gaze as an object'. In *Reading Seminar XI*, pp. 139–49 (eds R. Feldstein, B. Fink, M. Jaanus). Albany: State University of New York Press.

Sara Murphy

Ideal Ego

In Seminar I (1953–54, p. 282), Lacan explicitly ties the ideal ego to the specular image, grounding it in an illusion of unity, a point he develops in *Écrits* (1977, Chapter 1). Because it is a gestalt, it functions as a primordial unifying ego and, because it is an image, it is ideal.

In this latter meaning, Lacan builds on the work of Freud in this area, tying the ideal ego to the narcissistic operation of idealization and aggrandizement, the ideal ego being an ideal of narcissistic omnipotence constructed on the model of infantile narcissism. Thus, the ideal ego has its basis both in narcissistic idealization and in a specular image of unity.

This theme is reiterated by Lacan in Seminar II (1954–55, p. 166) where he writes about the ideal of unity which is evoked in the perception of ourselves at the mirror stage, but which constantly escapes us. This ideal of unity is essential to perception; its absence produces enormous anxiety, especially in the form of imaginary decomposition.

Following the line of thought adumbrated by Lacan in the mirror stage, it could be said that the subject constitutes him-/herself in his/her imaginary reality, but has, as his/her reference point, the other who looks at him/her. In this sense, the ideal ego is the ego which is loved by the other. This places a demand on the ideal ego to satisfy the other or, rather, the internalized representation of the other in the ego. Thus the subject will feel both satisfactory (because of the illusion of unity and the idealized sense of omnipotence) and loved, as long as it fulfils the demands of the other.

It seems then, that the ideal ego remains anchored in the narcissistic aspect of the mirror phenomenon, locked into the imaginary realm. It is linked, through narcissistic identification, to he/she who looks at the subject in a mirror – the ideal ego being that point at which he/she desires to gratify him-/herself in him-/herself.

The ideal ego relates to the ego-ideal in a narcissistic love relation, the subject seeing him-/herself in relation to his/her ideal images; or as Lacan points out in Seminar VII (1959–60, p. 98), the subject is placed in a dependent relation to an idealized image of itself. In the same seminar, he defines the ideal ego as 'the imaginary other who faces us at the same level' (p. 234).

Ego-Ideal

In *The Four Fundamental Concepts of Psycho-Analysis* (1978, p. 144), Lacan comments on both the ideal ego (in which the subject constitutes him-/herself in his/her imaginary reality) and the ego-ideal, but does not elaborate on the difference between them.

However, in this work in any case, Lacan presents the ideal ego as the object of the other's demands, whereas the ego-ideal is presented as an agency of unification and social cohesion (pp. 256–8). The conceptual vagueness inherent in his works about these two notions is not unique to Lacan's work, but is reminiscent of Freud's confusion of the two terms.

Following Freud, Lacan describes the kernel of the ego-ideal as being formed through both identification (of a non-narcissistic kind) and idealization. Whereas the ideal ego has as its reference point the other who looks at him/her ('it is in the Other that the subject is constituted as ideal', in *The Four Fundamental Concepts of Psycho-Analysis*, 1978, p. 144), the ego-ideal is based on the idealized image of unity, though not exclusively in the imaginary register, since Lacan sees the ego-ideal as occurring 'in the reign of the signifier' (p. 256).

Again in line with Freud, in Seminar VII Lacan distinguishes between ego-ideal and ideal ego, reminding us that this distinction coincides with Freud's distinction between object-libido and ego-libido, respectively.

We can extrapolate from Lacan's extension of Freud's concepts in this area that the ego-ideal is an agency resulting from the coming together of narcissism and identification with parents, their substitutes or with collective ideals. The subject then attempts to conform to the ego-ideal model.

Although its origin is narcissistic, the ego-ideal can be collective and forms the bond of human groups. That is, there is a double aspect to the ego-ideal – the social and the individual. As part of the psychology of the group, it reflects an ideal with which all members identify, and is thereby part of the shared symbolic order. As an individual phenomenon, it is an extension of primary narcissism and a standard of perfection.

If the ideal ego satisfies the ego-ideal, the ego-ideal will return the ideal ego's love; in this case, the subject is the beloved of the ego-ideal. But the ego-ideal is an exacting or demanding (persecutory) image; it expects satisfaction and perfection, not only love. Thus the ego-ideal is linked to demand, which is insatiable and addressed to the pre-Oedipal omnipotent or phallic mother.

Another function fulfilled by the ego-ideal is introduced by the process of separation which produces object a. Through the function of object a, the ego-ideal is implicated in the separation which constitutes the subject and joins him/her to the symbolic order. We master our lack through an attachment to our specular image.

In summary, the ideal ego remains a narcissistic phenomenon, modelled on a love relation with the self, where it is the part of the ego which is loved by the ego-ideal. The ideal ego thus remains in a narcissistic loop with the ego-ideal.

The ego-ideal, by contrast, though stemming from the unified mirror image and involving idealization (a process shared with the ideal ego), is linked to the symbolic system through identification. It always remains in relation to the Other and is the signifier to which the ideal ego relates and on which the ego models itself.

Thus it can be seen that Lacan places the ideal ego squarely in the imaginary and narcissistic realms, while the ego-ideal is situated in the symbolic and object relation worlds.

See also: **imaginary, mirror stage, symbolic**

References

Lacan, J. (1977) [1959] 'On a question preliminary to any possible treatment of psychosis', *Écrits: A Selection*. London: Tavistock.

Lacan, J. (1978) *The Four Fundamental Concepts of Psycho-Analysis* (trans. A. Sheridan). New York: W.W. Norton.

Lacan, J. (1988) [1954–55] Seminar II, *The Ego in Freud's Theory and in the Technique of Psychoanalysis* (ed. J.-A. Miller, trans. S.

Tomaselli, notes by John Forrester). Cambridge: Cambridge University Press.

Lacan, J. (1991) [1953–54] Seminar I, *Freud's Papers on Technique* (ed. J.-A. Miller, trans. with notes by J. Forrester). New York: W.W. Norton.

Lacan, J. (1992) [1959–60] Seminar VII, *The Ethics of Psychoanalysis* (ed. J.-A. Miller, trans. D. Porter). New York: W.W. Norton.

Huguette Glowinski

Imaginary

The imaginary in Lacan's theory immediately invokes a set of characteristic terms, most of which are already present in his article on the mirror stage (1949).

This set comprises the notions of Gestalt (ideal), ego and identification, lure and *méconnaissance*, reciprocity, counterpart, object, (paranoiac) knowledge and aggressivity. Of the three registers (or orders) of the subject, the imaginary is the first to enter on stage both in Lacan's writings and teachings. It dominates his thinking until the mid-1950s.

The imaginary as such is not a Freudian concept, although Lacan cautions us not to think that the function of the imaginary is absent in Freud's texts. In his elaboration of the imaginary, Lacan makes use of at least three major references, namely the notion of Gestalt, animal ethology and Freud's early theory on narcissism.

For Lacan, the function of the Gestalt in animal behaviour, which presents itself par excellence in the behaviour of the animal couple, allows a much clearer structuring of the function of the imaginary in man than was possible for Freud. To illustrate this function of the imaginary in animal behaviour, Lacan takes the example of the stickleback (Seminar I, 1953–54, p. 137). Gestalten come into play in releasing the complementary sexual behaviour of the male and the female stickleback; the male or the female is captivated by a Gestalt. Typical for animal behaviour is that the animal subject is completely identical to the image governing the release of a specific motor behaviour. Man's relation to the unitary image (Gestalt) is fundamentally different. This is linked to the fact that man comes into the world in a structurally premature state, which is mastered at an early stage – the mirror stage – by means of the identification with the unitary image of the body.

The mirror stage constitutes a first structuring moment for the human subject. It also functions as the prime reference in distinguishing between the imaginary relation in animal and in man. 'In man, the imaginary is reduced, specialized, centred on the specular image' (Seminar I, 1953–54, p. 282).

The assumption of the unitary image of the body, meaning that the human subject recognizes the specular image as being its own, presents the anticipation of real mastery. Both anticipation and recognition are crucial in man's relation to the specular image. Combined, they typify the imaginary as illusory and alienating – one recognizes and assumes an attainable totality. It is important to add that this recognition of the specular image is a function of something outside the imaginary relation, namely the symbolic.

Lacan accentuates the difference between animal and man in still another way:

> For the animal there is a limited number of pre-established corre-spondences between its imaginary structure and whatever interests it in its Umwelt … In man, by contrast, the reflection in the mirror indicates an original noetic possibility, and introduces a second narcissism. Its fundamental pattern is immediately the relation to the other. (Seminar I, 1953–54, p. 125)

This takes us back to the Freudian reference of narcissism, including both the formation of the ego and the object. In Lacan's view, the specular image as a total unity functions as a primordial form of the ego, which 'simply because it is an image … is ideal ego' (Seminar I, 1953–54, p. 282).

At this point, Lacan also refers to the notion of specular *Urbild*. Conceived as such, the ego is constituted by an alienating identifi-cation with a Gestalt – of the body or the other – functioning as an ideal image. The ego is an imaginary function serving (imaginary) mastery. In linking the constitution of the ego to the relation to the other, the ego is defined as the identification with the other. This has a certain implication for the relation to the object:

> … [man] only perceives the unity of this specific image [of the body] from the outside, and in an anticipated manner. Because of this double relation which he has with himself, all the objects of his world are always structured around the wandering shadow of his own ego. (Seminar II, 1954–55, p. 166)

Hence, the specular image (of the other) is both the framework of the ego and the object.

Lacan's further development of the dialectics between ego, other and object as being a function of rivalry and competition is clearly influenced by Hegel. Here the (Hegelian) notion of desire comes into play. Since the ego is constituted in reference to the other, whatever the ego is oriented towards will depend on what this other is oriented towards. 'An apprehended, desired object, it's either he or I who will get it, it has to be one or the other. And when the other gets it, it's because it belongs to me' (Seminar II, 1954–55, p. 51). All this implies that the object of man's desire is essentially an object desired by someone else.

Thus far, it has become apparent that the imaginary relation is always a (specular) relation between similar or equal others. This means that in a certain sense the notion of 'sameness' is central. This is also invoked in the characterization of the imaginary in terms of reciprocity, and symmetrical and interchangeable positions. Lacan illustrates this by means of what he calls the phenomenon of transitivism, in which the infant takes as equivalent his own action and that of the other. For instance, an infant saying 'Paul hit me', whereas it was he who hit Paul. In discussing transitivism, Lacan refers to the well-known 1927 study by Charlotte Bühler.

With all this, the coordinates of the relation between the imaginary and aggressivity are given. Aggressivity always refers to the imaginary register. In his 1948 article on aggressivity, Lacan posits that aggressivity is the 'correlative tendency of a mode of identification that we call narcissistic' (Écrits, 1977, p. 16), thus linking aggressivity to the imaginary relation. This link can be interpreted in two ways.

First, the constitution of the ego implies a certain satisfaction as compensation for the original organic disarray of the human subject. However, the tension implied in the relation between the initial fragmentation (original disarray) and the unifying image also becomes a source of aggressivity in the sense that the image that shapes the subject also structures the subject as rival for himself. Furthermore, since the narcissistic identification mediates the imaginary relation, rivalry is at the core of the imaginary relation to the other as well. Thus, aggressivity is always present in the relation to the similar other, which is perceived as ideal. The other is always one step ahead of the subject, and is thus seen as a rival. At this point we can more clearly refer to animal ethology to render the functioning of aggressivity, as essentially different from aggression. The function of the imaginary in animals makes it possible that a struggle between two males, that is, between two rivals, is not turned into a real struggle which would lead to the destruction of one of the animals. By transposing the conflict on to the imaginary plane, real destruction is prevented. Here it becomes clear that aggressivity has nothing to do with aggression. 'At the limit, virtually, aggressivity turns into aggression ... aggression is an existential act linked to an imaginary relation' (Seminar I, 1953–54, p. 177).

Second, aggressivity emerges in the situation of the ego encountering another subject like itself, giving rise to a desire for the object of this other's desire. Here also, the potential struggle is a function of something the other has, namely the object of his desire. Thus, aggressivity is linked to the object which is always the object of a counterpart, and therefore in the logic of the imaginary, an object that belongs to the ego. According to Lacan, the human object differs fundamentally from the object of the animal in that it is 'originally mediated through rivalry, through the exacerbation of the relation to the rival ... man's desire is the desire of the other' (Seminar I, 1953–54, pp. 176–7). Hence, aggressivity, rivalry and desire are closely linked within the frame of the imaginary relation.

The imaginary is also linked by Lacan to knowledge (*connaissance*). This link, which is a function of Lacan's critique of the Cartesian *cogito*, is centred on the ego's relation to reality and is typified by Lacan as miscognition (*méconnaissance*) and as being paranoiac in nature.

Although based on the recognition of the specular image, the ego can be conceived as 'a capacity to fail to recognize (*méconnaissance*)' (Seminar I, 1953–54, p. 153). Indeed, one of the fundamental characteristics of the specular image is that the reflection in the mirror is an inversion of what stands before the mirror. This implies that there is a primitive distortion and thus miscognition in the ego's experience of reality. Another way to understand this miscognition, is to link it to the alienating nature of the ego. In identifying with the image of the other, the subject inevitably fails to recognize many things about itself. In the same sense, all knowledge deriving from the imaginary relation – the ego's relation to the world of objects and similar others – is a function of miscognition, since this very relation is based on the ego's miscognition of its own alienating nature.

In his article on the mirror stage, Lacan speaks of human knowledge as paranoiac in nature. The term 'paranoiac knowledge' refers to what is found in paranoia (e.g., in the external persecution and observation) and which is also detectable in the imaginary relation, especially in the phenomenon of transitivism. It concerns the captivation by the image of the other – one recognizes the image of the other as one's own – and thus again reinforces the imaginary alienation of the ego.

During the period 1953 to 1974, the imaginary maintained importance, especially in relation to the signified and its effect; see for example, 'The function and field of speech and language in psychoanalysis' (1953); 'On a question preliminary to any possible treatment of psychosis' (1955–56); 'The agency of the letter in the unconscious or reason since Freud' (1957); 'The direction of the treatment and the principles of its power' (1958). All are published in the English translation of *Écrits* (1977) and *The Four Fundamental Concepts of Psycho-Analysis* (1978).

However, from the late 1950s onwards the ideas of the symbolic relation or the radical Other and the subject as subject of the signifier occupy a more central position. This does not mean that Lacan suddenly ceases to acknowledge the importance of the imaginary, or that the imaginary is depreciated or pushed aside. This should be stressed, since the imaginary is often regarded in a pejorative way for being pure 'illusion'. Although the imaginary is indeed essentially linked to miscognition, to mirage and thus also to 'false reality', it is nonetheless a 'verified reality' (Seminar II, 1954–55, p. 244), mediating man's relation to similar others and to the objects of his desire.

One thing is certain: without the imaginary there can be no human reality as such. Moreover, the imaginary is the only 'consistency' man has. This is developed by Lacan in one of his later seminars, on *R.S.I.* (1974–75). As far as the imaginary is concerned, Lacan here refers to his earliest formulations on the subject, by defining it as essentially departing from the body as a reflection of the organism. This seminar also illustrates that Lacan's conception of the imaginary does not fundamentally alter over the years. In this sense, it indeed functions as a consistency.

The function of the imaginary is always related to the other two registers used by Lacan, namely, the symbolic and the real.

See also: **aggressivity, desire, ideal ego, mirror stage, real, symbolic**
Other terms: ego, identification

References

Lacan, J. (1975–76) [1974–75] 'Le Séminaire de Jacques Lacan, Book XXII: Réel, symbolique, imaginaire (Real, symbolic, imaginary)'. In *Ornicar?* (2, 3, 4) 1975, (5) 1975–76.

Lacan, J. (1977) [1948] 'Aggressivity in psychoanalysis'. In *Écrits: A Selection* (trans. A. Sheridan). London: Tavistock.

Lacan, J. (1977) [1949] 'The mirror stage as formative of the function of the I as revealed in psychoanalytic experience' in *Écrits: A Selection* (trans. A. Sheridan). London: Tavistock.

Lacan, J. (1977) [1953] 'The function and field of speech and language in psychoanalyis'. In *Écrits: A Selection* (trans. A. Sheridan). London: Tavistock.

Lacan, J. (1977) [1957] 'On a question preliminary to any possible treatment of psychosis'. In *Écrits: A Selection* (trans. A. Sheridan). London: Tavistock.

Lacan, J. (1977) [1957] 'The agency of the letter in the unconscious or reason since Freud'. In *Écrits: A Selection* (trans. A. Sheridan). London: Tavistock.

Lacan, J. (1977) [1958] 'The direction of the treatment and the principles of its power'. In *Écrits: A Selection* (trans. A. Sheridan). London: Tavistock.

Lacan, J. (1978) *The Four Fundamental Concepts of Psycho-Analysis* (trans. Alan Sheridan). New York: W.W. Norton.

Lacan, J. (1988) [1975] *The Seminar of Jacques Lacan, Book I. Freud's Papers on Technique 1953–1954.* (ed. J. A. Miller; trans. J. Forrester). Cambridge: Cambridge University Press.

Lacan, J. (1988) [1978] *The Seminar of Jacques Lacan. Book II. The Ego in Freud's Theory and in the Technique of Psychoanalysis. 1954–1955.* (ed. J. A. Miller; trans. S. Tomaselli). Cambridge: Cambridge University Press.

Katrien Libbrecht

Infantile

The infantile is first and foremost a Freudian term. It is less a concept as such than that which denotes a mixture of notion and phenomenon: the recording of a series of clinical facts collected in the analytical treatment, a resource in the doctrine which enables this recording. The infantile is also the site of a misunderstanding between a certain idea of 'development' and an essential feature of the subjectivation process.

With the treatment of neurosis, we know that Freud had no problem acknowledging that the symptom acquires meaning in analysis only when referred back to some sexual aetiology. In other words, the cause of the patient's symptom is his/her confrontation with sexuality, or perhaps even with the other sex, since both are ultimately traumatic for everyone, and since both occur at the origin for all human beings, that is, in their dependency on the other.

In this respect, Freud changes direction for the first time when he stresses that it is sexuality as such which is inherently traumatic and fundamentally infantile, rather than particular events in the subject's life or childhood. Indeed, such events only provide occasions or reasons for neuroses and symptoms. Thus, in contradistinction to psychologizing theories, the infantile cannot be considered as the pathological after-childhood in the neurotic's life (regression or cessation in the development), but as that which persists in any case (contrary to the symptom), never ever to develop in the subject's history, and as the trigger of this history.

This lack of development, this 'immaturity' would thus be inherent in, and constitutive of, modern subjectivity. This is what Lacan echoes when he speaks of 'universal childhood' and sparseness of 'grown ups' in scientific civilization. Here is not, however, a mere psychological feature of our contemporaries, but a structural fact, even though this fact is only highlighted as such under the constraining power of the discourse of science peculiar to our times. Freud defines this structural fact by relating it to his breakthrough (to the coordinates of the treatment as well as the components of his doctrine) and to the fundamental concepts in so far as these are destined to account for the analytical praxis. First, he refers it to the unconscious, and then, to repetition.

The infantile and the unconscious

The treatment of neurosis and of the symptom – albeit revised in analysis through the interpretation of dreams, shows that what underpins the subject's problematic relationship with him-/herself (posthumous desire, writes Freud) is always an infantile wish: as origin and reason for desire, since this desire is unconscious. The infantile is thus the ultimate trigger of desire that makes it indestructible while maintaining the irreducibility of the unconscious. This means that at this level there is some kind of equivalence between the infantile and the unconscious. Here, but also later, Freud explains through both his clinical practice and doctrine, the reasons for this privileging of the infantile; they are predicated on the determining circumstances of human life. In other words, on the predicament of the 'little man' who must relate to his parents, with the ensuing dependency – more definitely so in modern societies where the nuclear family prevails, until the subject manages to react against this state of affairs; hence, the installation of the Oedipus complex as place and time of the relaying of desire. What Freud locates in his clinical practice as 're-editing' of the infantile, before expressing it in terms of the action of repetition in his doctrine is, however, not so much the mere reconstructing of some determining circumstance. (All children have in one way or another something to do with mothers and fathers, and, as Lacan notes, it is not the same thing to have such a father, or mother, rather than another one.) Rather, it is the insistent question covered by the neuroses, that is, to find out what the subject decides to do or not with this determining circumstance. The subject must choose what position to take, which choices to make, how to respond, given these particular contingencies. Thus, contrary to common preconceptions, the meaning and outlet of what determines the infantile are to be found within its confines. For instance, it can exist in the family saga, where the child learns how to use his/her parents to finally become self-reliant. The question is how to go about this, if not in order to achieve separation from the infantile, then at least in order to use it satisfactorily.

Infantile neurosis

We know the difficulties entailed in the resolution of the Oedipus, even when everything points to its disappearance. Witness the existence of a neurosis. The subject is confused about how to transpose Oedipal solutions in his/her relationship with the other and the world, where these solutions have become irrelevant. Now, analysands implicated in a transference relationship during the treatment itself might then find it necessary and inevitable to recognize the Oedipal identifications to which they are subjected. This, however, is not enough for them to use these identifications to free themselves. In other words, releasing repression or opening up the unconscious in the analytical process is not enough for removing the Oedipus from the path of the patient's destiny, despite the displacement of the subject this entails.

The persistence of the infantile and its effects, however, is not the same thing as a mere postponement of the Oedipus: for this persistence goes far beyond the action of the Oedipus complex, and it can equally persist when the Oedipus is resolved or maintained. In the name of common sense, psychologists inevitably invoke the normal and banal passage from childhood to adulthood. This makes it hard for psychoanalysts to respond in pointing out the Oedipal contamination – which is all too obvious in most 'adult' behaviour, in the most firmly rooted social relationships – if not in the treatment, then in the psychopathology of daily life. Were a woman to stand up and claim a position of nanny on the grounds of her own experience with children since she was once a child, Freud would object, saying that it is precisely because we were once children that, subjected to Oedipal repression, we do not know what a child is.

How then to articulate continuity and crossing-over? Is it just a matter of degree – quantitative threshold or qualitative hurdle? According to Freud and Lacan, it is the role of psychoanalytic inquiry (praxis and doctrine) to survey the process of subjectivation in what is called normal development, as well as in information available from the treatment, in a kind of 'after education'.

This is how Freud and Lacan – albeit using different contexts and vocabularies, first point to the gap between the child whose play is predicated on concrete relationships borrowed from the parental universe, and the adult (the analysand, at least) who is asked to break away from them and can do without them, notably in creative activities, in order to give 'some support to the most effective realizations and poignant realities'. Thus, Freud's stroke of genius, which is also the distinctive feature of psychoanalysis, is to have found in the exclusive recourse to the treatment and taking into account the impediments this entails, the intermediate point, the point of leverage, which makes moving from 'universal childhood' to 'grown up' possible.

This movement, no doubt, anticipates quite a few more swings – that is, an intervention at the level of fantasy which is best effected by psychoanalysis. There is one paradox though: this procedure is a kind of *Aufhebung* (lifting and conserving – 'sublation' is the term used by Lacanians) of the infantile. This means that the infantile is not a fact in some development, but rather the result, and the end produced by one of the subject's decisions.

What are the prerequisites and outcomes of this procedure? Infantile desire, as we have seen, reveals itself so promptly through interpretation early in analysis (and early should be stressed here, relevant as it is to both the history of Freud's breakthrough and any treatment) because some opening in the unconscious proves to be impossible to reduce during the course of the treatment. Once identified as such, this desire can neither be diminished nor fulfilled: set in and encrusted in neurotic formations through Oedipal normalization or normativization (the latter remaining to some extent resistant to an interpretation of the unconscious) it seems to resist analysis – no need to say that resistances are potent here.

The work of the treatment is impeded by the indestructible character of infantile desire at some moment of closing up of the unconscious while a realm heterogeneous to the unconscious opens up. This alternating between opening and closing of the unconscious implies that history cannot be reduced to development, nor the existence of the infantile to childhood.

In other words the mishaps in the treatment show that the infantile Oedipal desire remains untouched, come hell or high water during the course of development, and remains unresolved because the subject keeps it at bay. Herein lies the tour de force of fantasy: that through which the subject maintains the infantile link of Oedipal desire (incestuous and parricidal) while making sure that it does not return. Obviously, adolescence is the time when the subject seeks to take advantage of this ambiguity of fantasy in his attempts to make sense of sexual encounters and acts. It is, however, as consequence of, and conclusion to the failure of the Oedipal solution that fantasy first constitutes itself and positions itself by proxy.

Infantile neurosis, in point of fact, as Freud discovered when studying neurosis, is the prehistory of the latter. Infantile neurosis is the time when the child asks what his/her mother wants. In order to come up with an answer, a hasty and premature answer at that, it is the phallus, until it is time for the child to think through his/her own relationship with the phallus and how he/she is likely to use it as subject, starting with a willingness no longer to be it – the relinquishment to be it.

Strictu sensu, infantile neurosis is but an equivalent, a replacement, a proxy of fantasy. Fantasy makes its conclusions stronger and takes over: fantasy maintains the response derived from infantile neurosis while distancing the subject from his/her relationship with the parental authority once he/she has confronted the prospect of his/her own castration. Fantasy is thus both bound to the Oedipus and to the scar of castration.

In the subjective apparatus, fantasy is the formation without which the infantile establishes and maintains itself as deadlock of the Oedipus and stumbling block of castration, leaving the child in a state of subjection, and the subject struggling with the alienation of desire. This is why the infantile begs for developments in psychoanalysis. These are foreshadowed, if not pointed out, in Freud's work, then confirmed and followed up by Lacan.

The Infantile as home of fantasy

The infantile means the existence of fantasy, which is not necessarily true for every subject. It is the presence of fantasy, whose action may be recognized or acknowledged by the analysand. Finally, it is the use of fantasy that can be altered or changed in analysis.

It should thus be conceded that the subject's relationship with the Other is structured like a fantasy – since psychotic parents do not necessarily have psychotic children. From Freud to Lacan, psychoanalysis has attempted to locate the manifestations of fantasy and to find ways of transmuting it. The Lacanian way consists in a return to Freud and his doctrine which, by changing direction, stresses gaps and paradoxes. This is particularly so with respect to the infantile.

Transference in the treatment is as resistant as the infantile. Contrary to prejudices inherent in ideologies of development and progress, transference does not manifest itself as mere relic or reserve, but rather as the 'kernel of being' for the subject. For if the infantile produces the strongest kind of resistance in the treatment, it is in fact, according to Freud and Lacan, because the infantile is the time and place where everything happens for the analysand. Here all inner resistances must be conquered, here was the subjectivized, and here must 'the unfathomable decision of being' be re-subjectivized. Indeed, the analysis of the infantile is the only way to entice the consent – to desire, to the drive, to *jouissance* – where the subject happens as subject.

Analysing the infantile begins with invoking the ghost of the cause at the onset of the treatment and proceeds to direct all biographical events back to the reasons for the Oedipus complex, and more importantly to subject this complex to the action of structure: from family saga to individual myth and primal fantasies. But the analysis of the infantile proceeds with the constructing of primal fantasy in an attempt to identify the subject's own formula: the axiom of desire involving the divided subject, truth signifying the object cause, and the type of *jouissance* involving a subjective position.

The infantile takes part in the main paradox of the fantasy where it is located: it is consonant with the phallic register, for it is the logical consequence of going through castration, while accommodating that which escapes castration, that is, according to Freud, instinctual residues and perverse remainders. For Lacan, who goes further with this logic, the drive cannot be constituted if there is no fantasy (in infantile neurosis), and fantasy cannot be constituted without generating some perverse attribute. Similarly, constructing and going through fantasy in the treatment, is concomitant with acknowledging the drive and taking into consideration one's 'duties', isolating the perverse attribute and its uses.

To conclude, the infantile is not an original phenomenon, but rather results from the encounter between the structure and the consequence of a specific response to this original phenomenon. Not only does this mean that the infantile – this stumbling block in analysis – is correlated to fantasy as the real support of the symptom, but also that the infantile is the very core of fantasy: it corresponds to the masochistic kernel (primary kernel for Freud), which supports fantasy all along. This is also that which is left alone in analysis, or even given logical consistency as support for the existence of the subject.

The analysis of the infantile aims at the point and moment where a particular subjective position in a human being decides to face the primary condition and the object of *jouissance*, which is indeed the child's – in other words a decision to take responsibility for it. Thus, the infantile as hearth of fantasy is the component of *jouissance* which escapes castration, or rather, that which remains as *jouissance* in the aftermath of castration.

The infantile is the foundation of desire because it is that which is caused by the signifier as *jouissance*, and hence cannot be incorporated in the signifier. This is why Freud virtually identifies the infantile with the drive, and correlates it with the feminine, a register that exceeds Oedipal normalization as well (beyond the Oedipus). Now what Freud calls 'the superimposition of the infantile and the feminine' would then point to a surpassing of the infantile, a Freudian term for going through fantasy for Lacan.

See also: **castration**, **desire**, *jouissance*, **subject**
Other terms: neurosis, other, repetition, transference, unconscious

Further Reading

Freud, S. (1951) [1905] 'Three Essays on the Theory of Sexuality', *Standard Edition of the Complete Psychological Works of Sigmund Freud.* Volume 7, pp. 135–243. London: Hogarth Press.

Freud, S. (1951) [1909] 'Analysis of a Phobia in a Five-year-old Boy'. 10: *S.E.* pp. 5–148.

Freud, S. (1951) [1918] 'From the History of an Infantile Neurosis' 17: *S.E.* pp. 7–104.

Freud, S. (1951) [1924] 'The Economic Problem of Masochism' 19: *S.E.* pp.159–70.

Lacan, J. (1974) 'Le Mythe individuel du Névrosé, ou poésie et fiction dans la névrose', *Ornicar?* No. 17–18, 287–307.

Lacan, J. (1977) *Écrits: A Selection* (trans. A. Sheridan). London: Tavistock.

Lacan, J. (1994) [1956/57] *Le Séminaire Livre IV: la relation d'objet.* Paris: Seuil.

Sauret, M.-J. (1991) *De l'infantile à la structure.* Toulouse: P.U.M.

Michel Lapeyre, Christiane Alberti, Sidi Askofare,
Marie-Jean Sauret
(trans. Dominique Hecq)

Jouissance

Jouissance, and the corresponding verb, *jouir*, refer to an extreme pleasure. It is not possible to translate this French word, *jouissance*, precisely. Sometimes it is translated as enjoyment, but enjoyment has a reference to pleasure, and *jouissance* is an enjoyment that always has a deadly reference, a paradoxical pleasure, reaching an almost intolerable level of excitation. Due to the specificity of the French term, it is usually left untranslated.

Lacan refers to the subject of *jouissance* as 'this fathomless thing capable of covering the whole spectrum of pain and pleasure in a word, what in French we call the *"sujet de la jouissance"'* (Lacan, cited in Macksay and Donato, 1970). There is an element of horror present in *jouissance* connected with the erotics of the death drive and offering terrible promises, going beyond the pleasure principle.

Jouissance is fundamentally linked with excess. This excess refers to a pure expenditure which serves no purpose and is of a negative order, an excess of sexuality and death which Freud and Lacan increasingly addressed as they encountered it in their work.

From where does this excess, this *jouissance* beyond the pleasure principle, come? Excess, in relation to sexuality and death, is situated in language. It is a function of the operation of language. Lacan makes it clear that the signifier is both the cause of *jouissance* and what creates a limit to it. *Jouissance* is produced by the encounter with the fundamental lack in language to say everything, that place beyond language which is pointed to through this lack of a signifier to say it all: that real which points to the impossibility of a fit between the sexes, of a fit between the drive and the object around which it circulates, of a fit between what is said and the thing itself. This impossibility creates a push to repeat, a repetition which is founded on a return of *jouissance* and which always produces a failure, a loss. It is in the encounter with this aspect of repetition that Freud discovers the death instinct.

Jouissance is not a Freudian term. It is a term increasingly referred to by Lacan, especially in his later works. However, it is possible to point to the Freudian concept which serves as a foundation for the function of *jouissance* in Lacan's works.

Freud spoke of the death drive at work in those clinical moments encountered in the negative therapeutic reaction, masochism, an unconscious sense of guilt and in every encounter with the drive. The main Freudian reference is, therefore, that of the drive, from *The Three Essays on Sexuality* (1905) to the end of his work, with the emphasis on the death drive which he had begun to outline in *Beyond the Pleasure Principle* (1920).

What Freud presents as a duality, an opposition between two types of drive, sexual and death drive, Lacan presents as an internal antimony, a knot of satisfaction and suffering. In this sense, *jouissance* is a type of satisfaction that includes its contrary, exquisite pain. The drive's satisfaction is a mode of what is beyond the pleasure principle, a determination by the subject to suffer.

Lacan emphasises two slopes of the death drive, that of the signifier, and that of *jouissance*. The slope of the signifier refers to the way in which death can be thought of, anticipated. Language assures the subject of a margin beyond life. The slope of *jouissance* is that which is harmful to the subject in the sense that it disturbs the equilibrium aimed at by pleasure. *Jouissance* is therefore not desirable, and is presented in the clinic as an incomprehensible suffering.

In outlining the limits to *jouissance*, Lacan refers to the signifier, pleasure and desire as placing barriers to *jouissance*, commenting that 'The organism seems made to avoid too much *jouissance*' (Macksay and Donato, 1970). The pleasure principle, which aims at a minimum level of excitation, maintains a limit in relation to *jouissance*. Desire, which aims at dissatisfaction, does not go beyond a certain limit in *jouissance*. What lies beyond it is *jouissance*, and the drive of which *jouissance* is the satisfaction.

A mapping of *jouissance* in Lacan's work

1953 until 1960

Jouissance is not a central preoccupation during the first part of Lacan's teaching. *Jouissance* appears in Lacan's work in the seminars of 1953–54 and 1954–55, and is referred to in some other works (*Écrits*, 1977). In these early years *jouissance* is not elaborated in any structural sense, the reference being mainly to Hegel and the master–slave dialectic, where the slave must facilitate the master's *jouissance* through his work in producing objects for the master.

From 1957 the sexual reference of *jouissance* as orgasm emerges into the foreground. This is the more popular use of the term *jouissance*, with *jouir* meaning 'to come'.

In his seminar of 1959–60, *The Ethics of Psychoanalysis*, Lacan deals for the first time with the Real and *jouissance*. Although the Real of the 1960s is not the same as his use of the Real in the 1980s, the first concepts emerge in this seminar. Here *jouissance* is considered in its function of evil, that which is ascribed to a neighbour, but which dwells in the most intimate part of the subject, intimate and alienated at the same time, as it is that from which the subject flees, experiencing aggression at the very approach of an encounter with his/her own *jouissance*. The chapters in this seminar address such concepts as the *jouissance* of transgression and the paradox of *jouissance*.

1960s

It is in the text 'The subversion of the subject and the dialectic of desire in the Freudian unconscious' that a structural account of *jouissance* is first given in connection with the subject's entry into the symbolic (Lacan, 1977).

The speaking being has to use the signifier, which comes from the Other. This has an effect of cutting any notion of a complete *jouissance* of the Other. The signifier forbids the *jouissance* of the body of the Other. Complete *jouissance* is thus forbidden to the one who speaks, that is, to all speaking beings. This refers to a loss of *jouissance* which is a necessity for those who use language and are a product of language. This is a reference to castration, castration of *jouissance*, a lack of *jouissance* that is constituent of the subject. This loss of *jouissance* is a loss of the *jouissance* which is presumed to be possible with the Other, but which is, in fact, lost from the beginning. The myth of a primary experience of satisfaction is an illusion to cover the fact that all satisfaction is marked by a loss in relation to a supposed initial, complete satisfaction. The primary effect of the signifier is the repression of **the thing** where we suppose full *jouissance* to be. Once the signifier is there, *jouissance* is not there so completely. And it is only because of the signifier, whose impact cuts and forces an expenditure of *jouissance* from the body, that it is possible to enjoy what remains, or is left over from this evacuating. What cannot be evacuated via the signifying operation remains as a *jouissance* around the erotogenic zones, that to which the drive is articulated.

What is left over after this negativization (–) of *jouissance* occurs at two levels. At one level, *jouissance* is redistributed outside the body in speech, and there is thus a *jouissance* of speech itself, out-of-the-body *jouissance*. On another level, at the level of the lost object, object a, there is a plus (+), a little compensation in the form of what is allowed of *jouissance*, a compensation for the minus of the loss which has occurred in the forbidding of *jouissance* of the Other.

The Freudian Oedipus refers to the father prohibiting access to the mother, that is, the law prohibiting *jouissance*. Lacan refers not only to a *jouissance* forbidden to the one who speaks, but the impossibility in the very structure itself of such a *jouissance*, that is, a lack of *jouissance* in the essential of the structure. Thus, what is prohibited is, in fact, already impossible.

The lack in the signifying order, a lack in the Other, which designates a lack of *jouissance*, creates a place where lost objects come, standing in for the missing *jouissance* and creating a link between the signifying order and *jouissance*. What is allowed of *jouissance* is in the surplus *jouissance* connected with object a. Here *jouissance* is embodied in the lost object. Although this object is lost and cannot be appropriated, it does restore a certain coefficient of *jouissance*. This can be seen in the subject repeating him-/herself with his/her surplus *jouissance*, *plus-de jouir*, in the push of the drive.

Plus-de jouir can mean both more and no more; hence the ambiguity, both more *jouir* and no more *jouir*. The drive turning around this lost object attempts to capture something of the lost *jouissance*. This it fails to do, there is always a loss in the circuit of the drive, but there is a *jouissance* in the very repetition of this movement around the object a, which it produces as a *plus-de jouir*. In this structural approach, there is a structuring function of lack itself, and the loss of the primordial object of *jouissance* comes to operate as a cause, as seen in the function of object a, *the plus-de jouir*.

Jouissance is denoted, in these years, in its dialectic with desire. Unrecognised desire brings the subject closer to a destructive *jouissance*, which is often followed by retreat. This destructive *jouissance* has a Freudian illustration in the account of the case of the Ratman, of whom Freud notes 'the horror of a pleasure of which he was unaware' (Freud, *S.E.* 10, pp. 167–8).

1970s

Seminar XX, *Encore*, given in 1972–73, further elaborates Lacan's ideas on *jouissance* already outlined, and goes further with another aspect of *jouissance*, **feminine *jouissance***, also known as the Other *jouissance*.

The speaking being is alone with his/her *jouissance* as it is not possible to share the *jouissance* of the Other. The axiom that Lacan has already given in earlier seminars, **there is no sexual rapport**, comes to the foreground in *Encore* as male and female coming from a very different *jouissance*; different and not complementary. It is a difference in the relation of the speaking being to *jouissance* which determines his being man or woman, not anatomical difference.

Sexual *jouissance* is specified as an impasse. It is not what will allow a man and a woman to be joined. Sexual *jouissance* can follow no other path than that of phallic *jouissance* that has to pass through speech. The *jouissance* of man is produced by the structure of the signifier, and is known as phallic *jouissance*. The structure of phallic *jouissance* is the structure of the signifier. Lacan proposes a precise definition of man as being subject to castration and lacking a part of *jouissance*, that which is required in order to use speech. All of man is subjected to the signifier. Man cannot relate directly with the Other. His partner is thus not the Other sex but an object, a piece of the body. Man looks for a little surplus *jouissance*, that linked with object a, which has phallic value.

The erotics embodied in object a is the *jouissance* that belongs to fantasy, aiming at a piece of the body, and creating an illusion of a union linking the subject with a specific object. The *jouissance* of man is thus phallic *jouissance* together with surplus *jouissance*. This is linked to his ideas of the 1960s outlined above.

Woman is phallic *jouissance* with something more, a supplementary *jouissance*. There is no universal definition of woman. Every woman must pass, like man, through the signifier. However, not all of woman is subjected to the signifier. Woman thus has the possibility of the experience of a *jouissance* which is not altogether phallic. This Other *jouissance*, another kind of satisfaction, has to do with the relation to the Other and is not supported by the object and fantasy.

Increasingly, in his works of the 1970s, Lacan points to the fact that language, in addition to having a signifier effect, also has an effect of *jouissance*. In *Television*, he equivocates between *jouissance*, *jouis-sens* (enjoyment in sense) and the *jouissance* effect, the enjoyment of one's own unconscious, even if it is through pain (Lacan, 1990). The unconscious is emphasized as enjoyment playing through substitution, with *jouissance* located in the jargon itself. *Jouissance* thus refers to the specific way in which each subject enjoys his/her unconscious.

The motor of the unconscious *jouissance* is *lalangue*, also described as babbling or mother tongue. The unconscious is made of *lalangue*. Lacan writes it as *lalangue* to show that language always intervenes in the form of *lallation* or mother tongue and that the unconscious is a 'knowing how to do things' with *lalangue*. The practice of psychoanalysis, which promotes free association, aims to cut through the apparent coherent, complete system of language in order to emphasize the inconsistencies and holes with which the speaking being has to deal. The *lalangue* of the unconscious, that which blurts out when least expected, provides a *jouissance* in its very play. Every *lalangue* is unique to a subject.

Jouis-sens also refers to the super-ego's demand to enjoy, a cruel imperative – enjoy! – that the subject will never be able to satisfy. The super-ego promotes the *jouissance* that it simultaneously prohibits. The Freudian reference to the super-ego is one of a paradoxical functioning, secretly feeding on the very satisfaction that it commands to be renounced. The severity of the super-ego is therefore a vehicle for *jouissance*.

In 'La Troisième', presented in Rome in 1974 (*Écrits*, 1977), Lacan elaborates the third *jouissance*, *jouis-sens*, the *jouissance* of meaning, the *jouissance* of the unconscious, in reference to its locus in the Borromean knot. He locates the three *jouissances* in relation to the intersections of the three circles of the knot, the circles of the Real, the Symbolic and the Imaginary. The Borromean knot is a topos in which the logical and clinical dimensions of the three *jouissances* are linked together: the Other *jouissance*, that is the *jouissance* of the body, is located at the intersection of the Real and the Imaginary; phallic *jouissance* is situated within the common space of the Symbolic and the Real; the *jouissance* of meaning, *jouis-sens*, is located at the intersection of the Imaginary and the Symbolic. It is the object a that holds the central, irreducible place between the Real, the Symbolic and the Imaginary.

Jouissance and the clinic

Lacan's contribution to the clinic is paramount in regard to the operation of *jouissance* in neurosis, perversion and psychosis. The three structures can be viewed as strategies with respect to dealing with *jouissance*.

The **neurotic subject** does not want to sacrifice his/her castration to the *jouissance* of the Other (*Écrits*, 1977). It is an imaginary castration that is clung to in order not to have to acknowledge Symbolic castration, the subjection to language and its consequent loss of *jouissance*. The neurotic subject asks '*why me, that I have to sacrifice this castration, this piece of flesh, to the Other?*' Here we encounter the neurotic belief that it would be possible to attain a complete *jouissance* if it were not forbidden and if it were not for some Other who is demanding his/her castration. Instead of seeing the lack in the Other the neurotic sees the Other's demand of him/her.

The Pervert imagines him-/herself to be the Other in order to ensure his/her *jouissance*. The perverse subject makes him-/herself the instrument of the Other's *jouissance* through putting the object a in the place of the barred Other, negating the Other as subject. His/her *jouissance* comes from placing him-/herself as an object in order to procure the *jouissance* of a phallus, even though he/she doesn't know to whom this phallus belongs. Although the pervert presents him-/herself as completely engaged in seeking *jouissance*, one of his/her aims is to make the law present. Lacan uses the term *père-version*, to demonstrate the way in which the pervert appeals to the father to fulfil the paternal function.

The practice of psychoanalysis examines the different ways and means the subject uses to produce *jouissance*. It is by means of the *bien dire*, the well-spoken, where the subject comes to speak in a new way, a way of speaking the truth, that a different distribution of *jouissance* may be achieved. The analytic act is a cut, a break with a certain mode of *jouissance* fixed in the fantasy. The consequent crossing of the fantasy leaves the subject having to endure being alone with his/her own *jouissance* and to encounter its operation in the drive, a unique, singular way of being alone with one's own *jouissance*. The cut of the analytic act leaves the subject having to make his/her own something that was formerly alien. This produces a new stance in relation to *jouissance*.

In **psychosis**, *jouissance* is reintroduced in the place of the Other. The *jouissance* involved here is called *jouissance* of the Other, because *jouissance* is sacrificed to the Other, often in the most mutilating ways, like cutting off a piece of the body as an offering to what is believed to be the command of the Other to be completed. The body is not emptied of *jouissance* via the effect of the signifier and castration, which usually operate to exteriorise *jouissance* and give order to the drives.

In Schreber we see the manifestation of the ways in which the body is not emptied of *jouissance*. Shreber describes a body invaded by a *jouissance* that is ascribed to the *jouissance* of the Other, the *jouissance* of God.

The practice of psychoanalysis with the psychotic differs from that of the neurotic. Given that the psychotic is in the position of the object of the Other's *jouissance*, where the uncontrolled action of the death drive lies, what is aimed at is the modification of this position in regard to the *jouissance* in the structure. This involves an effort to link in a chain, the isolated, persecuting signifiers in order to initiate a place for the subject outside the *jouissance* of the Other. Psychoanalysis attempts to modify the effect of the Other's *jouissance* in the body, according to the shift of the subject in the structure. The psychotic does not escape the structure, but there can be a modification of unlimited, deadly *jouissance*.

See also: **Borromean knot, castration, psychosis**
Other terms: death, drive, ethics, neurosis, perversion, super-ego

References

Freud, S. (1951) [1905] 'The Three Essays on Sexuality'. *S.E. 7*: pp. 125–244. In: *Standard Edition of the Complete Psychological Works of Sigmund Freud*. London: Hogarth Press.

Freud, S. (1951) *Notes upon a Case of Obsessional Neurosis*. *S.E. 10*: pp. 153–319.

Freud, S. (1951) [1920] *Beyond the Pleasure Principle*. *S.E. 18*: pp. 3–64.

Lacan, J. (1970) 'Of structure as an inmixing of an otherness prerequisite to any subject whatever' in *The Structuralist*

Controversy, Richard Macksay and Eugenio Donato (eds). Baltimore: Johns Hopkins University Press, p. 194.

Lacan, J. (1975) Seminar XX, *Encore* (1972–73). Text established by Jacques-Alain Miller. Paris: Seuil, p. 10. Now translated by Bruce Fink (1998) under the title of *On Feminine Sexuality, The Limits of Love and Knowledge 1972–1973, Encore. The Seminar of Jacques Lacan. Book XX*. New York: W.W. Norton, p. 3.

Lacan, J. (1958) 'The youth of A. Gide', April, 1958; 'The signification of the phallus', May, 1958; 'On the theory of symbolism in Ernest Jones', March, 1959, in *Écrits*. Paris: Seuil.

Lacan, J. (1977) [1960]. 'The subversion of the subject and the dialectic of desire in the Freudian unconscious' in *Écrits: A Selection* (trans. A. Sheridan). New York: W.W. Norton.

Lacan, J. (1990) *Television*. New York: W.W. Norton. (note 5), p. 325.

Carmela Levy-Stokes

Mathème

Lacan first introduced the notion of mathème (matheme) in 1973: in his seminar, of course, but more particularly in 'The Twit' ('L'Étourdit'), his last major piece of writing. That was the year of *Seminar, Book XX, Encore,* and p. 108 of the transcript reads: 'Formalization is our goal, our ideal. Why? Because formalization as such is a mathème: it can be fully transmitted.'

In 'The Twit', he says that he has mathematized his discourse so that it could be taught: 'the unteachable, I turned into a mathème' (*Scilicet* 4, 1973, p. 39).

But what exactly is a mathème? What does Lacan have in mind? Is he thinking of the formulas that punctuate his teachings, such as the formulas for metaphor and metonymy, for instance, or the formulas for sexuation? Or is he rather thinking of the topological constructions on the torus and the cross-cap that he had just introduced, not as metaphor, but as structure itself?

If one tracks down the word 'mathème' in 'The Twit', it first appears to be intertwined with the topological construction presented as contributing to the analytical discourse, to its fabric: 'No other fabric to endow it with but the language of a pure mathème, in other words, the only teachable discourse' (1973, p. 28). The definition, which identifies the mathème with the teachable, supersedes the mathematizable itself, since the Real can only be apprehended through mathematics, except the real of the impossible sexual relation, which, in point of fact, cannot be transcribed by any mathematical relation: 'This is why the mathèmes which are transcribed as dead-ends by the mathematizable, that is, the teachable in the Real, are likely to be coordinated to this "impossible" from the Real' (p. 35).

How is the mathème apprehended in the structure of our language? The first mathèmes, the arithmetical figures, are on the border of language, in its fringe: 'The mathème is a product of the only real which is first recognized in language: the arithmetical figure' (1973, p. 37). The arithmetical figure is on the border between common language and mathematical discourse. The first figures are signifiers, but these quickly become meaningless.

In *L'Oeuvre Claire* (1995), J. C. Milner attempts to define the mathème on the basis of the definitions of phoneme (the linguist's phonetic unit) and mytheme (part of a myth). Milner proposes that the mathème is an 'atom of knowledge'. But, apart from mathematical objects, there is no such thing as an atom of knowledge in mathematics. This is in fact what J. A. Miller means when, talking about the mathème in the *Revue de la Cause Freudienne* No. 33, he says that the aim of the analytical experience is to 'know one's own mathème' (1996). What is important then, is less to formalize the knowledge achieved during the cure, than to identify with one's own mathème.

Miller gives the witty example of the triangles and the spheres, but it is obvious that in this particular context the mathèmes are mathematical objects, such as the triangle or the sphere, but also the Borromean knot, the torus, the Möbius strip, and the geometrical projection. These objects are no longer at the edge of language, but rather at the point where the real, the imaginary, and the symbolic intersect. Rather than being atoms of knowledge, each one of these objects is a concentrate of knowledge: that which governs the subject's relation to the Real.

This means that, as J. A. Miller makes clear in the above-mentioned article, the knowledge which is formalized in the mathème (and intertwined with satisfaction), represents a stake for the ending of the cure:

> This is what Lacan has reformulated when he suggested that the experience be carried on to the point when the subject accedes to his own mathème, and more particularly the mathème of the primary fantasy, since this fantasy conditions, indeed, determines, whatever keeps Mr So and So going all through his existence. (p. 11)

The stakes of the mathème are many. After the fundamental stake, which has to do with the aim of the cure, there is teaching, as my first allusions to the mathème and its definitions make clear; then there is a political stake and a clinical one.

If the only valuable teaching is the one that can be transcribed into a mathème, then the teacher's role is reduced to the ultimate: to transmit an elaboration without having anything to do with it.

The consequence is the same with all writing: *Scilicet*, the journal where 'The Twit' ('L'Étourdit') was first published is – except for Lacan's texts – a collection of unsigned articles after Bourbaki's style of presentation, Bourbaki being one of the collective and anonymous mathematical writers of the time. As J. C. Milner points out in his book on Lacan, the master's figure disappears with the mathèmes: we are left with professors.

If one takes Lacan's topology and mathèmes seriously, the clinical scene changes too. That which makes the symbolic ensnare and bump into the impossible of the real becomes clearer in the light of what Lacan called the topology of signifiers, which taps in the general topology of kinship between signifiers, a topology which, according to Lacan, is budding, if not born, in Freud's 'Project' (*Esquisse*, see *Ornicar?* 36). Inasmuch as it can be separated from the clinic of signifiers, the clinic of the object is spotted in, by, and through, the topology of surfaces, just as Lacan shows in 'The Twit' and in some of his later seminars.

Later, J. A. Miller took up the clinical stake. He focused on interpretation. There is a trace of this concern in *Revue de la cause Freudienne*, No. 34. The classical interpretation that focused on meaning is no longer convincing; we are witnessing what S. Cottet would describe as 'the decline of interpretation'. This led J. A. Miller to devise a conception of interpretation aiming at the level of the Real where 'it is loving it' (*ça jouit*) rather than at the level where 'it speaks' (*ça parle*). If the analytical interpretation is that through which the Real is asserting itself, then interpretation is a matter of formalization – supposing that the mathematical formalization is the only one that can reach the Real. This is what Lacan explores (1996, p. 18).

The Borromean knot provides an illustration of what Lacan was striving to achieve with a 'mathematical clinic'. This knot consists of three 'loops of string': two of these loops are loose while the third is tied. Thus, when one loop becomes undone, all three become undone. This first enabled Lacan to illustrate the solidarity of the three registers, that is, the Imaginary, the Real, and the Symbolic, in the knot which defines the human subject. But in the year of his seminar on Joyce, which is when the question of the structure of the writer arises, Lacan devises a knot with three untied loops that would collapse unless a fourth loop ties them all together. Lacan identifies this fourth loop with the symptom – spelled *sinthome* in Joyce's case. Thus, Joyce's psychosis never manifested, because his writing acted as a substitute that held together the three registers, despite Joyce's obvious lack of the paternal function. One could therefore generalize the question of the real of the symptom as being equivalent to the Father, as father version (or to invert elements in the pun, *père-version*), that holds the knot together. It might now be possible to differentiate between types and to outline a clinic.

See also: **Borromean knot, formulas, imaginary, real, symbolic, topology**
Other terms: fantasy, interpretation, symptom, torus

References

Lacan, J. (1973) 'L'Étourdit' (The Twit). *Scilicet*, 4.

Lacan, J. (1975) [1972–73] *Le Séminaire XX Encore*. Paris, Seuil.

Lacan, J. (1976) *Le Sinthome, Séminaire XXIII* (1975–76), *Ornicar?* 6, 7, 8, 9, 10, 11 [Provisional transcription].

Lacan, J. (1986) [1945–46] *Esquisse. Ornicar?* 36.

Miller, J. A. (1996) '*Retour de Granade: Savoir et satisfaction*'. *Revue de la cause Freudienne*, 33: 7–15.

Miller, J. A. (1996) '*Le monologue de l'appard*'. *Revue de la cause Freudienne*, 34: 7–18.

Milner, J. C. (1995) *L'Oeuvre Claire*. Paris: Seuil.

Nathalie Charraud (trans. Dominique Hecq)

Mirror Stage

The theory of the 'mirror stage' was one of Lacan's major early original contributions to psychoanalysis. While less prominent in his later thinking it continued to provide a reference point for his thinking concerning the organization of the register of 'the imaginary'. The theory was developed during the 1930s and his most central paper on the subject, 'The mirror stage as formative of the function of I as revealed in psychoanalysis' (1949) has been available, in English, as one of the collection of papers in *Écrits* since 1977.

Subsequent discussions of the mirror phase are to be found, in translation, in 'Some reflections on the ego' (1953 [1951]), 'The neurotic's individual myth' (1979 [1953]), *The Seminar of Jacques Lacan: Book II* (1988 [1954–55]) and in 'On a question preliminary to any possible treatment of psychosis' (1977 [1959]).

Among untranslated or unpublished works in which are to be found major statements concerning the 'mirror stage' are his contribution to the *Encyclopédie Française* titled 'La famille' (1938), which is essential reading for the person who wishes to appreciate the context in which the theory was developed, and 'The Seminar of Jacques Lacan: Book V, Formations of the Unconscious' (unpublished).

In his 1949 account of the mirror stage Lacan took as his reference points both child and ethnological observations to describe a stage in human development which had links with more archaic forms of behavioural transmission, such as imprinting, but which in the human had a most distinctive characteristic which allowed it to become the prototype for the ego.

It is evident that what he had in mind here is not the Freudian ego as he used the term *je* (I) rather than *moi* which is the French rendering of Freud's *ich*. Later he abandoned the distinction and referred to the *moi*, which suggests that he believed that his theory of the ego and its links to the mirror stage should replace the Freudian ego.

He proposed that during a certain period of development (six to eighteen months usually), the child exhibits a fascination with and delight in his/her image as reflected either in the mirror or in his/her perception of another child of similar age who acts as a reflection of his/her own body or a double.

In his later references to the mirror stage he adopted a less empirically developmental perspective using it rather as a metaphor to describe aspects of, in particular, the mother–child relation, a polar relation constructed around a specular fascination. Lacan suggested that the power of this image derives from its quality as a Gestalt, an integrated form; a perception which stands in such contrast to what has up until then been experienced co-aesthenically, as a fragmented body. The integration is an illusion, but a captivating one which promises much and provides, according to Lacan, the prototype for the ego.

He argued that the fascination of the infant with the visual Gestalt is not a definitively human phenomenon, but one which can be observed in a range of animals in which a visual signal provides a necessary impetus for development.

He referred to the instance of the female pigeon whose gonad will develop only following the sight of another pigeon. However, what is most distinctive in the human is his/her 'specific prematurity of birth', by which the development of mental functioning precedes in some respects the development of physical functioning.

What the infant experiences, according to Lacan, when he/she catches sight of him-/herself in the mirror or recognizes him-/herself in the other is an image of perfection and completeness at marked variance from the impression which his/her other senses have provided. At the same time it is a glimpse of the future, of what he/she will become or at least imagines he/she will become. From this point the duality of the ego becomes established in his/her psyche, as represented in the ideal form of the specular other, the mirror image or what Lacan termed the 'ideal ego' on the one hand and on the other hand the fragmented body which gazes upon the 'ideal ego' and which Lacan designates as the 'ego'.

Although the 1949 article remains the central reference point for the English language reader, his 1938 *Encyclopédie Française* entry 'La famille' which appeared just two years after he had first introduced the theory of the mirror stage at the Fourteenth International Psychoanalytic Congress provided an elaboration of the full theoretical context within which the mirror stage theory is located.

This article contained a pungent critique of certain strands of Freudian theory. Whereas Freud had, by the latter stage of the development of his metapsychology, either manifestly or implicitly spliced together the biological and the cultural factors in psychical organization, Lacan emphasized their independence. At the core of his argument, he insisted on the structural distinction between 'instinct' and 'complex', the former being a biological structure and the latter a cultural structure which is specific to the human.

Lacan suggested that the complex has an 'organizing' function in psychical development and defined the 'imago' as the unconscious part of the complex. He proposed three broad complexes corresponding to stages of psychical and physical development: complexes of weaning; complexes of intrusion; and the Oedipus complex. Freud and Lacan share a common biological starting point for their conception of psychical development. This is the general observation that the human is notable for the 'specific prematurity of birth'. The baby is both physically and psychologically immature and remains so for many years.

Whereas Freud placed the emphasis on sexual immaturity and the effects of changes in the location of the organization of erotogenic experience, Lacan placed the emphasis on the effects of discrepancies in the progress of psychical and physical maturation.

Lacan's argument was that the infant was able to apprehend the integration and maturation of his or her body at the level of image prior to its achievement at the level of lived experience. The consequence was a division within the psyche between a registration at the level of lived experience of the body as immature and fragmented, and a registration at the level of the imaginary of the body as mature and integrated. This division, which was manifest in but not confined to the mirror stage, is, according to Lacan, central to the formation of the various infantile complexes associated with weaning, rivalry, sexual orientation to the parent, and castration.

These complexes were, according to Lacan, best understood as cultural solutions to the social problems engendered by the specific prematurity of birth, solutions which in other species are instinctual or pre-established. The tension between the biological and the cultural would later be organized by Lacan into psychical registers which he terms 'imaginary' and 'symbolic', the term imaginary giving recognition to the powerful psychical effects of the unifying operation of visual perception and its product, the image.

Twenty years later, in his unpublished Seminar of 1957–58 ('Formations of the unconscious'), Lacan employed the theory of the 'mirror stage' in a discussion of that most elusive of psychical phenomena, comedy. He distinguished the comic from the joke or witticism which Freud had effectively analysed in his *Jokes and Their Relation to the Unconscious* (1905). The effect of the latter turned on its capacity to open up the field of the unconscious through the operation of linguistic devices and to thereby release and structure quanta of pleasure hitherto barred. Comedy on the other hand was not so intimately linked to the operation of language. Lacan pointed out that the sight of a beheaded duck walking around may be quite comic. Similarly the Chaplinesque antics and poses which form the basis of the repertoire of a certain field of comedy have their effect quite independently of language.

It is, according to Lacan, precisely the tension between the degraded figure of fun and the elevated triumphant figure that we hold in our mind as the image of contrast, which provides the origin of laughter in this form of comedy. This tension is the fundamental tension of the ego, structured in accordance with the mirror stage, and released in laughter. Just as the joke permits through its structuration, the realization of pleasure that previously is consciously experienced only as anxiety, comedy of the slapstick kind organizes in a fashion which enables pleasure, the aggressivity aroused by the presence of the image of the specular other.

See also: **aggressivity**, **ideal ego**, **imaginary**, **symbolic**
Other terms: instinct, complex, ego, image, structure.

References

Freud, S. (1960) [1905] 'Jokes and their relation to the unconscious', *S.E. 8*. London: Hogarth.

Lacan, J. (1938) 'La famille'. In De Monzie (ed.*) Encyclopédie Française*, vol. 8. Paris: Monzie.

Lacan, J. (1977) [1949] 'The mirror stage as formative of the function of the I', *Écrits: A Selection* (trans. A. Sheridan). London: Tavistock.

Lacan, J. (1977) [1958] 'On a question preliminary to any possible treatment of psychosis', *Écrits: A Selection* (trans. A. Sheridan). London: Tavistock.

Lacan, J. (1953) 'Some reflections on the ego', *International Journal of Psychoanalysis*, 34: 11–17.

Lacan, J. (1979) [1953] 'The neurotic's individual myth', *Psychoanalytic Quarterly*, 48: 405–25.

Lacan, J. (1988) [1954-55] 'The ego in Freud's theory and in the technique of psychoanalysis', *Seminar of Jacques Lacan: Book II*, (trans. S. Tomaselli). Cambridge: Cambridge University Press.

Lacan, J. [1957–58] Seminar Book V: 'Formations of the unconscious' (trans. C. Gallagher). Unpublished.

Robert King

Name-of-the-Father

Lacan's interest in the question of the father goes back to his article on the family, written for the *Encyclopédie Française*, where he linked the contemporary forms of neurosis, and the social conditions that made possible the very emergence of psychoanalysis, to the problematic position of the father in our culture (Lacan, 1938). He pursued this line of thought in his 1953 article on 'The neurotic's individual myth':

> At least in a social structure like ours, the father is always in one way or another in disharmony with regard to his function, a deficient father, a *humiliated* father, as Claudel would say [...] In this divergence lies the source of the effects of the Oedipus complex which are not at all normalising, but rather most often pathogenic (Lacan, 1979, p. 423).

In the 'Rome Report', of 1953, the expression 'name of the father' appears for the first time (Lacan, 1977, p. 67). Over the following years Lacan devoted much of his research to the elaboration of the concept, first, in relation to the psychoses (when he presented the thesis of the foreclosure of the Name-of-the-Father as the specific mechanism that produces psychotic phenomena), then to the object relation and phobia, and finally, in the context of his revision of the Oedipal structure. This resulted in his postulating the constitution of the subject as a metaphorical operation (Lacan, 1977, pp. 177–225; 1993; 1994; 1998).

Over the same period (the 1950s) Lacan developed the correlative categories of the three registers of the subject (symbolic, imaginary and real), metaphor and metonymy and the paternal metaphor. Thus, he distinguished the symbolic father from the imaginary father and the real father, and the concept of the Name-of-the-Father, which is a signifier, and intimately connected to the function of the father as **symbolic** father.

The French homophony of *nom du père* (name of the father) with *non du père* (the 'no' of the father) must be borne in mind, as the two senses are present in Lacan's conception of the paternal function: the father operates as a signifier, that is, in the name of a symbolic, ideal position; and he also represents the law and its prohibition – more specifically, in the context of the Oedipal normative structure, the prohibition of incest.

The introduction of the signifier Name-of-the-Father makes possible the institution of the paternal metaphor. The Name-of-the-Father therefore substitutes for the desire of the mother, thus giving a new signification to the subject. As a result of this operation the subject ceases to be the phallus of the mother, while for the mother it is no longer possible to have the child as her phallus (Lacan, 1977, pp. 199–215; 1994, pp. 151–408; 1998, pp. 143–212).

Psychosis is the failure of this metaphorical operation, that is, the failure of the constitution of the Oedipal structure: the signifier Name-of-the-Father is not repressed but foreclosed.

During the 1950s and 1960s the concept of the Name-of-the-Father appeared to be pivotal in Lacan's conception of the constitution of the subject. Without abandoning its significance, he later developed some properties of the concept which places it in a somewhat different position within the theoretical framework. It retains its status as a knot, a notion already discussed in the 1955–56 seminar on the psychoses (Lacan, 1993, pp. 310–23).

It is however possible for the subject to 'go beyond it' – yet only 'on the condition of making use of it' (Lacan, 1976–77 [*Ornicar?* 10: 10]). Lacan's development of the concept (and the clinic) of the symptom resulted in his establishing an equivalence between the symptom and the function of the father: ' … after all the Father is nothing but a symptom, or a sinthome'.

The Name-of-the-Father retains its function as 'the father of the name', which provides a support for the whole signifying order, but this 'does not make the symptom less necessary' (Lacan, 1976–77 [*Ornicar?* 6: 9]).

See also: **psychosis, imaginary, real, symbolic, phallus, Borromean knot**

References

Lacan, J. (1938) 'La famille', in *Encyclopédie française*, vol. 8, sections 40 (3–16) and 42 (1–8). Paris: Monzie; republished as *Les*

Complexes familiaux dans la formation de l'individu. Paris: Navarin, 1984.

Lacan, J. (1976–77) *Le Sinthome, Séminaire XXIII* (1975–76). *Ornicar?* 6, 7 and 8 (1976); 9, 10 and 11 (1977).

Lacan, J. (1977) *Écrits: A Selection* (trans. A. Sheridan). London: Tavistock.

Lacan, J. (1979 [1953]) 'The Neurotic's Individual Myth', *Psychoanalytic Quarterly* 48: 405–25.

Lacan, J. (1993) *The Seminar, Book III, The Psychoses,* 1955–1956. New York: Norton.

Lacan, J. (1994) *Le Séminaire, Livre IV, La relation d'objet,* 1956–1957. Paris: Seuil.

Lacan, J. (1998) *Le Séminaire, Livre V, Les formations de l'inconscient,* 1957–1958. Paris: Seuil.

Leonardo S. Rodriguez

Object a

L'objet petit a, the object cause of desire, has occasionally been translated into English as 'object a' or 'object petit a'. Lacan considered it to be his most significant and influential formulation, and it can be seen as one that distinguishes psychoanalysis as a mode of investigation in similar ways that number or quantity distinguish mathematics or physical phenomena. It is inextricably linked to the formulation of fantasy, and as much as the 'uncanny' in Freud's work can be seen as a theoretical panoply, perhaps even the theoretical precursor to object a, the latter may be seen as the Lacanian theoretical panoply. It is crucial in the gradual elaboration and revision of his work, although its definitions are arguably complex, and at times seemingly aleatory. It is a fundamental concept, but more than any other it possesses atavars and antinomies (Fink, 1995). This becomes evident mapping its conceptualizations over years of theorizing, despite the fact that Lacan's work is not characterised by major epistemological shifts. It is salutary for the reader of Lacan to note that his work and the understanding of it implies 'work in progress'; this is truly the case with object a. Nevertheless, to follow the way it has been introduced in the Lacanian opus in relation to, for example, the advent of the subject, the mediation between the subject and the Other, the logic of the fantasy, repetition, desire … it is possible to provide a tentative account of object a – tentative because it cannot be exhausted. Much explanation would involve commentary on algebraic formulation and topography; furthermore, a considerable amount of Lacan's work remains untranslated, indeed unpublished.

Importantly however, the distinction should be made at the outset between an object of desire and an object that *causes* desire. Object a can be introduced as the object cause of desire. It is not what is desired but it sets desire in motion, and because desire is metonymical it may move, it may be displaced from object to object.

> … any more than to say that man's desire is a metonymy. For the symptom *is* a metaphor whether one likes it or not, as desire *is* a

metonymy, however funny people may find the idea. (Lacan, 1977, p. 175)

The distinction is crucial and will become clear as this very nuanced concept that Lacan elaborated in the 1950s to the 1970s is discussed, particularly in terms of its relation with desire.

Its conceptual origin can be found in the work of Karl Abraham and his theoretical contribution to the notion of the part-object. Lacan makes reference to this and to Winnicott's transitional object in the essay 'The direction of the treatment and the principles of its power' (Lacan, 1977). However, it is to Freud that Lacan is most indebted for the theorisation of object a, because what was implicit in his work, particularly in *Beyond the Pleasure Principle*, was that *something lies beyond the symbolic* (Freud, *SE, XVIII*). Additionally, there is no doubt of Heidegger's influence on Lacan's evolving conceptualization about desire and knowledge, where object a – in different guises – assumes a central position.

One can see specifically in Lacan's work early elaborations of the symbol a in Schema L – the scheme where the dialectics of inter-subjectivity are laid down. In this scheme Lacan developed the imaginary axis a–á where one's own ego is represented by a and that of another á. Its development is through the theorization represented in the mirror stage and the figure of the ego. The mirror stage, appropriately designated a structuring stage rather than a chronological stage, describes the relationship of identifications that exist between the ego and the other, or the ego and its coun-terpart, where the relations with the specular image are inextricably bound up with speech. The effect of the relationship a–á is to open up a gap that alienates the subject from his/her own image, but it

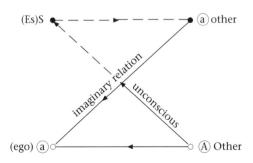

Figure 7: Schema L
Source: Lacan (1978).

is a necessary gap notwithstanding, because it provides a base that Lacan states permits the operation of the symbolic relation:

> ... but rather that without this gap that alienates him from his own image, this symbiosis with the symbolic in which he constitutes himself as subject to death, could not have occurred. (Lacan, 1977, p.196)

The symbolic mediation of the mother–child relation is further developed in Schema R, where the subject-child as desiring, is produced as split between the I – ego-ideal and the S-phallus axis. The subject identifies with the imaginary phallus as he/she projects him-/herself in the position of object of desire for the Other, in this case the mother:

> ... the child, in his relation to the mother, a relation constituted in analysis not by his vital dependence on her, but by his dependence on her love, that is to say, by the desire for her desire, identifies himself with the imaginary object of this desire in so far as the mother herself symbolizes it in the phallus. (Lacan, 1977, p. 198)

Therefore, the subject as desiring is produced as split between S and I but through the field of the Real, that is, what is understood as the zone that occurs between I-e and i-M. What falls from this moment is called **object a**.

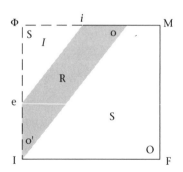

Figure 8: Schema R
Source: Lacan (1977), *Écrits*, p. 197.

Thus, considered in the earliest Schema L and further developed in Schema R, 'a' may be seen as an instance of mediation between the subject and the Other, and for the subject to the ego-ideal, respectively. Its development in both schemas also serves to demonstrate what Jacques Alain Miller in his *Commentary on the Graphs* contends:

> ... the straight line I M cannot refer to the relation between the subject and the object of desire: the subject is simply the cut of the strip, and what falls from this is called the object *o*. The subject is caused by the desire of the Other but it is a desire that cannot be articulated by the subject, a desire which keeps being displaced. (Miller, cited in Lacan, 1977, p. 334)

Continuing elaborations of object a can be seen in the algorithm $\$\lozenge$a, the logical articulation of fantasy. Specifically, the $\$$ represents the barred subject – irremediably divided by the signifier in its relation to object a, the primal object, and conceptually, the fantasy can be seen as a structure that constitutes the subject. Desire is founded in the division of the subject caused by language. Object a lies beyond the signifier, it cannot be expressed in signifiers but it can be distinguished as the object cause of desire precisely because desire endlessly shifts through a chain of signifiers; it never co-incides with them.

In Seminar V, *Formations of the Unconscious* (1957–58), the graphs of desire, which map the functioning of the signifier in the object assume a central position; however, a more concise elaboration takes place in *Subversion of the subject and dialectic of desire* (Lacan, 1977). In an explication of the subject of psychoanalysis, that is, the subject of the unconscious, Lacan claimed that the subject is merely 'the place of the "inter-said" (*inter-dit*), which is the 'intra-said' (*intra-dit*) of a between-two-subjects, ... the very place in which the transparency of the classical subject is divided and passes through the effects of "fading"' (Lacan, 1977, p. 299). According to Marini's reading and interpretation, the fading is linked to 'the suspension of desire', to the 'eclipse' of the subject in the signifier of demand, and to the fascination of the fantasy (1992, p. 175).

The object a is the remainder from the operation of being constituted as a speaking being; it cannot be assimilated because it is Real.

A further development of object a can be seen in Lacan's reading of Plato's *Symposium* in Seminar VIII, *Transference* (1960-61). In this seminar the metonymic and metaphoric structure of object a is revealed (Green, 1983, p. 169). The *agalma*, the hidden, precious object, the golden ornament contained in Silenus-like figures but actually seen by Alcibiades as depicting Socrates, the object of his desire, represents the object a, the missing object that is sought in the Other. It is precisely because this object is perceived as one of lack in the signifying process and in the Other that one becomes a subject of desire. Socrates, according to Lacan, produces the function of lack, but his method extracts knowledge (*Savoir*), knowledge of the truth of unconscious desire. But there is an inescapable division between the subject and knowledge at the moment the process of knowledge comes into play, at the moment of knowing that something is lost. This object of lack represents '*the nonspecularizable nature of the (a)*' (Green, 1983, p. 169).

A residue that stems from the desire of the other affects the Other – the locus of the word – to the extent that something takes on the value of a privileged object. It is in the measure of the subject's identification with this object, the object a, that the fundamental fantasy is constituted and around which desire is designated and follows its metonymic pathway.

Lacan's work continues an elaboration of object a following Seminar VIII but vestiges of earlier encounters with it are evident. This recognition supports the early contention that this is a truly pivotal concept. It marked his work and defined the object of psychoanalysis. Seminar X, *Anxiety* (1962–63), for example, may be seen as the work of refinement of object a, particularly in its relation to anxiety, and its links with desire and fantasy. However, its elaboration in this work depended upon the earlier formulation of the graphs of desire that structure the relationship of the subject to the signifier. In Seminar X, there is a clear distinction between Lacan's interpretation of the object and that of Freud. For Lacan, the object is beyond symbolization, and anxiety occurs not because of its loss but precisely because something appears in its place. Furthermore, the articulation of the object that sees anxiety as constituted by 'something' that appears in the place occupied by the object of desire moves it beyond the imaginary status – specifically more so by Lacan's invocation of the *Unheimlich*. It is here that some theoretical links can be made to Freud's Uncanny and its unquestionable theoretical intimation of Lacan's Real. The function of object a is that of cause of desire and in Seminar X 'Anxiety is the signal of its appearance' (Marini, 1992, p. 188).

Object a is paradoxically the object of anxiety, *the thing*, yet it is the cause of desire. Notwithstanding, it is a desire related to a lack not an object, as Lacan insists, 'man's desire is the desire of the Other' (Lacan, 1981, p. 38).

In Seminar XI (1964), object a, the privileged object that Lacan states is discovered by psychoanalysis, is purely topological. It is the object around which the drive moves, and it is in this seminar that object a refers more specifically to the Real, something outside the signifying system of language that produces an effect. This is the very position the analyst should uphold, as Socrates did, to move the subject to discover his desire.

The elaboration of the four discourses in the seminar 'The other side of psychoanalysis' (1969–70) presents object a as what, in the effects of discourse, is most opaque, yet essential. It assumes the place of knowledge in the discourse of the analyst, it is the cause of desire, and it sets the subject to work. The work thus produced – through knowledge as a means of enjoyment – is truth, and as Lacan claimed we are not without a relationship with truth (Lacan, unpublished). However, it may present as *Unheimlich* inasmuch as we may not know the truth of our desires.

In the seminars given between 1969 and 1981 (e.g., *Encore, Le Sinthome*), Lacan continued to focus on object a as the focus of the psychoanalytic act. This was evident in the important interview 'Radiophonie' (1979), which assessed the contribution and the place of psychoanalysis. Lacan stated in this interview that 'the unconscious is the condition of linguistics' but linguistics has no hold over the unconscious because it leaves as a blank that which produces effects in the unconscious – the object a. Specifically, at this point, he alluded to the fact that object a is the focus of the analytic act (Marini, 1992, p. 225).

The traversing of the fundamental fantasy (that which constitutes one's subjectivity in relation to the desire of the Other) in the course of analysis, represents the process whereby the subject comes to the place of a different relation with the cause of desire – object a.

Object a plays a unique role in the construction of fantasy and the determination of linguistically structured subjectivity. It is at the junction of the *Symbolic*, the *Imaginary* and the *Real* and it represents a point of impossibility; it is unknowable yet it has effects: **Object a is no being**.

The subject of religion, that is, the subject who is sustained by a belief in religion accepts a God as the Other. The subject of psychological science is conscious and rational, and may or may not have a belief in God, but the subject of Lacan's discourse is a subject of the unconscious and the other is object a.

To appreciate the full implication of this term, being cognisant not only of Lacan's desire not to fix meaning, but to appreciate its many movements and formulations, is to recognize precisely how significant a contribution object a has been in Lacan's psychoanalytic knowledge.

See also: **agalma**, **desire**, **imaginary**, **mirror stage**, **the Real**, **schema**, **symbolic**
Other terms: signifier

References

Fink, B. (1995). *The Lacanian Subject*. New Jersey: Princeton University Press.

Freud, S. (1955) [1920] *Beyond the Pleasure Principle, SE 18. The Standard Edition of the Works of Sigmund Freud*. London: Hogarth Press.

Green, A. (1983) 'The logic of Lacan's *objet a* and Freudian theory: Convergences and questions'. In: *Interpreting Lacan*, Vol. 6. Edited by J. H. Smith and W. Kerrigan. New Haven: Yale University Press.

Lacan, J. Seminar XVII. 'The other side of psychoanalysis'. Draft translation by Russell Grigg, unpublished.

Lacan, J. (1977) *Écrits: A Selection*. Trans. Alan Sheridan. New York: W.W. Norton.

Lacan, J. (1981) *The Four Fundamental Concepts of Psycho-Analysis* (ed. J.-A. Miller, trans. A. Sheridan). New York: W.W. Norton.

Lacan, J. (1998) (1975) *The Seminar, Book XX, Encore 1972–1973, On Feminine Sexuality, The Limits of Love and Knowledge* (ed. J.-A. Miller, trans. B. Fink). New York: W.W. Norton.

Marini, M. (1992). *Jacques Lacan: The French Context* (trans. A. Tomiche). New Jersey: Rutgers University Press.

Zita M. Marks

Pass (*Passe*)

The pass is a procedure instituted by Lacan in the 'Proposition of 9 October 1967 on the Psychoanalyst of the School', 1995. The moment of the pass is the moment of conclusion and resolution of an analysis and the verification of the passage from analysand to analyst with the emergence of 'the desire of the analyst'. The pass makes the transmission and verification of that desire possible.

Lacan's proposition was written three years after founding *L'École Française de Psychoanalyse* (*Television*, 1990, p. 97). Shortly after that, the school was known as *L'École Freudienne de Paris* (EFP). Lacan dissolved the school, the EFP, in 1980 because, according to him, it was not faithful to the project: 'since I have missed the boat with the school, for having failed to produce analysts within it who would be of the requisite level' (p. 33).

After the dissolution, *L'École de la Cause Freudienne* (ECF) was founded in January 1981; the pass was placed at the centre of its creation. This was the response to the Act of Foundation and the Proposition of 9 October 1967.

The procedure of the pass in the school of Lacan is the way in which the school guarantees the nomination of an analyst as AS or analyst of the school.

The category of membership in the school, *gradus analyst* of the school, is the result of successfully completing the pass. In the pass, the passant discusses the crucial moments in the treatment and its end with two members in analysis, the passers, who in turn transmit that testimony to 'the cartel of the pass'.

There is another *gradus*: AMS or analyst member of the school – the recognition by the school of those who have proved themselves. The status of *gradus* is for life.

In the Proposition of 9 October 1967, Lacan states one of the key principles of the pass when he says that the psychoanalyst derives his authorization only from himself. This does not mean that it is legitimate for anyone to authorize himself as analyst. On the contrary, the 'Proposition' and the 'Italian note' show the need for this new desire to be put to the test, to be proved (*Ornicar?* 1982). It also means that the analyst's authorization does not come from the Other, that is, not from a diploma, or a title, or from an authority.

Analysis is a necessary condition to become an analyst, although it is not enough. The analyst can neither be authorized by his analyst, nor by his analysands. For Lacan, the pass is the occasion when the candidate analysed has to give a testimony of the end of analysis, and of the motivation which leads a subject to authorize him-/herself as a psychoanalyst.

Lacan's principle is in opposition to the training of analysts as it is carried out in some psychoanalytic institutions. Lacan's proposition is contrary to the tradition of the institutions affiliated with the Institute of Psycho-Analysis (IPA), in which candidates are authorized as analysts as a result of their didactic analyses with analysts assigned by the institutes in a standardized way.

The principle of the pass in which 'a psychoanalyst derives authorization from him/herself' is a rethinking of what is called the formation of the analyst in the school of Lacan, putting the emphasis on the particularity of the transmission of knowledge of the analytic experience, and the new link between truth and knowledge which psychoanalysis produces. This knowledge is characterized by the not-all in its inconsistency and incompleteness.

The pass demonstrates that there is no standard or universal psychoanalyst. It means that the psychoanalyst does not exist, so the authorization that he/she derives from him-/herself is found in the singularity and particularity of his/her desire to be an analyst. What justifies the procedure of the pass is that of examining in each case if 'there is an analyst' ('Italian note').

The existence of analysts is demonstrated in each case, one by one, by what Lacan called 'the desire of the analyst'. At the end of Seminar XI of 1964, Lacan refers to 'the desire of the analyst as a desire to obtain absolute difference' which is in opposition to the idea of identification with the analyst as a person, or to the analyst's ego or super-ego.

The procedure authenticates this moment; however, there is no obligation that this moment should be verified in each case. The 'desire of the psycho-analyst' is the pivotal point around which the movement turns (Lacan, 1978). This new desire is deduced from the end of analysis, and it can be verified in the pass as an *après-coup* of the treatment.

The emergence of this new desire as the 'desire of the analyst' has an aim, which is that of offering the possibility of analysis to others. In the passage from analysand to psychoanalyst, the analyst consents to become *semblant* of object a, cause of desire. It is the support of the analytic discourse *a/S2*.

> From this moment, he must know he is rubbish. This is what an analysis, must at least, make him feel. And if by this,he is not carried by enthusiasm, there might have been an analysis but there is no analyst. ('Italian note', p. 8)

The analyst must know the consequences of the discourse that his/her practice supports. In offering his/her being as support of the analytic experience, the analyst knows that his/her final destiny in the analytic journey is to consent to be rubbish.

The pass is a structure of four parts:

- The *passant* or candidate
- Two passers
- Cartel of the pass
- The secretariat

The *passant*

The one who wants to go through the pass is called *passant*. The *passant* approaches the secretariat of the school to ask for the pass.

The testimony of the *passant*, transmitted by each passer to the cartel of the pass, constitutes a privileged instrument to know what an analytic treatment consists of, its crucial moments, the obstacles, the interruptions, the end, what changes and what does not change, how it affects the relationship of the subject with the fantasy in its crossing over and to the symptom in its identification, as well as the emergence of the 'desire of the analyst'.

The outcome of the pass must be a contribution to knowledge. In the 'Italian note' Lacan writes that the subject wants to believe, but does not want to know. Knowledge is the effect of subjective destitution, and this implies the traversing of the fundamental fantasy which gave the subject a frame of security for what he believed he was for the Other.

The 'horror to know' is transformed into 'desire to know'. The knowledge of the existence of analysts is a knowledge that cannot be universalized in the sense of determining being. The procedure of the pass, which is done 'one by one', will put that knowledge to the test. However, the knowledge that is transmitted is not standard but contingent on the subjects' presentation of the process of their analyses. The pass gives a proof of the existence of analysts by their testimony.

The two passers

The practice of the procedure establishes an encounter between the *passant*, the one who asks for the pass and the two passers separately. The passer is nominated by his/her own analyst if the analyst considers that he/she is at the moment of subjective destitution, that is, the crossing over of his/her fantasy.

The nomination designates a function, a fleeting function, that lasts the time of passing to another function, that of making another analysand go through the pass. By this designation the passer first meets the school, then the *passant*.

For the passer, who is still in analysis, this experience which is marked by chance, can be pointing to the end of his/her own analysis. The passer is a pure tool of the school, indispensable as the device. As witness he/she has the responsibility to transmit the *passant*'s testimony to the cartel of the pass. It is necessary for the *passant* to trust the passers and the cartel. The passer is susceptible to being able to imprint, through his/her own analysis, the singularity of any other analysis. There is no standard discourse, there are no rules or knowledge a priori that would establish the passer's meetings with the *passant*. The testimony is transmitted to the cartel of the pass through the operative deductions of the passer's own analysis. The passer is not at the same point in his/her own analysis as the *passant*. The former is a step behind. The passer can listen to the testimony of the *passant* from the empty space that this destitution has left. The difference between passer and *passant* is that they are not at the same point of their unconscious elaboration.

The passer, as Lacan says, is the pass. The passer registers at the secretariat of the school after being designated by his/her own analyst, and from that moment on he/she will become part of the pool of names available to be selected by the chance of the draw. It can happen that the draw falls several times to the same person, so the secretariat of the pass may receive the suggestion from the cartel of the pass to withdraw this name from the pool.

The cartel of the pass demands that the passer be ready for the experience of the 'accurate' testimony ('Proposition', 1995). The testimonies of the two passers are essential.

The decision of the 'jury' (cartel) depends on each passer's 'accurate' communication, which is not merely information. It needs a reduction of a whole existence of an analysis, the testimony of the *passant*, reduced to the brevity of the presentation of the passer to the cartel in only an hour. The object of the transmission to the cartel of the pass is the structure that has supported the analytic experience: the moments of subjective mutation, the clinic of the symptom, the traversing of the fantasy, and the fluctuations in the transference.

Cartel of the pass

The cartel is the third part of the structure and has the function of a 'jury'. It does not have a preconceived idea of how an analysand becomes an analyst as there is no standard solution to the production of the desire of the analyst. The cartel has to identify how the desire of the psychoanalyst is deduced from the analytic operation. What is verified at the end of analysis is the complete operation. Its result is the desire of the analyst. The cartel has to judge the result from the material produced in an analysis by the function of the unconscious.

The secretariat

Apart from selecting the *passant*, the secretariat is in charge of appointing the two *passers* and then of communicating to the waiting *passant* the nomination of AS.

After the nomination, the AS, has to teach the analytic community about his/her pass. The transmission will not be the same as the previous elaborations at the meetings with each of the passers.

The one who demands the pass knows that the possible nomination as 'analyst of the school' by the cartel of the pass implies a commitment to the school at the level of transmission. It is a responsibility towards the school to contribute to the progress of psychoanalysis with work and testimony.

The nomination of AS is not a stable position, but a precarious one. It is a function with the responsibility of testifying about the logical moments of an analysis for three years. This active contribution is the achievement of making of the pass something transmissible; communicating the most crucial moments of each analytic experience. The desire of saying belongs to what is called the desire of the analyst.

The analysts of the school can become members of the cartel of the pass. Their own experience of the pass will have taught them that this does not constitute the measure to judge the others.

See also: **desire**, **object a**, **subject**
Other terms: analysand, analysis, analyst, ethics, fantasy, *semblant*, transference, unconscious

References

Lacan, J. (1978) [1973] *The Four Fundamental Concepts of Psycho-Analysis*. New York: W.W. Norton.

Lacan, J. (1982) 'Note Italienne' (Italian note), *Ornicar?* 25: 8.

Lacan, J. (1990) [1964] 'Founding act', *Television*. New York: W.W. Norton.

Lacan, J. (1990) [1980] 'The Other is missing', *Television*. New York: W.W. Norton.

Lacan, J. (1995) 'Proposition of 9 October 1967 on the Psychoanalyst of the School', *Analysis* 6.

Susana Tillet

Phallus

In Freud

The term 'phallus' occurs in Freud on very few occasions and usually in reference to the use antiquity makes of a figurative representation of the male member as object of veneration. However, Freud makes use of the adjective 'phallic' by means of which he develops his ideas on infantile sexual theories, particularly in reference to the phallic stage or the phallic mother, who is endowed with having a phallus.

In Freud's early work, both the boy and the girl are described as relating to the universality of the penis, producing castration fear on the side of the boy and penis envy on the side of the girl. In 1923 Freud posed the primacy of the phallus, which was a decisive step for psychoanalysis. He opposed the penis and the clitoris as organs that symbolize the one phallus. Here it can be said that although Freud described the phallus in direct relation to the penis, the reference is to the penis as lacking or potentially lacking. However, he reduced the phallus to the real categories of male and female, which eventually led to the impasse of analysis without end.

Freud considered the phallic organization as a stage of libidinal development for both the girl and the boy. The pair of opposites – activity/passivity – operating during the anal stage, is transformed into the polarity of phallic and castrated. The choice offered the subject is between having the phallus or being castrated, that is, at this stage, both sexes only really relate to one genital organ, the male organ.

It can be noted that it is not entirely correct to characterize Freud as making an equivalence between penis and phallus. What is symbolized cannot be reduced to the male organ in its anatomical reality. Laplanche and Pontalis (1983) point out that what really characterizes the phallus and reappears in all its figurative embodiments is its status as a detachable and transformable object. Freud (1917) particularly shows this with female sexuality, where the wish to have the phallus is transformed into the wish to have a child by the father.

The centrality of the phallic stage functions in the dissolution of the Oedipus complex, where the threat of castration for the boy focuses him on preserving the narcissistic investment in his penis. For the little girl, her discovery of the lack of a penis and potential penis envy, lead her to turn away from the mother and to await the reception of a baby in the form of a symbolic substitute for the penis, from a man. Both of these developments, for the girl and for the boy, are centred around the phallic organ and its substitutes.

In 1925, Freud's unique contribution was to set out the different ways in which the primacy of the phallus is revealed for each sex. The discovery of the phallus is inscribed in the register of lack for the boy. It is dealt with by means of signifying the lack with the phallus. The discovery for the girl is inscribed in the register of the veil. She sees and understands instantly that she is without it and wants to have it. The sign of the penis as a sexual identification, which she is without, serves as a screen to veil the nature of her lack (Andre, 1999).

In Lacan

Phallus as signifier and lack
It was Lacan who made of the phallus a signifier and a lack, in stating that the only way of comprehending the symbolism of the phallus is through its specific function as signifier of lack.

In his 1958 paper, 'Signification of the phallus', Lacan arrives at the following:

> [...] the phallus is not a phantasy, if by that we mean an imaginary effect. Nor is it as such an object (part-internal, good, bad, etc.) in the sense that this term tends to accentuate the reality pertaining in a relation. It is even less the organ, penis or clitoris, that it symbolises. And it is not without reason that Freud used the reference to the simulacrum that it represented for the Ancients. For the phallus is a signifier, a signifier whose function, in the intrasubjective economy of the analysis, lifts the veil perhaps from the function it performed in the mysteries. For it is the signifier intended to designate as a whole the effects of the signified, in that the signifier conditions them by its presence as signifier. (p. 285)

Lacan thus stresses that the phallus is never anything but a signifier. It is the signifier of desire and, as desire is always correlated with a lack, the phallus is the signifier of lack. Its displacements and shifts in discourse indicate the movement of lack within the structure as a whole. The main emphasis is on the speaking being as a divided subject marked by the lack which makes him or her desire.

Prior to this, Lacan had established his work on the Symbolic, Imaginary and Real registers, the unconscious structured as a language and the paternal metaphor. Each of these notions plays a fundamental and structuring role for the operation of the phallus.

Paternal metaphor

The establishment of the Name-of-the-Father stabilizes the structure of the unconscious through the correlative establishing of the phallus. The Name-of-the-Father substitutes for the Desire of the Mother, and the phallus is established as signifier of this desire in the subject's unconscious. It is fundamentally the repression of the phallus as signifier that constitutes the unconscious as language. The phallus is the name given to what the mother lacks. The assumption of the phallic signifier enables the subject to adopt a position in relation to sexual differentiation. This then makes it possible for the subject to normalize his or her relation to the phallus, as someone who will be able to provide it, in the case of a male, or as someone able to receive it, in the case of a female. Lacan's distinction between the penis as sexual organ, and the phallus as signifier of sexual desire and castration are important here. The possession of a penis does not guarantee possession of the phallus. A biological male may be completely identified with not having the phallus, for instance.

From penis to phallus

Lacan preserves the term penis for the male genital organ whereas phallus is used for the imaginary and symbolic dimensions. The penis is only the phallus in so far as it can lack, and it is the symbolic alone that can create a lack.

Lacan never stopped revising his definitions in order to make the phallus a fundamental concept of psychoanalysis. In this light, he continues to refer to the Symbolic, Imaginary and Real registers throughout his work in order to justify his use of the phallic reference.

In 1966–67, he returns to the idea of the 'negativising' that is brought to bear on the *jouissance* of the organ of copulation, the penis. It is this negativizing that gives a limit to a *jouissance* that would otherwise be excessive and interfere with a desire which is necessarily based on lack. It does so on the basis of the function of detumescence.

> And why does the penis find itself symbolising it? Precisely because of that which, in the form of detumescence, materialises this flaw, this lack in jouissance, materialises the lack which derives or, more exactly, which appears to derive, from the law of pleasure. (Seminar of 8 March 1967)

This refers to the fact that pleasure has a limit and that too much pleasure is an unpleasure. Here the phallus is the signifier of lost *jouissance* and, as it is the signifier of desire, desire implies lack of *jouissance* (-phi).

In the seminar of 1956–57, when Lacan first introduces the distinction between penis and phallus, the phallus refers to an imaginary object perceived by the child in the pre-Oedipal phase as the object of the mother's desire, referring to that which she desires beyond the child and with which the child seeks to identify.

To re-emphasize, Lacan refers to the phallus as a signifier. One signifier comes to signify that part of the parents' desire that goes beyond the child. It is this aspect that becomes the principal element of Lacan's theory of the phallus – the signifier of the desire of the Other.

It is also in this seminar that Lacan articulates the notion of the phallus on different levels. He illustrates, with the case of Little Hans, how Freud introduces the phallus as a third imaginary term between the mother and the child, and this phallus plays a major signifying role. Lacan distinguishes three structural moments in the constitution of the subject:

- the moment of frustration, which refers to the imaginary damage done to a real object – the penis as organ;
- the moment of privation, which refers to the real lack created by the loss of a symbolic object – the phallus as signifier;

- the moment of castration, referring to the symbolic debt in the register of the real and the loss of the phallus as imaginary object.

Each subject must renounce the possibility of being the phallus for the mother, opening the way for a relation to the symbolic phallus, where the relation is different for each sex. Having the phallus or not is going to act as localization of *jouissance*. The effects of the phallic function on the relations between man and woman produce different effects in both sexes in terms of love and desire. In 'Signification of the phallus', Lacan describes how for women, love and desire converge on the same object. In men, the demand for love is satisfied in one woman, where the signifier of the phallus 'constitutes her as giving in love what she does not have', and the desire for the phallus leads to another woman, who signifies the phallus in other ways, for example as virgin or prostitute. This basic idea comes from Freud (1912), with Lacan introducing to the structure a fourth element, the masquerade of having or being the phallus.

> Paradoxical as this formulation may seem, I am saying that it is in order to be the phallus, that is to say, the signifier of the desire of the Other, that a woman will reject an essential part of femininity, namely, all her attributes in the masquerade. It is for that which she is not that she wishes to be desired as well as loved. But she finds the signifier of her own desire in the body of him to whom she addresses her demand for love. Perhaps it should not be forgotten that the organ that assumes this signifying function takes on the value of a fetish. (p. 289)

In 1972–73, Lacan makes use of the phallic function in his formulae of sexuation. The phallus is required for sexuation because the object involved in the drive is asexual. Thus, the unconscious as locus of repression of the drives does not know the difference between the sexes as such. It is the phallus, as signifier, which introduces this dialectic for the unconscious, where the object can thus take on phallic signification for what is lacking. The Name-of-the-Father, functioning in the paternal metaphor to substitute for the Desire of the Mother, gives to the object of the drive a phallic identification. This renders the objects that come and go from the body the capacity to function as substitutes for the phallus.

In the formulae of sexuation, the phallic function is equivalent to the function of castration, referring to the fact that sexuality is marked by the sign of a lack, the phallic lack. This is brought about by the fact that a human subject is required to speak and use the signifier, thereby losing a part of his or her complete *jouissance*. The difference between man and woman comes about through the different relation to the phallic signifier and the different forms of *jouissance* thereby experienced. Man, completely subjected to the phallic signifier, experiences phallic *jouissance*. Woman, not-all subjected to the phallic signifier, experiences phallic *jouissance* plus the possibility of another form of *jouissance*, the Other *jouissance*.

The clinic

The most controversial question in relation to the phallus is how its function can be justified. The answer given by Lacan is that it is the clinic that gives the evidence which attests to its function.

In 'Signification of the phallus', Lacan points out that clinical facts reveal 'a relation of the subject to the phallus that is established without regard to the anatomical difference of the sexes'. He cites the clinical fact that both sexes consider the mother to possess the phallus and that the signification of castration shows its effects 'only on the basis of its discovery as castration of the mother'. In the case of women, Lacan cites the commonly presented problem of the girl regarding herself as castrated, first by her mother and then by her father. These circumstances lead to the question of the phallic stage, which is characterized by 'the imaginary dominance of the phallic attribute and by masturbatory *jouissance*'. This *jouissance* for the woman is localized in the clitoris, thus raising it to the function of the phallus.

A few examples can be cited to give some manifest clinical indications.

A common presentation of the neurotic is a subject who wants to be the phallus, thinking that he or she has to show the possession of it. From this there follows a fear that the Other wants to take it. However, the phallus can be nothing material, even though something can represent it. The neurotic makes the mistake of trying to be the phallus for the Other by having it. The phallus has to be a sign of lack and the object can represent the phallus only in so far as it lacks.

Lacan comments that one of the conditions of 'frigidity' is that of the woman identifying herself with the phallic object. Lacan elaborates the position of woman in the sexual relation as being placed as the phallus. It is a question, however, of being the phallus of the Other and does not involve a phallic identification with the standard, as happens in the case of 'frigidity'.

Some little girls defend themselves against the sexual difference by way of compulsively displaying the non-existent penis. This avoids having to find a substitute for the missing penis. However, this abolition of lack can lead to the abolition of sexual life, since without lack there is no desire to seek satisfaction.

In the case of psychosis, the foreclosure of the primordial signifier has a direct impact on the rest of the chain of signifiers, producing two holes in the Other, in the places where the Name-of-the-Father and the phallus should be. This produces catastrophic consequences for the psychotic's relation with the signifier and with his/her own body. In a number of cases of psychosis, the penis is not marked by symbolization and is therefore unable to accede to functioning as phallus in the dialectic of desire. Where this occurs, the organ, in its real dimension, suffers from being experienced as 'too much'. What often ensues is a real self-mutilation taking the place of what has not been symbolized.

The clinic presents the evidence that the phallus is the principle of the desire of the mother, of the function of the father and of the signification of the child. Neurosis, perversion and psychosis are the clinical consequences of the position that the child will take, depending on whether or not the dialectical movement between the mother's desire and the paternal function has occurred. The conception of the child is as the subject to whom the question of the unconscious concerning the mother's desire is addressed. The answer to this question lies in its reference to the phallus, the discovery of which leads to a neurosis. If, in spite of finding the answer, the subject enjoys occupying the place of object of the Other's desire, he or she becomes perverse. 'He becomes psychotic when he realises the presence of the object plugging the lack that is specified in the desire of the mother, and when he incarnates the object of the prohibited jouissance. We could say that neurosis is related to desire, whereas psychosis concerns jouissance.' (DiGiacomo, 1998: 52).

See also: **castration**, **desire**, **imaginary**, ***jouissance***, **Name-of-the-Father**, **psychosis**, **real**, **sexuation**, **symbolic**
Other terms: clinic, lack, neurosis, other, perversion

References

Andre, S. (1999) *What Does a Woman Want?* New York: Other Press.
DiGiacomo, E. (1998) 'Sexuality in the structure of childhood psychosis', *Analysis* 8: 48–58.
Freud, S. (1912) [1957] 'On the universal tendency to debasement in the sphere of love'. *SE 11*:177. *Standard Edition, Complete Psychological Works of Sigmund Freud.* London: Hogarth Press.
Freud, S. (1917) [1955] 'On the transformations of instinct, as exemplified in anal erotism'. *SE 17*:127.
Freud, S. (1923) [1961] 'The infantile genital organization'. *SE 19*:14.
Freud, S. (1925) [1961] 'Some psychical consequences of the anatomical distinction between the sexes'. *SE 19*: 243.
Lacan, J. (1966–67) Le Séminaire, Livre XIV. 'La logique du fatasme' (The logic of the fantasy). Unpublished.
Lacan, J. (1977) [1958] 'Signification of the phallus'. In *Écrits: A Selection.* London: Tavistock.
Lacan, J. (1994) [1956–57] *Le Séminaire, Livre IV. La relation d'objet.* (*The object relation*) (ed. J.-A.-Miller). Paris: Seuil.
Laplanche, J. and Pontalis, J.-B. (1983) *The Language of Psychoanalysis.* London: Hogarth Press.

Carmela Levy-Stokes

Quilting Point (*Point de capiton*)

The concept of a quilting point (also translated as 'anchoring point') was first introduced by Lacan on 6 June 1956 in his seminar on the psychoses (Seminar III, Lacan, 1993). In the first instance the term refers to a type of speech occurrence in which a given signifier has a crystallizing effect that ramifies throughout entire chains of signifiers. This effect is in part semantic, in that it can have a radical meaning effect upon a chain of signifiers, either by making clear what is vague and nebulous or by radically altering the meaning of an entire discourse. The quilting point can also have an ontological effect, producing a modification of or displacement in, the subjective position of one or more subjects. Lacan's theory of the quilting point thus reflects both the experience of analysis, particularly the place of interpretation in that experience, and also the more general phenomenon of language use. It is also, in part, his response to the question of how meaning emerges in speech.

The term 'quilting point' is additionally used in a more specific sense, related to its origins in Lacan's first theory of psychosis. In this sense 'quilting' is an outcome of the successful foundation of the paternal metaphor, which accomplishes a knotting between signifier and signified; indeed the paternal metaphor has itself come to be regarded as the primordial quilting point, and certain speech and language phenomena in psychosis are a direct consequence of its absence (see, for just one example, the discussion of code phenomena and message phenomena in 'On a question preliminary to any possible treatment of psychosis', Lacan, 1977, pp. 184–7).

Ferdinand de Saussure had promoted the view of a synchronic unfolding of signifier and signified in speech, whereby the signified unfolds at the same rhythm as the signifier.

This view followed directly from Saussure's claim that the sign comprises a signifier and a signified and that there is a one-to-one correspondence between the two. The meaning of a sentence or a locution then follows relatively easily: it arises from the mere concatenation of signs, each with its own signified. Thus, the only

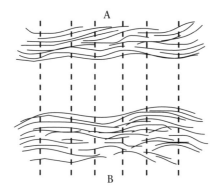

Figure 9: Saussure's schema
Source: Saussure, F. de (1905) *Courte in General Linguistics*.

real question for Saussure here was how the mutual delimiting of signifier and signified occurs. This is not unlike the question of how it is that speakers generally manage to disambiguate words with more than one meaning when they occur in the context of a sentence. It was thought that the mutual interaction between the signs of a language forced one meaning to be chosen over another.

The approach is too simplistic, as linguists themselves came to see. With examples such as 'The shooting of the hunters was terrible', Noam Chomsky showed that ambiguity could be generated by an underlying syntactic complexity that could not be explained by treating grammar as mere concatenation of individual words.

Lacan also questioned the Saussurian approach in the 1950s, in his enquiry into the nature of psychosis and the elaboration of the concept of foreclosure and in the subsequent reflections on language that appeared in 'The Agency of the Letter'. Lacan's views about the nature of the relationship between the signifier and the signified follow from the basic point that there is a constant sliding of the signifier over the signified (Lacan, 1977, pp. 146–78; 1993, chapter 21). There is no 'pinning' of one signifier to a signified; at best one can pin one signifier to another and see what happens (Lacan, 1998). And what happens is that as the signifier unfolds in speech it both anticipates meaning and has a retroactive impact upon meaning. Hence Lacan's observation in 'The agency of the letter' that 'it is in the signifier chain that meaning *insists*, but ...

none of the chain's elements *consist* in the signification it is capable of at any given moment' (Lacan, 1977, pp. 146–78).

The notion of an incessant sliding of the signified under the signifier Lacan regarded as 'unavoidable' and he rejected Saussure's illustration which reminded him of 'the wavy lines of the upper and lower Waters in miniatures from manuscripts of Genesis: a twofold flood [*double flux*] in which the landmarks – fine streaks of rain traced by vertical dotted lines that supposedly delimit corresponding segments – seem insubstantial' (Lacan, 1977, p. 154; trans. modified).

Lacan, because psychoanalytic experience runs counter to this, introduced the quilting point, required 'to account for the dominance of the letter in the dramatic transformation that dialogue can effect in the subject' (Lacan, 1977, p. 154).

In a discussion of *Athaliah* in his seminar on the psychoses already referred to, Lacan takes the signifier 'the fear of God' to illustrate the *point de capiton* (see Seminar III, pp. 262–8, 297–304, especially p. 289, fn. 6). The play opens with a dialogue between an officer in the army of the queen, Abner, and the High Priest. Each is unsure of the intentions of the other and the exchange between them corresponds to the 'amorphous mass of thoughts' in the upper level of Saussure's schema. Abner declares, 'I tremble with fear … that Athaliah should … wreak upon you her dreadful revenge.' However, as Lacan observes, the status of the remark is thoroughly ambiguous: is Abner making a threat, uttering a warning, giving a counsel of prudence, or calling for discretion? As the dialogue unfolds, what crystallizes his remarks, and indeed decides his own position, is the High Priest's words, 'I fear God, dear Abner, and have no other fear.' This reply transforms the 'zeal' of the outset into the 'faithfulness' of the conclusion, and in doing so, transforms Abner from a somewhat purposeless/abstract zealot into a committed and faithful supporter of the plot to overthrow the Queen. This 'transmutation' is brought about by 'the intervention of the signifier'. The phrase, 'fear of God', as the agent of this transformation, is the quilting point.

Two comments on this discussion should be made. The first is that the transformation is brought about by the intervention of a signifier, not of a meaning or signification. The second is that the transformation has not only a semantic and epistemological function, but also, crucially, it produces a subjective transformation or subjective rectification.

It is this latter development that echoes the effect of analytic interpretation. This can be seen in Freud's intervention in the case of Dora when, faced with her litany of reproaches against her father and his lover, Frau K, and her husband, Herr K, he asks about the self-reproaches that are its other side. This has the effect of referring Dora to her own complicity in the arrangement and produces a subjective reversal: from innocent victim of the machinations of others to complicit conspirator in the intrigues that are unfolding.

'Quilting point' (Chomsky, 1971) has a more specific use stemming from its origin in Lacan's first theory of psychosis. It is an aspect of a successful outcome of the paternal metaphor, which is absent in psychosis, where the knotting between signifier and signified is accomplished. In the absence of this knotting there arise a number of psychotic phenomena that include linguistic ones.

See also: **discourse**, **Name-of-the-Father**, **signifier**

References

Chomsky, N. (1971) *Syntactic Structures*. The Hague and Paris: Mouton.

Lacan, J. (1977) 'The agency of the letter in the unconscious or reason since Freud'. In: *Écrits: A Selection*. London: Tavistock.

Lacan, J. (1993) *The Seminar of Jacques Lacan, Book III, The Psychoses 1955–1956* (chapter 21). New York: W.W. Norton.

Lacan, J. (1998) *Le Seminaire, Livre V, Les Formations de l'inconscient, 1957–58*. Paris: Editions du Seuil.

Saussure, F. de (1966) [1905] *Course in General Linguistics*. C. Bally and A. Sechehye in collaboration with A. Reidlinger (eds) (trans. W. Baskin). New York: McGraw-Hill.

Russell Grigg

Psychosis

Psychosis is a nosological category distinct from neurosis and perversion. It is brought about by the foreclosure of a primordial signifier, the Name-of-the-Father.

In his seminar of 1955–56 (Seminar III, *The Psychoses*), Lacan argues that there is a defence mechanism specific to psychosis on the grounds that the peculiarly invasive and devastating nature of psychotics' delusional systems and hallucinations indicates major structural differences between psychosis and neurosis.

It is true that Freud had found that the discourse of the psychotic and the apparently bizarre and meaningless phenomena of psychosis could be deciphered and understood, just as dreams can. Freud's analysis of the psychotic Schreber's memoirs thus broke with contemporary approaches to psychosis, which regarded psychotics as beyond the limits of understanding (Freud, 1951).

However, as Lacan points out, the fact that the psychotic's discourse is just as interpretable as that of the neurotic leaves the two disorders at the same level and fails to account for the major differences between them, thus the distinction between the two remains to be explained. It is around this issue of the different mechanisms in psychosis and neurosis that Lacan's major contribution to the study of psychosis revolves.

Freud claims that in both neurosis and psychosis there is a withdrawal of investment, or object-cathexis, from objects in the world. In the case of neurosis the object-cathexis is retained, but is invested in fantasized objects in the neurotic's internal world. In the case of psychosis the withdrawn cathexis is invested in the ego at the expense of all object-cathexes, even in fantasy. This turning of libido upon the ego accounts for symptoms such as hypochondria and megalomania. The delusional system, the most striking feature of psychosis, arises in a second stage. Freud characterizes the construction of a delusional system as an attempt at recovery in which the psychotic re-establishes a new, often very intense, relation with the people and things in the world by way of a delusional formation.

According to Lacan, psychosis cannot be the result of repression. He argues that Freud's classic studies on the unconscious, that is, *The Interpretation of Dreams, The Psychopathology of Everyday Life, Jokes and their Relation to the Unconscious,* indicate that the mechanisms of repression and the return of the repressed are linguistic in nature. That the unconscious is structured like a language implies that for something to be repressed it has to have been previously acknowledged by the subject, implying prior recognition within the symbolic register.

When the child's symbolic universe is created it is possible for a signifier to be excluded from the symbolic altogether and thus never to form part of it. It is this exclusion or foreclosure of a fundamental linguistic element, a key signifier, at the moment of the genesis of the symbolic that results in a psychotic subject. Foreclosure contrasts with repression, in that what is foreclosed is excluded from the symbolic system altogether; it has never been registered there and therefore, so far as the symbolic is concerned, simply does not exist. Yet what is foreclosed from the symbolic is not purely and simply abolished. It returns, but, unlike the return of the repressed, it returns from outside the subject, as emanating from his environment in one form or another – a phenomenon not to be confused with projection, which is not specific to psychosis.

Psychosis involves a form of regression – topographical rather than chronological – from the symbolic register to the imaginary. That is, what has been foreclosed from the symbolic reappears in the real, which is not the same as reality, and it is marked by the properties of the imaginary. In particular, relations with the other are marked by erotic attachment and aggressive rivalry. Thus, Professor Flechsig becomes an erotic object for Schreber but also the agent of Schreber's persecution. The homosexuality in Schreber that Freud highlighted is therefore treated not as a cause of Schreber's psychosis but rather as a symptom produced by the psychotic foreclosure.

Foreclosure may well be a normal psychic process; it is only when what is foreclosed is specifically concerned with the question of the father, as in Schreber's case, that psychosis is produced. Using a term to indicate that what is at issue is a signifier and not a person, and that this signifier is replete with cultural and religious significance, Lacan refers to this signifier that is missing in psychosis as the Name-of-the-Father. The Name-of-the-Father is a key signifier for the subject's symbolic universe, regulating this order and giving it its structure. Its function in the Oedipus complex is to be the vehicle of the law that regulates desire – both the subject's desire and the omnipotent desire of the maternal figure.

Since foreclosure of the Name-of-the-Father is an outcome of the Oedipus complex, it follows that the psychotic structure is laid down for a subject at the time of negotiating the Oedipus complex. This implies that the psychotic structure will have existed all along, like a hairline fracture, for many years prior to the clinical appearance of the psychosis when it suddenly and dramatically appears. And we can see this in Schreber, who, after all, had up until the age of fifty-one led a relatively normal life, enjoying a successful career, and carrying out quite demanding duties on the bench.

Lacan holds that it is a certain type of encounter, in which the Name-of-the-Father is 'called into symbolic opposition to the subject', that triggers psychosis (*Écrits*, 1977, p. 217). In the seminar on psychosis there is a discussion of the function of *l'appel*, the call, the calling, the appeal or the interpellation. The discussion is not related specifically to psychosis but rather to a quite general linguistic function. The basic idea is captured in the English distinction between, for example, the two statements: 'You are the one who will follow me', and 'You are the one who shall follow me.'

It is possible to take the first as a description of or prediction about something that will come to pass: 'I predict that you will follow me.' The second, on the other hand, can serve as an appeal, where the interlocutor is called upon to make a decision, to pursue a course of action that he must either embrace or repudiate. This latter case is for instance exemplified by Jesus of Nazareth's invocation to his disciples-to-be, where 'You are the ones who shall follow me' means something like this: 'I say to you, "You are the ones who shall follow me." Now, tell me, what is your reply, what do you say to this? Give me your answer, for now is the time to choose.' In this example Jesus is 'in symbolic opposition to' his disciples, he is asking them, for 'symbolic recognition', since his speech calls upon them to respond in a way that commits them to a decision, one loaded with practical consequences, as to whether they are to recognize him as the Messiah.

For Schreber there is a moment when he is called, interpellated, by, or better, *in* the Name-of-the-Father, and the lack of the signifier declares itself. This is sufficient to trigger the psychosis.

In psychosis this symbolic opposition, this call for symbolic recognition, is brought about by an encounter with 'a real father, not necessarily by the subject's own father, but by A-father' – a situation that arises under two conditions: when the subject is in a particularly intense relation with a strong narcissistic component; and when, in this situation, the question of the father arises from a third position, one that is external to the erotic relation.

It may occur, 'for the woman who has just given birth, in her husband's face; for the penitent confessing his sins in the person of his confessor, for the girl in love in meeting "the young man's father"' (*Écrits*, 1977, p. 217). It can also occur in analysis, where the development of the transference can precipitate a psychosis.

Once the psychosis is triggered, everything will have changed for good, but what about before the onset? It is in pursuing this question that Lacan discusses Hélène Deutsch's work, in which she refers to the 'as if' phenomenon, where, for example, an adolescent boy identifies with another youth in what looks like a homosexual attachment but turns out to be a precursor of psychosis. Here there is something that plays the role of a *suppléance*, a substitute, a stand-in, for what is missing at the level of the symbolic. Lacan uses an analogy to explain this notion of a substitute or stand-in for what is lacking in the symbolic:

> Not every stool has four legs. There are some that stand upright on three. Here, though, there is no question of their lacking any, otherwise things go very badly indeed … It is possible that at the outset the stool doesn't have enough legs, but that up to a certain point it will nevertheless stand up, when the subject, at a certain crossroads of his biographical history, is confronted by this lack that has always existed (Seminar III, *The Psychoses*, p. 265).

It is intriguing that some psychotics have been capable of making important scientific or artistic contributions. Cantor, the mathematician, is a famous example we know about because of the documented psychotic episodes he underwent. But Lacan also speculates that there may be cases where the psychosis never declares itself and the clinical phenomena never eventuate. Perhaps in these cases the (pre-)psychotic subject may find a form of substitute for the foreclosed signifier that enables the subject to maintain the minimum symbolic links necessary for normal, even for highly original and creative, functioning.

Lacan argues in *Le Sinthome* (1976) that there are a number of indications suggesting that James Joyce was probably such a case: a psychotic who was able to use his writing as an effective substitute that prevented the onset of psychosis. Though necessarily speculative, such a line of thought raises important issues here to do with the diagnosis of psychosis – could, for example, the so-called borderlines be situated here?

Lacan admonished psychoanalysts not to back away from the treatment of psychosis. Lacan received psychotics, and today most Lacanian analysts are prepared to work with psychotics. Indeed, there are psychoanalyst-psychiatrists in France and elsewhere who have instituted the regular and systematic treatment of psychotics in State psychiatric services – services, note, that receive no special funding vis-à-vis those employing more typical psychiatric approaches. Two major issues are raised by the treatment of psychotics: the handling of the transference and, the aim of the treatment, and these have been extensively addressed by Lacanian analysts.

The main points of Lacan's theory of psychosis can be summarized as follows:

- A specific mechanism, foreclosure of the Name-of-the-Father, produces psychosis. This key signifier is not admitted to the symbolic system, leaving a hole where this signifier would normally be.
- Foreclosure occurs, under circumstances not discussed here, at the moment of the Oedipus complex. It is one resolution of the Oedipus complex, and contrasts with neurosis and perversion.
- Onset of psychosis is triggered, years later, by a particular type of encounter, which Lacan calls an encounter with A-father.
- The psychosis eventually stabilizes into a delusional system, or 'delusional metaphor', involving imaginary phenomena in the place of the missing signifier.

See also: **aggressivity, Borromean knot, desire, discourse, fore-closure, imaginary, Name-of-the-Father, real, symbolic, treatment**
Other terms: neurosis, Oedipal complex, perversion, repression, structure, *suppléance*, symptom, transference, unconscious

References

Freud, S. (1951) [1911] 'Psycho-Analytic Notes on an Autobiographical Account of a Case of Paranoia (Dementia Paranoides)', (vol. 12, p. 3) *Standard Edition, The Complete Psychological Works of Sigmund Freud*. London: Hogarth Press.

Freud, S. (1986) [1900–01] *The Interpretation of Dreams* (*SE* vols 4, 5).

Freud, S. (1986) [1905] *The Psychopathology of Everyday Life* (*SE* vol. 6).

Freud, S. (1986) [1905] *Jokes and their Relation to the Unconscious* (*SE* vol. 7).

Lacan, J. (1993) [1955–56] *Seminar III: The Psychosis* (trans. R. Grigg). New York: W.W. Norton.

Lacan, J. (1977) [1959] 'On a question preliminary to any possible treatment of psychosis', *Écrits: A Selection* (trans. A. Sheridan). London: Tavistock.

Lacan, J. (1976) *Le Sinthome, Séminaire XXIII* (1975–76), *Ornicar?* 6, 7, 8, 9, 10, 11 [Provisional transcription].

Russell Grigg

The Real

During the early 1950s Lacan introduced his triad of the imaginary, the symbolic and the real as the elementary categories structuring psychic reality and psychoanalytic experience. As a component part of human experience, the Real is not simply equated with common reality, although Lacan did not always clearly distinguish these two terms during the early years of his teaching.

The meaning and relative importance of the categories of the real, the symbolic and the imaginary varied over the years, and the significance of each category always remained relative to that of the two others. This interrelation especially holds for the real, which was explicitly conceived as a <u>function</u> of the symbolic and the imaginary.

At first, Lacan considered the relevance of the real within psychoanalysis to be insubstantial. Yet its importance grew steadily from the 1960s onwards and it gained momentum in the 1970s, while as a category it kept the status of being deducted from the symbolic and the imaginary. The real thus remained that limit of experience resisting symbolization (Seminar I, p. 66; Seminar IV, p. 31). The other side of the story reads that the symbolic is the only go-between able to apprehend the real (Seminar II, p. 97; Seminar XI, p. 6).

In accordance with his project to re-establish the function of speech and the field of language in psychoanalytic treatment, Lacan initially emphasized the priority of the symbolic over the imaginary, and more particularly the distinction between a praxis founded on the symbolic and a praxis restricted to the imaginary (ego psychology). Within this framework, the real was considered 'residual with respect to the edifice which commands our attention in analysis' (Seminar I, p. 66).

Opposed to the gestalt character of the imaginary, which is ruled by (re)semblance, and distinguished from the discursive reality of the symbolic, which is grounded on the notion of difference, the real was primarily defined in a negative way. Since it is neither imaginary nor symbolic, the real is excluded from the realm of fantasy and does not take part in speech (Seminar I, p. 74).

From this it follows that the real also falls beyond the scope of analytic treatment, which is an experience of speech. This may explain why Lacan considered its relevance insignificant at that stage of his teaching.

Lacan's conception of the hallucination as a psychotic phenomenon can be situated in the same vein. For, '[i]n the subject's relationship to the symbol there is the possibility of a primitive *Verwerfung*, that is, that something is not symbolized and is going to appear in the real' (Seminar III, p. 81).

Additional indications of the real as being 'without fissure' (Seminar II, p. 97) and as always appearing 'at the same place' (Seminar II, p. 235) further designate it as the remainder or the residue of (psychoanalytic) experience not susceptible to any form of corrosion or change (*Variantes de la cure-type*, p. 350).

Despite its auxiliary character during the early years of Lacan's teaching, and despite its oblique description as an obstinate leftover of experience, the real was held to be antagonistic to a conception of reality that is unequivocal, external and cognizable.

Early on, the real's qualities of being unmediated and residual drew it close to the experience of anxiety. In his 1955 discussion of Freud's dream of Irma's injection, Lacan expressed this link aptly:

> [t]here's an anxiety-provoking apparition of an image which summarizes what we can call the revelation of that which is least penetrable in the real, of the real lacking any possible mediation, of the ultimate real, of the essential object which isn't an object any longer, but this something faced with which all words cease and all categories fail, the object of anxiety *par excellence* (Seminar II, p. 164).

The relation between the real and anxiety varied along with Lacan's conceptualization of anxiety. The early 1960s seminar on anxiety is an interesting reference in this respect.

Although not crammed with mentions of the real, Lacan's seminar on *The Ethics of Psychoanalysis* (1959–60), and, more specifically, his elaboration of the Freudian *Ding* (Thing), constitutes a seminal text for comprehending the real's paradoxical nature.

[T]he Thing is that which in the real, the primordial real ... suffers from the signifier – and you should understand that it is ... the real in its totality, both the real of the subject and the real he has to deal with as exterior to him. (Seminar VII, p. 18)

Throughout a lengthy comment on Freud's *Project for a Scientific Psychology*, Lacan demonstrated how human experience is organized around the Thing, which he depicted as an 'excluded interior' (Seminar VII, p. 101), 'intimate exteriority', and 'extimacy' (Seminar VII, p. 139).

The Thing's paradoxical nature is that it never existed as human experience, but was installed retroactively through the (Oedipal) law. The incest prohibition bars access to an object that was never available in the first place. More emphatically, the said prohibition (paradoxically) installs the forbidden object as the pivotal element of subjective experience.

The term extimacy invokes that peculiar blend of being both inaccessible and intimate, but also stresses the Thing's ambiguous position with regard to in- and outside. It is both internal and external to the subject's reality. The extimate Thing which can only be represented by something else also prefigures the status of the (sexual) object. 'The object is established in a certain relationship to the Thing and is intended to encircle and to render both present and absent' (Seminar VII, p. 141).

The above connection between the real and the function of the object persists in later years, through the concept of the object a as cause of desire, but even more conspicuously as object of the drive. In the mid-1960s, Lacan introduced a radical split between desire and drive, desire being on the side of the law (the Other), and drive on the side of the Thing.

The real Thing of the drive is *jouissance*. From that moment onwards, the relation between the divided subject and the object a, the fundamental fantasy, became important for defining the real. '[I]t is in relation to the real that the level of fantasy functions. The real supports the fantasy, the fantasy protects the real' (Seminar XI, p. 41).

The fantasy functions as a screen, as an illusion covering or masking the real. Reality is rooted in fantasy, the object a is a semblance of being, 'unable ... to sustain itself in approaching the real' (Seminar XX, p. 95).

Lacan's 1964 seminar the *Four Fundamental Concepts of Psycho-Analysis* (1978) constituted a pivotal point in Lacan's teaching, because he turned to tools other than language to formalize and transmit psychoanalytic experience. This shift to mathematics and logic was particularly germane to an approach of the real, which represents what is 'impossible' to catch in words.

This seminar indeed introduced the real as 'the impossible to say' (*l'impossible à dire*), the unsayable. However, instead of limiting the impossible to the quality of 'irreducible remainder', Lacan associated it with the possibility of something new.

Reminiscent of the lack in the symbolic order – not everything can be said – the real as the impossible to say opened up the contingency of the encounter (*tuché*) beyond the automaton (the endless repetition) of the symbolic.

'The real is distinguished ... by the fact that its economy ... admits something new, which is precisely the impossible' (Seminar XI, 167). It is the conceptualization of repetition as one of the four fundamental concepts that led Lacan to approach the real in terms of the encounter.

This encounter which happens by chance is always missed, because it happens either too early or too late. The real escapes. Its quality of being impossible to master or to understand highlights its fundamental traumatic effect.

During the early 1970s, for instance in his seminar *Encore* (1972–73), Lacan still emphasized the contingency of the encounter. 'The regime of the encounter is tantamount to contingency' (Seminar XX, p. 94). But by this time, the impossible of the real had obtained an additional epithet, in the format of the impossible sexual relation.

Thus, the impossibility introduced by the signifier (*l'impossible à dire*) and the inherently traumatic aspect of human sexuality were joined. The real of the *non-rapport sexuel* ('L'Étourdit') also drew on the experience that sex as such does not create social bonds. It is rather the other way round. Because sexual enjoyment or '*jouissance*' is never an indelible sign of love, there is such a thing as the love relationship in which the illusion of a sexual relation is cherished.

According to Lacan love is an excellent answer to the impossible sexual relation. In a way, this confirms the fantasy's function of

❙ masking the real. In establishing the illusion of a sexual relationship, as love does, the sexual object functions as an obstacle to the acknowledgement of the impossible sexual relationship, that is, that having sex does not establish a relationship between human beings.

In *Encore* Lacan also introduced 'that which does not stop not being written' (Seminar XX, p. 59) as the articulation of the modal category of the impossible. The impossible of the sexual relationship is that it 'cannot in any case be written' (in a symbolic formula for instance).

As such, the impossible is crucial to the organization of human sexuality. It casts a new light on the category of the necessary – 'which doesn't stop being written' or the automaton of the symbolic – that is, as a mere contingency or that 'which stops not being written'. Herewith Lacan affirms that it is the impossible which introduces the possibility of something new: the contingency of the encounter (Seminar XX, p. 94).

At that time, Lacan still had high hopes of formalizing psychoanalytic experience through topology and more specifically knot theory. The Borromean knot of the three categories of the real, the imaginary and the symbolic was very important for Lacan's thinking at the time, the Borromean knot being a set of three rings which are tied in such a way that when one of the three is severed, the other two also become separated. This is an alternative reading of the special interrelation of the symbolic, the imaginary and the real.

See also: **borromean knot, desire, imaginary,** *jouissance*, **object a, symbolic, topology**
Other terms: *das ding* (the thing), drive, extimacy

References

Lacan, J. (1973) 'L'Étourdit', ?*Scilicet*, Paris, Seuil, 4, pp. 5–52.

Lacan, J. (1978) [1964] *Seminar XI: The Four Fundamental Concepts of Psycho-Analysis* (trans. A. Sheridan). New York: W.W. Norton.

Lacan, J. (1988) [1954–55] Seminar II, *The Ego in Freud's Theory and in the Technique of Psychoanalysis* (ed. J.-A. Miller, trans. S. Tomaselli, notes by J. Forrester). Cambridge: Cambridge University Press.

Lacan, J. (1991) [1953–54] Seminar I, *Freud's Papers on Technique* (ed. J.-A. Miller, trans. with notes by J. Forrester). New York: W.W. Norton.

Lacan, J. (1992) [1959–60] Seminar VII, *The Ethics of Psychoanalysis* (ed. J.-A. Miller, trans. D. Porter). New York: W.W. Norton.

Lacan, J. (1993) [1955-1956] Seminar III, *The Psychoses* (ed. J.-A. Miller, trans. with notes by R. Grigg). New York: W.W. Norton.

Lacan, J. (1998) [1972–73] Seminar XX, *Encore, On Feminine Sexuality, The Limits of Love and Knowledge* (ed. J.-A. Miller, trans. with notes by B. Fink). New York: W.W. Norton.

Katrien Libbrecht

Schema

Schemata, like mathèmes and formulae, were used by Lacan as an economical means of representing major tenets of his theory. Although he made abundant use of such means of representation, he also gave due warning of their limitations. His own words provide the best definition of what is, and what is not, a schema. Talking of Schema L in Seminar II, he says: '[This] schema would not be a schema if it yielded a solution. It isn't even a model. It's just a way of fixing our ideas, called for by an infirmity in our discursive capacity' (1988, p. 243).

Again, talking of Schema I in *Écrits* he says: '... it would be better to confine this schema to the waste-bin, if, like so many others, it was to lead anyone to forget in an intuitive image the analysis on which it is based' (1977, p. 214).

Lacan's use of schemata (and indeed, mathèmes and formulae) arose from his great respect for, and the close relation his teaching had with, the science of logic. His use of logic, however, was in reference to the logic of the subject, of her/his speech, of the field of objects – *object a* and the big Other and of the internal registers of the imaginary and the symbolic. The use of logic was not about an ordering of ideas on the theory of psychoanalysis; it was never about something external to the subject. Rather, the structuring of the topology of the subject could, one might say, provide a means of understanding the rules of intuitive geometry as applied to the external world.

In the English version of *Écrits*, three of the schemas are presented: Schema L, R and I along with his graph of desire. The optical schema of the inverted bouquet (present in the French edition of *Écrits* but not in the English) was first presented in Seminar I (1953–54) in the chapter 'The Topic of the Imaginary' (which, rightly translated should read 'The **Topology** or **Topography** of the Imaginary') and again in Seminar VIII, 'Transference', chapter 11 (1960–61).

Schemas L, R and I were developed in the chapter on 'A question preliminary to any possible treatment of psychosis' presented in

1957–58. Schema L, however, was first presented in Seminar II, 'The ego in Freud's theory and the technique of psychoanalysis' (1954–55) in the chapter 'Introduction of the big Other'. It also made an appearance in Seminar III 'Introduction to the question of the psychoses' (1955–56) and in Seminar IV 'The object relation' (1956–57). It was, in fact, a schema that remained at a pivotal point in any discussion on the intersubjective dialectic of the subject. In Seminar IV, he refers to it as **the schema**. In this seminar, too, he made the point about the **topological** nature of the term schema. 'It is not a matter of localizations, but of the **relations between places**' (p. 2 of the unpublished translation).

Schema L

The ego, which would have the subject believe that she/he is in charge when speech is uttered to another (an other), actually speaks from quite a different place in the act of enunciation, the act being, as it is, underlined with a fundamental *méconnaissance*. The other, like the ego, is never really where the interlocutor thinks she/he is at. Nowhere can this fundamental deception be more realized than in the analytic situation where not only the analysand is prey to its effects, but the analyst as well – especially if the analyst in question honours the school of ego psychologists. It is in the context of understanding the ego and its imaginary relation with the specular other, that Schema L was introduced in Seminar II. Lacan used the accompanying illustration to 'fix our ideas'.

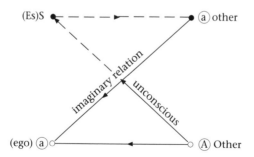

Figure 10: Schema L
Illustration taken from the English edition of *Book II*, p. 243.

The explanation of the schema in Seminar II is most clear. The *S* (*Es*) in the schema is the subject, not the 'whole' subject as he points out, but the subject **in its opening up**. The position, *S*, occupied in the schema, however, is not where the subject sees her-/himself, rather, it is at the position *a*, the position occupied by the ego – which is an imaginary construct; 'he may believe the ego is him', Lacan says with his usual mixture of irony and sagacity. Imaginary as it is, however, it holds an essential place in the life of the subject in the constitution of objects. Among these is the specular other, that 'fellow being' who has a very close relation to the ego and can be superimposed on it. It is written as *a'*. In the subject's world of objects there are many beings who fill the position. Hence we have *a, a'* (or, in English, *o', o''* ...).

Those whom we really address, however, are 'on the other side of the wall of language'. These are the true subjects, 'those we do not know', true Others, not the imaginary subjects of everyday discourse, whom we address. They are represented by A_1, A_2 (In English, *O*, for big Other). It is these (A_1, A_2) I seek to address every time I speak, but 'the subject is separated from the Others, the true ones, by the wall of language' (1988, p. 244), 'the wall' being represented in the schema by the solid line joining *a* and *a'*. This 'wall' is the imaginary relation between the ego and the other(s).

The passage to the Other (*A*) or (*O*), then, the one to whom one really speaks, is via the imaginary discourse with the other *(a–a')*, by finding a circuitous passage around the wall of language, back to the subject who speaks. This is the aim of analysis. Lacan points out the trap of the analyst's interposing her/his ego into the analytic discourse, keeping the discourse at the imaginary level of *a, a'*, causing an entrenchment, rather than a dismantling of the wall. What happens on these occasions is an identification with the specular other, the analyst, instead of the joining of the subject to another subject on the other side of the wall of language – 'the final relation of the subject to a genuine Other, to the Other who gives the answer one doesn't expect ...' (1988, p. 246).

In the next chapter in Seminar II, 'Objectified analysis', Lacan points out the limitations in trying to illustrate the concept, namely, the assumption that language is 'propagated like light, in a straight line'. However useful the schema may be, he points out, it is little more than a 'compasscard' by which his students find their way around Freud's teaching. The message is clear; nothing supplants 'the extensive reading of Freud's work'.

In chapter 6 of *Écrits*, many points of which were extracted from the seminar on 'Psychosis' delivered in 1955–56, Schema L is again referred to as an introduction to Schema R. If Schema L is a means of illustrating the imaginary in the dialectic of the subject, it is Schema R that illustrates the place of the symbolic, or rather, a marrying of the imaginary and the symbolic.

It is interesting that in this illustration in the English *Écrits* (and in the French edition as well) the positions of o and o' are reversed, with the o now in the top right-hand corner and the o' in the bottom left-hand corner. No explanation is offered for this. It may be that the reversal illustrates the similarity between the two positions and their capacity to exist in each other's place. It may be that as the handwritten sketch was taken down from the board, it was copied incorrectly. Regardless, the trajectory of the schema, S, o, o', O was to stay the same in later references.

Schema R

In Schema R, the bare bones of Schema L designate positions that can be taken up by the symbolic, creating over the original schema the 'imaginary triad'.

The 'imaginary couple' of the mirror stage takes up the o'–o line of Schema L, with o being occupied by M, the primordial object, namely the mother, and o' being occupied by I, the ego-ideal. The 'third term' of the imaginary triad, that position occupied by the subject, and from where the schema begins, is the phallic image.

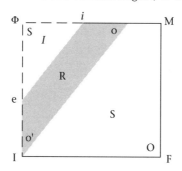

Figure 11: Schema R
Source: Lacan (1977), *Écrits*, p. 197.

The o'–o base is also the base of another triangle, the apex of which, in the position of O, is the Name-of-the-Father.

The phallocentricism of the schema derives from the child's relation to the mother – that river of desire into which the child is born. The 'vital dependence on her', which is actually a dependence on her love, on a desire for her desire, engenders an identification with the imaginary object of this desire 'in so far as the mother herself *symbolizes* it in the phallus'. The presence of the symbolic then, in the life of the subject, is present from this moment of awakening, is present from the mother's life, from her desire, from the motor engendering the conception itself. Lacan says in *Écrits*: 'Freud revealed this imaginary function of the phallus, then, to be the pivot of the symbolic process that completes *in both sexes* the questioning of the sex by the castration complex' (1977, p. 198).

Related to the notion of desire, both of the mother and the subject, and occupying a position central to it, is the paternal metaphor. The father's function in relation to the desire of the mother, 'the attribution of procreation' to him, is the effect of the *signifier*. This function is not about being a real father, but about occupying a symbolic function, hence its position in the schema.

Within the S–o(M)–o'(I) triangle, Lacan situates a quadrangle. Along the trajectory of the S–o relation is the S–i relation, i standing for specular image, one of the two terms of the narcissistic relation, (the other term is e, for ego). From i to M (that is in the position of o) are situated the 'extremities of the segments Si, So_1, So_2, So_n, SM ...', that is, all those other objects who hold shades of the primordial object.

Similarly, along the S–o' trajectory is the S–e relation. From e to I (occupying the position of o') lie the extremities of segments S–e, namely, Se, So'_1, So'_2, So'_n in which the ego identifies itself 'from its specular *Urbild* to the paternal identification of the ego-ideal'. (1977, p. 197).

The quadrangle Mie I thus contains within it 'the field of reality' designated in this schema as R. Looking at it in its purely representational form, one can see that, within the symbolic schema, it occupies a limited position, bound as it is by the 'wall of language' (o–o') and the two imaginary terms of the narcissistic relation e, the ego, and i the specular image.

Schema I

Again using the foundation structure of Schema L, Schema I was used by Lacan to illustrate the intersubjective dialectic of the psychotic subject, or rather the *structure* of that dialectic at the termination of the psychotic process – taking as a case example, the illness of Schreber. Later (1962–63), Lacan also used Schema I as the schema to illustrate the dialectic of perversion, which appeared in 'Kant avec Sade', published in the French edition of *Écrits*, not in the English edition.

Freud used the writings of Schreber's account of his own illness (1903), to illustrate his theory on paranoia. Freud's paper on Schreber was published in 1912. Lacan drew on the texts of both Schreber and Freud to illustrate his theoretical position regarding the psychoses. Lacan also used the writings of Sade in his theorizing on the perversions. The importance of the *text* in exposing the dialectic is thus demonstrated.

Schreber's fantasies involved homosexual fantasies of being a woman, of occupying the *position* of woman, in order to copulate with the great Other, God himself, and father supreme. The outcome would be a new race, freed from the baseness which is humanity's pitiful lot.

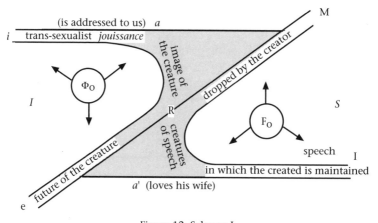

Figure 12: Schema I
Source: Lacan (1977), *Écrits*, p. 212.

Looking at the schema, one can see many more elaborations on the original Schema L. In the centre, the structural outline of the quadrangle – that is – the subject's 'field of reality', MieI, that was highlighted in Schema R can be seen. (There is still some ambiguity, at this point in his theorizing, about the register of the Real as opposed to 'reality'.) Either side of the central field, there is a 'double curve', each one swung around a hole, signifier of lack – both sides have their lack. On the left-hand side, the 'Imaginary' field, the 'creature' side of the delusion of copulation with the great Other, there are the two branches, 'that of narcissistic pleasure and that of the ideal identification'. Both are linked through 'the trap of imaginary capture' (1977, p. 211).

With a note of caution about schematizing the dialectic, Lacan points out the linking centre area that joins the delusional ego to the divine other. (Note the trajectory of 'future of the creature' heads in the direction of the trajectory 'dropped by the creator'.) On the right-hand side of the schema, one of the two branches, M, still occupies the place of the primordial other, but the position of O, the big Other, is now occupied by the ego-ideal, I.

There are the captivating, but deceptive properties of the image on the left-hand side; on the right-hand side are the alienating properties of speech 'in which the ego-ideal has taken the place of the Other' – resulting in a partial delusion. (Note the position of I has changed from its position in schema R, from the bottom left-hand corner to the bottom right-hand corner. This makes for some confusion.) The maintenance of the trajectory Soo'O, is not disturbed with the displacing of the big Other. Lacan says (p. 214) '... the relation to the *other* ... is perfectly compatible with the unbalancing of the relation to the capital *Other* ...' (which is now occupied by I, ego-ideal). It is in the relation to the signifier wherein lies the drama of madness. He urges his audience: 'I hold that we must listen to the speaker, when it is a question of a message that does not come from a subject beyond language, but from speech beyond the subject' (1977, p. 214).

The schema thereby demonstrates that the terminal state of psychosis is not about chaos, but a state, brought about by speech, that has its own kind of logic – the logic of the dialectic.

The three schemas, L, R and I, in demonstrating the directional flow of the intersubjective dialectic, whether the subject be that of ordinary, everyday (imaginary) discourse, or the subject of delusions, illustrate the truth of the directional flow of all human discourse.

The optical schema of the inverted bouquet

In this schema, which underwent a development from his first seminar in 1953–54, 'Freud's papers on technique' through his 1960 paper 'Observations on the paper by Daniel Lagache' published in the French, not the English, version of *Écrits*, to Seminar VIII, 'Transference', delivered in 1960–61, Lacan draws on the science of optics as a means of illustrating a theoretical point. One can see the appeal. Just as the science of logic has a structural basis that has parallels with the structure of intersubjective relations, the laws of optics, like the laws of physics, have a certain immutability; they only operate by virtue of the position of the retina within a certain optical arrangement. Ways of seeing an image or a virtual image have these laws as their basis. Light rays emanate from the object and are absorbed by the retina in an order that is mathematically and symbolically defined – the 'cone' of optics. 'For there to be an illusion', says Lacan in the 1954 seminar, 'one condition must be fulfilled ... the eye must be in a specific position, it must be inside the cone' (1988, p. 80).

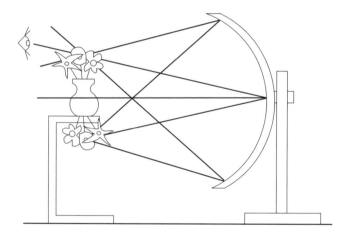

Figure 13: The experiment of the inverted bouquet
Source: Lacan (1988), Book I, p. 78.

The first presentation of the optical schema in which he demonstrates the well-known optical illusion of the reversed vase of flowers, is a continuation, in many ways, of his theory of the mirror stage. It was here that the topology of the imaginary and its relationship of the ego *o'*, the ego-ideal *I(o)*, and the ideal ego *i'(o)* 'the fascinating image' is mapped out. The deceptiveness of the image and confusion of the real and the virtual image have their parallels in the deceptive perceptions of oneself, of one's body, of the places occupied by the other(s) and the Other.

The various objects in the schema – the vase, the flowers, the box, the cauldron – all represent something: the imaginary vase containing the bouquet of real flowers 'is the image of the body'. Later, however, Lacan says: 'The box represents your own body, the bouquet, instincts and desires.' The reader is at risk of some confusion here. The point is, however, that the use of the concave mirror can **make** *appear* something that is not there. The final image of the complete vase of flowers is not even an image. It is a **virtual** image.

'Real' and 'reality' were still not differentiated at this point. What is important, however, at the early stages, is how he defines what is represented by the eye. 'The eye is here, as so often, symbolic *of the subject'* (1988, p. 80). It is an important stage in his theorizing on the subject. Here the subject is represented as *S*. It is not represented as *$, the barred subject. That was to come later in the response to the Daniel Lagache paper delivered at Royaumont in July 1958 (but written by Lacan in 1960 and published in 1961). Cormac Gallagher and Mary Darby (1994) point out that there is a 'striking difference' between the presentations of the schema between 1954 and 1960, relating to the developments in the theorizing of the subject over that time.

In the early schema the subject is the subject of the mirror stage, the eye is the observing eye of the infant which finds in the mirror image promise of 'a certain reduction and normalization of the subject's tensions' as a result of the introduction of the Name-of-the-Father, thereby establishing the agencies of super-ego and ideal ego, which, in turn, modify the threatening flood of the real (or reality). The eye is, among many things, the subject.

The eye as the barred subject (*$*), however, was to emerge later. It evolved with the emergence of the plane mirror in the schema. Gallagher and Darby make the point that the **real** image of the vase in the plain mirror is missing. It remained missing from all future versions of the schema until the final one which illustrates what happens at the end of a successful analysis. The **real** image then, is called into question. What is reflected back to the observing subject? Nothing but what the ego wants to see. The question makes sense when one thinks of the disturbed body image of the anorectic; the image that is reflected back to her from the mirror is from where?

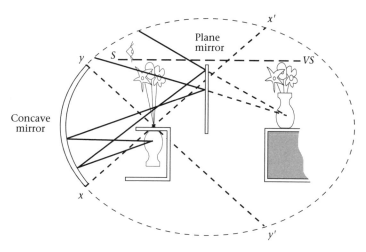

Figure 14: Later elaborations of the schema of the inverted bouquet
(note the position of the eye as *S*)
Source: Gallagher and Darby (1994), p. 95.

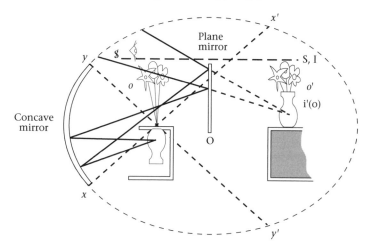

Figure 15: Later elaborations of the schema of the inverted bouquet
(note the position of the eye as *\$*)
Source: Gallagher and Darby (1994), p. 98.

The emergence in the symbolic order provides a buffer to the real through the subject's becoming a speaking being. The demand to the Other is thereby constituted (D → O). The plane mirror is the metaphor for the real Other who addresses the subject and with whom the subject interacts or *addresses his/her demand*. The reflection in the plane mirror through the intermediary of words, say Gallagher and Darby, 'allows the subject to form a new type of image of his body at a second remove' (1994, p. 94).

However, according to Gallagher and Darby, the most important modification of the later schema was the representation of the flowers as *object a* which, one can recall, was still not fully articulated in 1960. Quite possibly, it was the consideration of the internal logic of the schema that aided the progression towards the formulation of *object a* as a concept.

Although Lacan's response to the Lagache paper was not published till 1961, the ideas were presented in 1958. Thus the ground was set to apply the notions of the imaginary allocation of the position of objects in the subject's field – including that of the analyst – according to the metaphor of the schema. Lacan did this through the seminar on 'Transference', delivered in 1960–61.

Just what is transference? One could say that, among other things, it is a transferring on to the other, attributes that arise purely from the imaginary. There is ascribed to the other the possession of the **agalma**, that precise little something that is ungraspable precisely because it does not exist (see reference to Plato's *Symposium* in the entry on Agalma).

Lacan introduces the schema to demonstrate what precisely was happening with the elegiac merry-go-round at Plato's party. The intrasubjective interplay between Socrates, Alcibiades and Agathon, the aligning of positions of ego-ideal and ideal ego and the partial object, can be represented in the optical schema. The image of the vase in front of the mirror – a fantasized 'real image' – can be supported by the imaginary apparatus around it. It can be percieved as 'real' by virtue of the flowers which it holds. The positions are all reciprocating each other in an interplay that sustains and buttresses the image. At the centre of the image, then, is the precious thing, the flowers, which Lacan has designated *object a*. What happens in the Socratic dialectic, and which is formularized in the schema, is what Freud describes as the essential of being in love. But it is all a trick, an artifice, a **lure**. It is little wonder that in the discourse of Diotima we are told that love is not a god, but a demon.

The transference relationship between analyst and analysand can also be acted out in the interplay of ideal ego, ego-ideal and *object a*. It can also be represented in the schema. The knowledge of the lure of the imaginary is what provides the analyst with the tools to steer a safe course through dangerous fields.

See also: **agalma, ideal ego, imaginary, mirror stage, real, symbolic**
Other terms: big Other, ego, image (specular), transference

References

Gallagher, C. and Darby, M. (1994) 'The historical development and clinical implications of Jacques Lacan's "Optical Schema"', *The Letter*, Autumn, 87–111.

Lacan, J. (1956–57) The Seminar of Jacques Lacan, Book IV, 'The object relation' (ed. J.A. Miller) (trans. L. Roche). Unpublished manuscript. (Dates refer to years of seminar.)

Lacan, J. (1960–61) The Seminar of Jacques Lacan, Book VIII, 'Transference' (ed. J.A. Miller) (trans. C. Gallagher). Unpublished manuscript. (Dates refer to years of seminar.)

Lacan, J. (1966) 'Remarque sur le rapport de Daniel Lagache: "Psychanalyse et structure de la personalite"'. In *Écrits*. Paris: Seuil.

Lacan, J. (1977) 'On a question preliminary to any possible treatment of psychosis'. In *Écrits. A Selection* (trans. A. Sheridan). London: Tavistock, pp. 179–225.

Lacan, J. (1988) 'The topic of the imaginary'. In The Seminar of Jacques Lacan, Book I, *Freud's papers on technique* (ed. J.A. Miller) (trans. J. Forrester) (pp. 73–88). Cambridge: Cambridge University Press. (Original work published 1975.)

Lacan, J. (1988) 'Introduction of the big Other'. In The Seminar of Jacques Lacan, Book II, *The ego in Freud's theory and in the technique of psychoanalysis* (ed. J.A. Miller) (trans. S. Tomaselli) (pp. 235–47). Cambridge: Cambridge University Press. (Original work published 1978.)

Lacan, J. (1997) The Seminar of Jacques Lacan, Book III, *The psychoses* (ed. J.A. Miller) (trans. R. Grigg). New York: W.W. Norton. (Original work published 1981.)

Schreber, D.P. (1988) *Memoirs of My Nervous Illness* (trans. and ed. I. Macalpine and R. Hunter). Cambridge: Harvard University Press.

Sara Murphy

Sexuation

Sexuation refers to how the speaking being comes to acquire a sexual position from which to engage in a sexuality that never offers complete satisfaction. For both Freud and Lacan, the subject has to acquire his or her sexual position. This sexual position is not a given or a natural one and does not follow an inscribed or set course as it does for animals.

Sexuation involves a choice whereby a subject positions him- or herself within a particular sex. This is the radical level at which Lacan introduces the notion of sexuation or choice of sex and it operates at another level from biological sex. Thus, a subject with male anatomy may position himself on the side of woman, and a subject with female anatomy may position herself on the side of man.

Early Lacan

The first of Lacan's theories on how a speaking being becomes a sexed subject emerged in the 1950s and early 1960s and is mainly outlined in 'The signification of the phallus' (1958) and in the text on feminine sexuality in 'Guiding remarks for a congress on feminine sexuality' (1964) where he applies the theory of the signifier and the registers of the real, symbolic and imaginary to the debate on feminine sexuality.

In the 1950s Lacan adopted the position of Freud on the question of how a subject takes up a sexual position. Freud, in describing how a subject comes to acquire masculine or feminine psychical characteristics, refers to the Oedipus complex and its resolution. This requires the abandoning of incestuous objects following a prohibition, and the internalization of the cultural mandate to marry a subject of the other sex who is not of the family, that is, a prescription of exogamy.

The castration complex is considered by Freud to be the key to the outcome of the Oedipus complex. He argues that there is no access to a subjective position other than that which passes through the castration complex, a necessary structural foundation upon which the subject can assume a sexed position. For the woman (contrary to the man), it does not lead to the Oedipus complex being destroyed, but rather, created.

Freud posed the primacy of the phallus in 1923, referring to the idea that the subject of the unconscious is phallocentric. This was a decisive step even though it created something of an impasse. This impasse is due to the fact that on the male side, fear of castration is the bedrock, and on the female side, penis envy which creates an interminable repetition.

While his teaching was still strictly Freudian, in the 1950s, during which time he emphasized the primacy of the phallus and the part played by the castration complex, he later stressed that the phallus is not equivalent to an organ or an image, but operates as a signifier. Lacan referred to the phallic function as that which institutes lack in relation to the alienating function of language. This implies that the access to sex for the speaking being has to pass through language and speech which necessarily involves a loss of the real *jouissance* of the body. For the speaking being there can be no access to the complete *jouissance* of the Other. For each sex, the phallus provokes a loss and a choice, with choice of sexual position being the result of that loss.

Lacan reworked the Freudian Oedipus complex and developed the paternal metaphor, which is the operation by which the Name-of-the-Father substitutes for the Desire of the Mother and produces the phallus as signifier of desire. Applying this symbolic operation of the paternal metaphor to the castration complex allows Freud's development to be viewed in the light of a symbolic process for both male and female.

Symbolic castration creates a universal paradigm of neurotic desire, where desire moves from the lack that has been constituted, towards objects given phallic value through the signifier phallus, which thus marks them as desired. Sexuality therefore refers to the subject of the unconscious, the field of language, and not to man or woman as biological or social beings.

The phallic function is an essential notion in Lacan's definition of the structure of man and woman, because man and woman are defined differently in terms of the way in which the splitting by language brings about a loss. Sexuality, within the field of language, implies that there is no sexuality in the human being other than that of speech.

By giving a prime place to the effects of the signifier on the speaking being, Lacan can restate the question, not at the level of the psychic effects of the anatomical difference between the sexes, but at the level of what this difference becomes in the signifying network.

Lacan introduced a thesis that sexuality for human beings is a *semblant*, that is, a make-believe. Lacan's emphasis is that, in defining sexuality in reference to the function of the phallus, all human sexuality is located in the field of *paraître*, appearing or seeming. Thus, the woman seems to the man to be the phallus that he lacks, and a man seems to have the phallus that the woman lacks.

Sexuality as appearing to have or appearing to be, indicates that there is no further truth behind the protection of masculinity or the mask of femininity. What we have here is the relation between two phallic positions: the feminine and the masculine, although castration, which is structurally involved for both man and woman, is masked in two different ways. In psychoanalysis, the phallic function dominates both partners equally, but it does not make them different. The difference has to be looked for elsewhere.

Lacan of the 1970s

In the 1970s Lacan elaborated different modes of *jouissance* for man and for woman. This was a new and radical development in which it is not a question of male and female sexuality, but a logic of sexuation which produces two sets of speaking beings with different conditions of *jouissance*.

One kind of *jouissance* is linked to the phallus, phallic *jouissance*, which Lacan founds in the *jouissance* of speech, that is, in the signifier and to its signification, to which every speaking being is subjected. The Other *jouissance*, other than phallic *jouissance*, is that experienced by woman and relates to the Other as such. It is a *jouissance* that goes beyond that which can be signified, and it is in the texts of mysticism that best describe this *jouissance* which goes beyond the phallus.

Lacan addressed a question that Freud raised and failed to answer: 'What does a woman want?' Where Freud preserved the class of men and the class of women, Lacan posed that the woman does not exist and that there is no sexual relation. This is a radical change from Freud's position. From his assertion that there is no signifier of the feminine sex in the unconscious, Lacan argued that the only place where a woman receives her certainty is in her *jouissance*. This is the only thing that defines woman.

In 1969–70, Lacan developed the four discourses in his Seminar XVII, *L'envers de la psychanalyse*. In his discussion of the discourse of the hysteric, Lacan tried in this seminar to situate what woman is in relation to the truth of the hysteric. The outcome, however, was that it is not through the hysteric that the woman is reached.

It is in the 1972–73 seminar *Encore* that Lacan introduced the formula, ~~The~~, after having developed his formulae of sexuation in the two preceding seminars, '… ou pire' (1971–72) and 'L'Étourdit' (1973). In '… ou pire', Lacan grounds his propositions in logic, contesting and revising Aristotle's categories, **the possible, the impossible, the contingent, the necessary**. He added **the impotence** to write the sexual relation.

Lacan also referred to the modern logic of Frege, Cantor and others. Lacan was constructing the equations to define man and woman and finding in logic the means to articulate the different ways in which man and woman are split by the signifier and therefore defined differently in relation to language and the symbolic order.

In 'L'Étourdit', Lacan elaborated his proposition, 'there is no sexual relation', around logic and topology, and asserted his theory of femininity that he based on the 'quantic formulas' of the two sexes. It is in this seminar that Lacan stated his thesis of the feminine as supplement to the masculine, specifying that a woman 'is the only one whose *jouissance* exceeds that of coitus'.

Concepts necessary to the logic of sexuation

'There is no sexual relation': '*il n'y a pas de rapport sexuel*'. Lacan was not saying here that people are not engaging in sexual acts. His use of the word *rapport* refers, rather, to the idea of proportion, that is, that there is no proportion between the sexes, no direct relationship between man and woman. There is nothing complementary about their relationship. For Lacan, male and female are not two complementary parts of a whole. Each position results from a failure of symbolization to say it all, where symbolization encounters an impossibility. Sexual difference emerges at the point where symbolization fails.

Sexual relations are impossible because the very notion of joining together to make 'one' ignores the fundamental gap that is the cause of the subject's desire and the origin of his demand for love. Instead of relating to each other, each sex relates to the Other, or to the lack in the Other, to castration. Each sex will take up a different position in relation to the castration of the Other.

Lacan elaborated the psychoanalytic idea of the impossibility of the sexual relation because the *jouissance* of the Other, taken as body, is always inadequate. The horizon of *jouissance* is to enjoy the Other, the body of the Other, but the *jouissance* called sexual, opposes it.

This is because the sexual comes to us from language, from where it gets its phallic determination. This refers to the fact that, because the human being has to use language, the *jouissance* of the signifier comes between the subject and the body of the Other, barring the subject from having direct access to this body. This is the law of castration, to which every subject is submitted. The sexual act, therefore, will always have to figure as a missed act, missing in relation to being able to reunite with the body of the Other. The resulting satisfaction is defined in relation to the failure of the *jouissance* of the body. Phallic *jouissance* makes it impossible for man to enjoy the body of woman taken as Other. 'All the needs of speaking beings are contaminated by the fact of being involved in another satisfaction [...] that those needs may not live up to' (*Encore*, Lacan, 1998, p. 51).

This other satisfaction, other than the *jouissance* of the body, is phallic *jouissance*, from its connection with the phallic function which produces the *jouissance* of speaking. The body, at the very level of the drive, is effected by the signifier, and it is in Seminar XX that Lacan will argue that it is the signifier which both causes *jouissance* and puts a limit to it. The Other is structured around this limit as traumatic impossibility, that which bars access to a complete *jouissance*.

At the point at which the Other is barred, the point of the hole in the Other, there is no signifier with which to write the sexual relation between man and woman. If a relation can be written, it is the relation between mother and father, the paternal metaphor.

In the unconscious there is a relation between mother and father, which is the relation producing castration and the phallic process of signification, where the mother desires the phallus. The mother can be represented in the unconscious as object of desire because she is forbidden. However, this symbolic process cannot produce a signifier of Woman.

The impossibility of writing the relation between man and woman is because 'analytic discourse [...] brings into play the fact that woman will never be taken up except *quoad matrem*. Woman serves her function in the sexual relationship only qua mother.' If Woman does not assume her function in the sexual relation except as mother, then woman does not exist.

The woman does not exist

Lacan is not saying here that women do not exist, but that the universal woman does not exist. Where man can be defined by the universality of the castration function, there is no universal function which can define woman, who can thus only be taken one by one. This is because not all her characteristics can be given meaning by the phallus.

There is no signifier to designate woman. Here woman is taken as that point in the Other that corresponds to the lack of signifier, that failure of symbolization to say it all, where symbolization encounters an impossibility to produce a signifier of sex, of woman. In psychoanalysis, femininity is another name for the Other, the Other's sex, which no signifier can designate.

Making up for the absence of the sexual relation

Sexual *jouissance* is conditioned by the impasse caused by the Other, with each sex missing its target in a different way. The question addressed by Lacan is that of how each sex makes up for the absence of sexual relation.

The male manner of failing the sexual relation and falling short of the *jouissance* of the Other, the body as such, provides him with a *jouissance* called phallic. In the symbolic order, the proper sexual partner of the subject is the Other. However, as this Other is barred, the subject can never reach his sexual complement except via an object, that object which falls from the Other in the process of barring, which is that of symbolization and separation.

This is the *object a* which is left over as a remainder after and outside of symbolization, and operates as cause of desire, providing a fundamental relation with the divided subject in the construction of the fantasy and with a *jouissance* which is phallic. It is phallic *jouissance* which is referred to as sexual *jouissance*.

Thus man, who cannot have direct access to the Other, has for his partner *the object a*. A woman's role in man's fantasy life is that of being the *object a*, that which provides some compensation or value of *jouissance* in the face of man's castration through language.

On the feminine side, something other than the object of fantasy comes to make up for this lack. The Other in question in feminine *jouissance* is not the Other of speech, where phallic *jouissance* is situated. Feminine *jouissance* is linked to another side of the Other, to the Other that is non-existent at the level of the signifier, to the sexed Other, to the Other as the Other sex. It is other than what can be named by the signifying chain organized by the law of the phallus and of castration. It is what places Woman at the level of the radical Other, of the sexed real Other, of which the unconscious can say nothing except lack.

The reasoning followed by Lacan is that because there exists in the Other, as the place of speech, a signifier S(Ø) that says that there is some hole, this hole can be assumed to be real and can be identified, because language includes words such as 'unutterable' and 'unnameable'. This is why feminine *jouissance* is conceived by Lacan as supplementary relative to phallic *jouissance*, that is, to *jouissance* of speech.

Lacan argued that in her *jouissance* that transcends the phallic reference, a woman can only want as a partner a being who is himself placed beyond the law of the phallus, a supreme being. Where the man responds to the hole in the Other with the object of his fantasy, a woman responds with a mode of *jouissance* related to a love without desire, without reference to the objects of fantasy. She relates herself to the lack and find her *jouissance* in this very lack.

It is this absence in the Other that the woman enjoys and the absence of the signifier of woman helps her to reach it. Thus the woman covers up the emptiness of the Other with this *jouissance* of the lack. Lacan relates this to religious ecstasy and to a kind of bodily *jouissance* which is not localized in the genitals the way that phallic *jouissance* is. For Lacan, the Other *jouissance* is asexual, involving a form of sublimation through love, in contrast to phallic *jouissance*, called sexual, because it involves the organ as instrument of the signifier. In sexuality there is a gap between the One, referring to phallic *jouissance* connected with the fantasy, and the Other, connected with S(Ø).

A key signifier which Lacan evoked in '... *ou pire*' and in *Encore* is the signifier 'One'. ' '*Y'a d'l'Un*', there is something of One, is what creates the illusion of the possibility of union between the sexes. Love aims at identity and fusion, at the relation of like to like. Freud set out the concept of Eros defined as fusion, making one out of two.

The demand for love is the demand to fill this gap, to cover over or fill the hole that is made by the separation from the Other. Love is also an attempt to hide the Other's castration, since it is the recognition of the lack in the Other that establishes the subject's own castration. Love can be conceived of as a fantasy of unity, as a fantasy of Oneness with the Other, that serves to supplement what is lacking for the subject, the sexual relation.

Another way of attempting to make up for the missing sexual rapport, as a consequence of 'there is something of One', is the fantasy, which makes the subject think that it is possible to have sexual relations. However the fantasy is not a relation between a subject and the Other sex. It is a relation between a subject and an object which comes in place of the Other sex, covering up the gap in the Other.

Schema of Sexuation

Lacan provides the schema in Seminar XX (*Encore*, Lacan, 1998, p. 78).

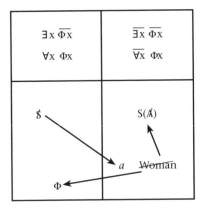

Figure 16: Schema of sexuation
Source: Lacan (1998), Seminar XX, p. 78.

In the upper section of the schema, Lacan writes the logical propositions which he had introduced in 'L'Étourdit', specifying both man and woman as speaking beings, defined differently in relation to language and the symbolic order and referring to the different ways of being split by the signifier. Every speaking being situates him- or herself on one side or the other, on the side of man or on the side of woman, regardless of anatomy.

On the side of man, $\forall x \Phi x$, where x stands for any given subject, Φx stands for the phallic function, and $\forall x$ refers to the whole of x. The universal definition of man is as a product of symbolic castration where the whole of a man falls under the phallic function. Thus the essence of man is castration. Above this is $\exists x \overline{\Phi} x$, referring to the existence of an x through which the phallic function is negated. The operation of the paternal metaphor to constitute subjects of language and the phallic law is closed, on the side of man, because of the existence of an exception, which constitutes an outside of the set. Freud gave mythic form to this exception as the primal horde father, the one who has not succumbed to castration, which he elaborates in *Totem and Taboo*. Thus $\exists x \overline{\Phi} x$ is known as the father's function. Being outside the set implies the possibility of the set itself. Every universal claim requires the existence of an exception which proves the rule.

The side of woman is not opposed to the side of man and is not complementary to it. Lacan used the term 'supplementary'. This is a completely new idea in psychoanalysis and allows Lacan to go further than the debates concerning the place of the clitoris or vagina which gained prominence in the 1920s and 1930s. What is revolutionary in Lacan is to find a way to write feminine sexuality, not only as defined by the use of fantasy or phallic signification, but as related to the principle of sacrifice of castration, Φ, by means of a different logical operator and using negating quantifiers which are never used in logic or mathematics. He uses them to define the feminine side of sexuation as functioning differently from the side of man with respect to the phallic law, while still being subject to it. $\overline{\exists} x \overline{\Phi}$ states that there does not exist an x which is not subject to the phallic function. There is, thus, a lack of an exception to the phallic law. As it is required to have an exception in order to constitute a set, women cannot be defined universally and can thus only be encountered one by one in an infinite series. This does not imply that the set does not exist but that it does not exist as a defined set in terms of universals and exceptions. Although what a woman is and what a woman wants cannot be universalized and the woman does not exist, it is possible to write feminine *jouissance*. In this sense, it is said to ex-sist, the Other *jouissance* thus opening the way to ecstasis, ecstasy, the being of non-existence.

While every subject, on the side of woman, is castrated and subject to phallic signification, not-all of her is subject to castration. Any time a speaking being places him- or herself on the side of woman, that being is situated within the phallic function as not-all. $\overline{\forall}x\Phi x$, not the whole of x, a given subject, is subject to the phallic law, and thus there is also a beyond. Her subjectivity to the signifier is all that can be said of a woman, but not all that she is. However, it must always be remembered that something that says no to the phallic function is still subject to it. The feminine position is not separated from castration but is related to it, not through the phallus and the object, cause of desire, but through the barred Other.

In the lower section of the schema

On the left side is the subject supported by the signifier of the phallus with an arrow going in the direction of the other side where the object cause of desire is written. This is a way of writing the fantasy. The arrow indicates the aim of desire. Every man is subject to fantasy which provides as his only partner, the *object a*. For men, women are nothing but objects of desire, and a piece of the body is what offers erotic consistency.

On the other side, where Lacan writes the woman with 'the', he puts in two arrows: one which aims at Φ and another which aims at the capital $\emptyset$. Lacan had already developed the link between feminine desire and the phallus, a Freudian thesis, where woman can have the phallus in the form of a child, a house and so on, or be the phallus for the man. What is new in Seminar XX, is the splitting of the feminine position between the phallus and the signifier of the barred Other or the lack of a signifier in the Other.

Woman's division is more radical than castration, as castration is not such an obstacle to be confronted. If woman is not-all, it is due to her division between the phallus and S($\emptyset$). The not-all is not equivalent to the S(Ø): it is the doubling between the phallus and the S(Ø) in terms of *jouissance*.

Clinical implications

The formulas of sexuation are applied to clinical practice. What is evidenced in the clinic is the possible encounter with subjects who have secondary male characteristics but present with a structure on the side of woman, and subjects with a female biology who present with a structure on the male side of sexuation. Thus, it is not anatomy which is crucial, but the signifier. What we learn from the clinic is to recognize each subject's relation to the signifier and to his or her particular mode of *jouissance*.

The clinic addresses the various attempts to reach the Other sex and to find a solution to make up for the absence of the sexual relation. Examples of this are evidenced in the form of motherhood or masquerade which are phallic answers via fantasy and desire, and homosexual love and the erotomanic form of psychosis which attempt to reach the Other through love as it touches the Real, by means of S(Ø).

See also: **castration**, *jouissance*, **object a**, **Name-of-the-Father**, **phallus**

References

Freud, S. (1951) [1912–13] *Totem and Taboo* (vol. 13, p. 1) *Standard Edition, Complete Psychological Works*. London: Hogarth Press and Institute of Psycho-Analysis.

Freud, S. (1951) [1923] 'The infantile genital organization' (*S.E.* 19: p. 141).

Jones, E. (1953–57) [1955] *Sigmund Freud: Life and Work* (3 vols). London: Hogarth Press.

Lacan, J. (1973) 'L'Étourdit', ?*Scilicet*. Paris: Seuil, 4, 5–52.

Lacan, J. (1977) [1958] 'The signification of the phallus', *Écrits: A Selection*. London: Tavistock, p. 281.

Lacan, J. (1982) 'Guiding remarks for a congress on feminine sexuality', in J. Mitchell and J. Rose (eds), *Feminine Sexuality*. London: Macmillan, p. 86.

Lacan, J. (1991) [1969–70] *Le Séminaire, Livre XVII, L'envers de la psychanalyse* (trans. R. Grigg, forthcoming). New York: W.W. Norton.

Lacan, J. (1992) [1959–60] Seminar VII, *The Ethics of Psychoanalysis* (ed. J.-A. Miller, trans. D. Porter). New York: W.W. Norton.

Lacan, J. (1998) [1972–73] Seminar XX, *Encore,* On Feminine Sexuality, The Limits of Love and Knowledge (ed. J.-A. Miller, trans. with notes by B. Fink). New York: W.W. Norton.

Carmela Levy-Stokes

Signifier

Freud's work abounds in references to language. Anna O, the very first analysand, referred to the technique Freud and Breuer had invented as 'the talking cure'. On virtually every page of Freud's early works – *The Interpretation of Dreams, Jokes and their Relationship to the Unconscious, The Psychopathology of Everyday Life* (in which Freud maps the nature and structure of the unconscious) – there are linguistic references and allusions that include jokes and puns, polysemy and ambiguity, tropes and figures of speech. From the outset Freud emphasizes the place of language in symptoms. In his first major publication, *Studies on Hysteria,* Freud (1895, p. 152) finds intimate verbal bridges linking, for instance, a patient's astasia-abasia to the pain of 'standing alone' and her inability to 'take a single step forward' in life. Yet despite this richness of linguistic material, and despite occasional recourse to those linguists whose work he knew, Freud was unaware of the most significant contributions in the field of modern linguistics that were being made, elsewhere in Europe, to the study of language.

In his 'return to Freud', and in particular in his writing and teaching of the 1950s, Lacan devotes considerable effort both to rekindling the interest in language that had disappeared from psychoanalysis and, to bringing modern linguistics to bear upon the field of the unconscious. The theory of the signifier is the name Lacan gives to a theory of language that, he believed, must be developed if the theory of psychoanalysis is ever to be adequate to the new experience opened up by Freud and the crucial role language plays within it.

The most important work by Lacan on this theory of the signifier occurs in two texts of the mid-1950s: 'The Agency of the Letter' (1957) and 'Seminar on "The Purloined Letter"' (1957). Both are crucial. They spell out a theory for which previous works had been mere preliminaries and, whatever the modifications Lacan subsequently makes to his views, the distinctive features of the conception of the signifier he develops in these texts remains present in subsequent work.

The term 'signifier' comes from the pioneering work of Ferdinand de Saussure in linguistics in the early twentieth century. Declaring that 'language is a system of signs', Saussure characterizes the sign as an entity made up of two components: a signifier or 'acoustic image' and a signified or 'sense'. Lacan captures this feature of the Saussurian sign in the following 'algorithm', which is to be read as 'signifier over signified':

$$\frac{S}{s}$$

But Lacan both is and is not Saussurian. He appears to be, and explicitly casts himself as, working with a Saussurian notion of signifier, yet his theory of the signifier diverges, and indeed diverges fundamentally, from the Saussurian view.

Saussure went on to compare the signifier and the signified, as the two components of the sign, with the front and back of a sheet of paper. Like the two sides of a piece of paper, signifier and signified exist together in an ontological indissolubility; neither can exist independently of its unity with the other. They exist together or not at all; the distinction between them is purely conceptual, and not real. Lacan rejects this conception of the sign and its account of the relationship between signifier and signified. Foregoing the view that there is an indissoluble unity between signifier and signified, he holds that the identity of the signifier depends solely upon its differences from all other signifiers: the identity of a signifier derives entirely from its being different and distinct from other signifiers. This so-called diacritical thesis of the nature of the sign is further developed by Roman Jakobson (1939), who thought that the basic units of language, its phonemes, consisted of bundles of ultimate differential elements which he called 'binary opposites'. This notion of binary opposites, which operates solely at the level of the phoneme, has often been mistakenly taken to imply that not only the signifier but also the signified is diacritical in nature. Ryan (1979) shows the claim is almost certainly a misinterpretation of Saussurian linguistics.

The Lacanian signifier, diacritical in nature, never exists on its own but always and only in relation to, and in opposition to, other signifiers. The thesis of the diacritical nature of the signifier is summed up in the following mathème:

$$S_1 \rightarrow S_2$$

where 'S_2' refers equally to 'any other signifier' and 'all other signifiers'.

As for the signifieds, there is not, indeed there cannot be, the same diacritical relationship between them, nor can there be a one-to-one relationship between signifier and signified. Thus, when Lacan refers to a 'sliding' of the signifier over the signified he has in mind two theses: that there is a barrier separating the signifier from the signified; and that this barrier has to be overcome for meaning to be produced. Meaning is thus produced episodically by what Lacan calls 'quilting points', moments at which meaning is produced or precipitated, typically accompanied by an effect of comprehension or understanding. This implies a different tempo from that of the unfolding of a chain of signifiers. Meaning is prospectively anticipated, and meaning is retroactively created (see entry on quilting point).

A more appropriate mathème for the relationship between signifier and signified might, for instance, look like this:

$$\frac{S_1 \qquad S_2 \qquad S_3 \qquad S_4 \qquad S_5 \qquad S_6}{\qquad s'' \qquad s''' \qquad s'''' \qquad s''''' \qquad}$$

The fact, then, that there is a barrier resistant to meaning (*la signification*) between the signifier and the signified means two things. First, that the production of meaning is episodic; and second, that there must be some particular event or process that produces meaning. The first point is clear enough. As to the second, something particular is required to produce meaning because meaning does not come about directly, or automatically, since the signified, understood as meaning, is not necessarily produced whenever a signifier is produced; at the very minimum, two signifiers need to be pinned together and, moreover, the semantic effect is never predictable. As Lacan comments, a meaning effect is never produced by a signifier alone but only by pinning two signifiers together and even then we have to 'see what happens'.

This process which crosses a semantic barrier that is resistant to signification, and thereby produces something new in meaning, Lacan calls metaphor. It contrasts with the metonymic process that maintains the impermeability of the bar and the otherwise permanent sliding of the signifier beneath the bar.

This contrast between metaphor and metonymy is part and parcel of a theory of metaphor and metonymy that Lacan develops and in which he finds the same mechanisms as those that go into the production of what Freud came to call condensation and displacement: condensation, where from a single element numerous chains of signifiers can lead off in different directions; and displacement, where meaning attached to one term can be displaced onto another, insignificant in itself.

The theory of the signifier is a crucial element in Lacan's return to Freud and his return to the sense of the Freudian discovery, since it alone makes sense of the structure of the unconscious as uncovered by Freud in his early work. The unconscious, the Freudian unconscious, is not a reservoir of biological instincts nor is it a remnant of some primordial archaic or primitive heritage, nor a vestige of early childhood left behind by a developmental process. Rather, the unconscious has the structure of language, and what Freud calls condensation and displacement turn out to be homologous to the rhetorical tropes of metaphor and metonymy respectively. These linguistic devices can be detected at work in a field of phenomena for which Lacan has coined the term 'formations of the unconscious', and which includes dreams, parapraxes (i.e., slips of the tongue or pen, bungled actions), jokes or *Witz* and, last but not least, neurotic symptoms. These are phenomena that exploit the particularities of the signifiers of a given language, its chance elements, coincidences of form and meaning, of sound and written form – all features of the so-called materiality of the signifier – as that which is unique and contingent in natural language. This is to take seriously Freud's thesis that there can be no dreambook, no manual for interpreting the meaning of a dream: even a spear in a dream need not be a phallic symbol but may instead be a chain of signifiers that goes from spear to spirit to spiritual leader, a chain which if followed will lead to a new series of connections to the dream.

There is a second range of issues that the theory of the signifier relates to. This has to do with the fact that the mere existence of signifiers introduces a new and autonomous realm. This realm of the signifier Lacan calls the symbolic, and its autonomy is captured in the notion of the big Other, which then comes to function in a number of different ways.

It initially marks the difference between other and Other, and the fact that speech is not only directed to the counterpart, the one to whom one is speaking, but also to the Other, as a locus beyond and external to the dyad. Behind this distinction is the thesis that the introduction of the signifier makes a difference at the level of intersubjectivity in a number of ways; indeed, the effect of the signifier is so radical that the term 'intersubjectivity' becomes misleading and eventually drops from Lacan's lexicon.

In any case, the fact that language introduces a new order of relations between subjects is an issue explored by Lacan in relation to the so-called 'language' of bees in 'The Function and Field of Speech and Language in Psychoanalysis', or the difference between deception and treachery sketched out in 'The Agency of the Letter'. The latter examples illustrate very well the point about the new order introduced by language. Language is not required for deception. One animal can deceive another: the bird pretends to have a broken wing to lure its predator away from the nest. Humans can perfectly well engage in the same deceptive behaviour: a battle plan may involve troop movements intended to deceive the enemy. But when the symbolic is invoked, as through a treaty drawn up with the enemy, a third place, the big Other, external to the two parties involved is introduced, with its new and autonomous order of relations. While in the presence of a treaty it is still possible to deceive the enemy, deception becomes betrayal, if not treachery (1977, pp. 172–3).

This line of thought has implications for the way in which the transference, the motor of psychoanalytic treatment, is to be understood also. Lacan initially construed transference in terms of the notion of intersubjectivity, as the relationship based on the pact or bond between subjects that true speech establishes. On this understanding the pact is construed as the overcoming of the imaginary relationship between ego and other described by Freud in his writings on narcissism, and subsequently developed by Lacan in his theory of the mirror stage. However, Lacan's thinking then moved him away from the intersubjective dimension of speech onto the more purely formal level of language conceived as a pure network of signifiers located in the locus of the Other. Henceforth small other and big Other are contrasted and the imaginary relationship is regarded as subordinate to the symbolic relationship of the subject to big Other. This is schematized in Schema L.

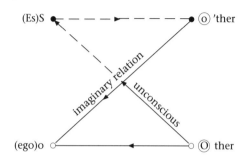

Figure 17: Schema L
Source: Lacan, Seminar III, p. 14.

Lacan characterizes the Other variously as the discourse of the unconscious; as the locus of good faith and the guarantor of truth; and as the treasure of signifiers upon which all speech acts must draw. The common element in all of these formulations of Lacan's is that the Other is a third place in discourse, radically external to both speaker and listener.

In urging a 'return to Freud' Lacan contended that the distinction between the symbolic as the order of language, and the imaginary as characterized by a dyadic interpersonal relationship, was already implicit in Freud. Post-Freudian analysis had come to focus on the imaginary and, as a result, psychoanalytic practice had failed to grasp the fundamental principles of psychoanalysis, which lay in the symbolic. This made it difficult to distinguish the essential in analytic practice from its contingent features, resulting in a conservatism that discouraged innovation and ritualized a technique misunderstood by its practitioners.

The theory of the signifier and the symbolic enabled Lacan to distinguish between the ego, as constituted by a series of imaginary identifications, and the subject, regarded as the result of the effect of language upon the human being.

While the concept of signifier derives from the field of linguistics, in Lacan's hands it becomes a key concept in the development of a theory of language adequate to the Freudian experience of psychoanalysis. When Lacan declares that the unconscious is structured like a language, it is the signifier that displays this structure. When he declares that the unconscious is the discourse of the Other, this Other and the radical consequences it brings in its wake are the outcome of the speaking being's relation to the signifier.

See also: **imaginary, mirror stage, quilting point (*point de capiton*), symbolic**
Other terms: metaphor, metonymy, other, unconscious

References

Freud, S. (1895) *Studies on Hysteria. SE* 2. *Standard Edition of the Complete Psychological Works of Sigmund Freud.* London: Hogarth Press.

Freud, S. (1900) *The Interpretation of Dreams. SE* 4 & 5.

Freud, S. (1901) *The Psychopathology of Everyday Life. SE* 6.

Freud, S. (1907) *Jokes and their Relationship to the Unconscious. SE* 8.

Jakobson, R. (1939) 'Observations sur le classement phonologique des consonnes'. In E. Blancquaert and W. Pee (eds) *Proceedings of the Third International Congress of Phonetic Sciences.* Ghent: Laboratory of Phonetics of the University.

Lacan, J. (1953) 'The Function and Field of Speech and Language in Psychoanalysis'. *Écrits: A Selection,* pp. 30–113 (trans. A. Sheridan). New York: W.W. Norton.

Lacan, J. (1973) [1957] 'Seminar on "The Purloined Letter"' (trans. J. Mehlman). *Yale French Studies,* 48: 39–72.

Lacan, J. (1977) [1957] 'The Agency of the Letter'. *Écrits: A Selection,* pp. 146–78 (trans. A. Sheridan). New York: W.W. Norton.

Ryan, M.-L. (1979) 'Is There Life for Saussure After Structuralism?', *Diacritics* 9: 28–44.

Saussure, F. de. (1966) [1905] *Course in General Linguistics.* C. Bally and A. Sechehaye in collaboration with A. Reidlinger (eds) (trans. W. Baskin). New York: McGraw-Hill.

Russell Grigg

Subject

For Lacan the subject is constituted by his/her subjection to speech and language, that is, the symbolic order or register. This subjection to language is unconscious and is materially supported by inscriptions (Freud's *Niederschriften*) arranged according to the normative axes of language: the metaphoric and metonymic axes, which for Lacan correspond to Freud's account of the mechanisms of the primary process – condensation and displacement.

These are the structural bases of the formations of the unconscious through which the subject reveals his/her truth: dreams, neurotic symptoms, parapraxes and jokes. In this sense, according to Lacan the subject is like a text. In his preface to the English translation of *The Four Fundamental Concepts of Psycho-Analysis*, Lacan wrote: 'I am not a poet, but a poem. A poem that is being written, even if it looks like a subject' (1978, p. 5).

What is written adopts different forms according to the various registrations in the three orders of the subject's experience: the symbolic, the imaginary and the real. 'Without these three systems to guide ourselves by, it would be impossible to understand anything of the Freudian technique or experience' (Seminar I, 1988, p. 73).

Freud and the unconscious

Freud did not use the term 'subject' systematically, but in his metapsychological works ('Project for a Scientific Psychology', Letter 52 to Fliess, chapter 7 of *The Interpretation of Dreams*, 'The Mystic Writing Pad' and *Papers on Metapsychology*) Freud attempted to give an account of what is constitutive for every subject: his/her singular unconscious **mnemic** inscriptions – the subject's unconscious knowledge, a knowledge that exceeds what is consciously known by the subject.

In particular, Freud mapped the paths by which unconscious inscriptions, the marks left by traumatic experiences, remained effective and produced patent manifestations while incapable of emerging themselves in consciousness. The psychoanalytic experience made Freud aware of that incongruity between the unconscious inscriptions and what the subject can consciously recognize as belonging to him-/herself.

The contradictions inherent in drives and desires lead the subject to choose, repress, deny or repudiate what is most intimately his/hers; as a result, the registrations of the subject's experience are never fully available to his/her consciousness.

In 'The Unconscious', Freud said that what is unconscious can only be known as conscious and yet the unconscious appears only fleetingly in consciousness and parts of it are never available to the subject. To overcome this problem and to make the unconscious conscious, is the aim of psychoanalysis.

Lacan: the subject, the other, the Other and object a

In his 1957 seminar *The Formations of the Unconscious*, Lacan introduced the notation of the subject as $, the barred subject, a mathème which concisely defines the human subject as radically divided. This established a fundamental difference with the use of the term 'subject' in other disciplines, such as philosophy or psychology.

Lacan's notation redefined in a mathematical expression what Freud attempted to formulate through his topographical models as the subject's division (conscious/preconscious versus unconscious; ego, super-ego, id and reality). For Lacan the term subject does not designate man, nor the human being, nor the individual in the sense of the indivisible psychobiological unit conceived of as possessing an undivided mind and (potentially at least) the master of his/her own thoughts and actions. The Lacanian subject is not the unified subject of knowledge, but the subject as it has emerged in the experience of psychoanalysis: divided, inconsistent, incomplete, punctuated rather than 'full'.

Lacan's use of the term emphasizes the state of subjection of the speaking being (*parlêtre*) in relation to the signifier. It is in and through the concrete experience of speech that the subject becomes the object of his/her own passions, drives, lines of fate, historical contingencies and, fundamentally, of his/her own desire, which is as such always the desire of the Other.

This is the indestructible desire, which Freud described as constitutive of the unconscious. Desire and subject can only exist at the price of a loss, a loss in and of *jouissance*, which Lacan called symbolic castration (Seminar IV, 1956–57). It is precisely the loss produced by the subject's immersion in speech and language that constitutes the unconscious and radically differentiates the human subject from the animal.

Between the subject and his/her desire, the ego stands as an obstacle. The ego is the product of an identification that provides the subject with an anticipatory sense of identity, unity and mastery. Lacan identified the first signs of its formation at the age of six months, with the advent of the mirror stage, manifested by the joy experienced by the *infans* subject when he/she recognizes in the Gestalt provided by the counterpart, the salutary image that gives him/her at once the sense of living in a unified body and of separation from the other's body.

This sense of unity has a structuring value, but it is nevertheless founded upon the relation with an image, with all the effects of illusion that this entails. The ego, as a precipitate of this primordial imaginary identification, will remain for life a deceiving and deceived agency which conceals from the subject the contradictory intricate components of its own genesis and structure. The ego is a 'rather impoverished point of synthesis to which the subject is reduced when he presents himself, but he is also something else, precisely from the point of beyond the pleasure principle' (Seminar I, 1988, p. 209).

The subject perceives his/her desire as that which he/she does not want. In order to defend him-/herself against it, the subject transfers to the ego the permanence of this desire – paradoxically, as it is the ego that is intermittent in its always failing mastery, and not desire (*Écrits*, 1977).

In Seminar I, Lacan borrows from physics an optical schema to illustrate some aspects of the constitution of the subject at the imaginary level and its presentations during the treatment, particularly in relation to the formation of the ideal ego and the ego-ideal.

Desire comes to the subject from the field of the Other, which is the treasure of all signifiers. The demands of the Other become the subject's drives and inscribe the signifiers that constitute the traits which form the subject's identifications. Once locked in the beginning of the signifying chain, the signifiers are used to question what the Other wants, what is the place of the subject in the Other's desire. This quest is one which every human being is forced to embark upon very early in life, as the human infant is marked by biological prematurity and a period of long dependence upon the parents. It is culturally ruled by the normative structure that Freud called the Oedipus complex (*The Four Fundamental Concepts of Psycho-Analysis*, pp. 292–324). In a similar vein Lacan said that the process of sexuation does not follow a natural maturational pattern. Humans are not provided by nature with any fixed instincts. The drives (*Triebe*, not instincts) are attached to the lines of fate of the subject, to his/her relation with the Other's desire. Lacan says that the sexual relationship **never ceases not being written** (Seminar XX, 1998). The symbolization of the drives for the subject remains always linked to trauma and the register of the Real.

Lacan elaborated in Seminar I and Seminar II his theory of the imaginary, in Seminar III and Seminar IV he developed his notion of the symbolic order. In Seminar III specifically, he proposed a theory of the psychoses, while Seminar IV elaborated the ideas of subject based on structure. Specific mechanisms will define the outcome for each psychopathological structure: foreclosure in the case of psychosis, repression for neurosis, and disavowal for perversion. These mechanisms are, in fact, three different forms of the subject's division, and are required for the construction of a subjective organization – the unconscious.

The idea of structure derives from studies on the structure of language, as proposed by Saussure, Jakobson *et al.*, which emphasized that in all languages the value of every elementary component is determined by opposition to, and difference from, other elementary components of language. In terms of the differentiation of the subject, the empty space of the subject becomes structured by identification with other/s, which become his/her objects. This is Lacan's conception of the mirror stage. But this first oppositional dyad only acquires meaning in the field of the Other. The subject is thus included in the symbolic order and the function of the law becomes apparent for the subject. The subject's drives are conditioned by the law; the subject arrives at a crossroads where his/her drives encounter the limit imposed by symbolic castration.

The Oedipal normative organization brings to each one, as a subjective drama, the structure of the prohibition of incest, the foundation of all culture. A major aspect of what Lacan proposes is the 'joining', the alienation in the signifiers of the Other. The subject is condemned to a meaning given by the Other, but Lacan insists that it is at the cost of a loss of his/her being. That is why Lacan considers the subject only appears in a gap between these two – signifier and being, or two signifiers. In his 1959 seminar 'Desire and its Interpretation', he places the pure being of the subject in the **cut**, in the gap left unsymbolized.

The symbolic pair present in the operation of alienation affects the imaginary dyad of the ego and its objects. The subject's enjoyment of his/her body and objects is only possible through a process of rejection of the original objects.

The dialectic of the operations of alienation and separation thus produces subject *qua* its own division: the division that results from being inextricably linked to a lost object, the object cause of desire, which Lacan named **a** in order to de-imaginarize it. (Historically, the concept of the object became impoverished in post-Freudian psychoanalysis as a consequence of its reduction to imaginary presentations, among which the mother's breast acquired prominence.) To the object described in analytic theory, breast, faeces, the phallus (imaginary object, the urinary flow), Lacan adds 'the phoneme, the gaze, the voice, the nothing' (*The Four Fundamental Concepts of Psycho-Analysis*, p. 315).

The concept of the subject is in co-relation with the concept of *structure*, but it was the structuralist, Claude Lévi-Strauss, who criticized Lacan in this respect, considering the concept of subject superfluous, and even a regression to the ideological need for an ego or agent of the structure. However, Lacan maintained that psychoanalysis could not do without the concept of the subject. In psychoanalytic experience – not only in psychoanalytic theory – the concept of the subject is indispensable as it concerns the assumption of responsibility for one's own structure, that is, for one's own desire. This principle informs the ethical dimension without which psychoanalysis cannot operate.

See also: **alienation and separation, desire, mirror stage, object a**

References

Freud, S. (1951) [1895] 'Project for a Scientific Psychology' (vol. 1). *Standard Edition, Complete Psychological Works*. London: Hogarth Press and Institute of Psycho-Analysis.

Freud, S. (1951) [1896] Letter 52, 'Extracts from the Fliess Papers', *S.E.* 1.

Freud, S. (1951) [1900] *The Interpretation of Dreams, S.E.* chapter 7, vol. 5.

Freud, S. (1951) [1915] 'Papers on Metapsychology', *S.E.* 14.

Freud, S. (1951) [1915] 'The Unconscious', *S.E.* 14.

Freud, S. (1951) [1924] ' Note Upon the Mystic Writing Pad', *S.E.* 19.

Lacan, J. (1959) 'Désir et son Interpretation' (24 June 1959), unpublished seminar typescript.

Lacan, J. (1977) *Écrits: A Selection* (trans. A. Sheridan). London: Tavistock.

Lacan, J. (1978) *The Four Fundamental Concepts of Psycho-Analysis* (trans. A. Sheridan). New York: W.W. Norton.

Lacan, J. (1988) [1957–1958] *Le Séminaire, Livre V, Formation de l'inconscient*. Paris: Seuil.

Lacan, J. (1988) [1953–54] *The Seminar, Book I, Freud's Papers on Technique, 1953–1954* (ed. J.-A. Miller, trans. J. Forrester). Cambridge: Cambridge University Press.

Lacan, J. (1988) [1954–55] *The Seminar, Book II, The Ego in Freud's Theory and in the Technique of Psycho-Analysis, 1954–1955* (ed. J.-A. Miller, trans. J. Forrester). Cambridge: Cambridge University Press.

Lacan, J. (1993) [1955–56] *The Seminar, Book III, The Psychoses, 1955–1956* (ed. J.-A. Miller, trans. R. Grigg). New York: W.W. Norton.

Lacan, J. (1994) [1956–57] *Le Séminaire, Livre IV: La relation d'objet*. Paris: Seuil.

Lacan, J. (1998) [1972] *The Seminar, Book XX, Encore* (ed. J.-A. Miller, trans. B. Fink) New York: W.W. Norton.

Silvia A. Rodriguez

Symbolic

The symbolic in the theory of Lacan is usually associated with the prime importance of language for the human subject. Expressions like 'the unconscious is structured like a language' and 'the subject is divided by language' are easily articulated in this context. However, both the role and the meaning of the symbolic evolve throughout Lacan's writings and teachings, implying that one can hardly speak of the symbolic. One way of describing this evolution is to note the shift in focus from the pre-eminence of speech and language over the supremacy of the signifier and language as structure, to the symbolic order as grounded by the signifier of the phallus, showing a fundamental lack. The symbolic as chain of signifiers constitutes the main logical thread.

The primacy of the symbolic, that is, of language and speech, explicitly comes to the fore in the article 'The function and field of speech and language in psychoanalysis', better known as 'The Rome discourse' (1953). This manifesto introduces Lacan's famous 'return to Freud'. Lacan considers it his task to 'demonstrate that the [Freudian] concepts take on their full meaning only when oriented in a field of language, only when ordered in relation to the function of speech' (*Écrits*, p. 39). This does not mean that the role of language enters the Lacanian stage at that precise moment in time. Already in his article on 'The Mirror Stage' (1949) Lacan writes that language is what 'restores to it [I], in the universal, its function as subject' (*Écrits*, p. 2). Subsequently, from the beginning of the 1950s, Lacan states that the symbolic relation – grounded on mutual recognition and the order of a law – is constituted prior to the structuring image of the ego, implying that the imaginary experience is inscribed in the register of the symbolic as early as one can think it.

In the initial invocations of the symbolic, the influence of structural anthropology, more particularly of Claude Lévi-Strauss' notion of elementary structure, is unmistakably present. At this stage the symbolic is intimately linked with the notions of law, pact, social and kinship structures. The law that encompasses the history of each individual and which is unconscious in its structure,

is the foundation of the symbolic (Seminar I, p. 179). 'This law ...
is revealed clearly enough as identical with an order of language'
(*Écrits*, p. 66). Here, the field of language and the structure inherent
to language are referred to. Important to accentuate though is that
the symbolic order conceived as law also implies the logic of mathematical combination and the whole pattern of social relatedness
(*Écrits*, p. 66).

When Lacan speaks of the symbolic in the early 1950s both
language and speech are implied. Speech is conceived as a means for
the subject to integrate itself into the symbolic system of language
and is thus linked to the 'realization' of the subject. The relation
between language and speech is that of a 'larger text' supporting the
individual discourse or speech. With the function of speech Lacan
also introduces the absolute, transcendent Other. 'Speech is founded
in the existence of the Other' (Seminar II, p. 244).

This implies an intimate connection between speech, Other and
language. This is developed at length in the seminar on the
psychoses (1955–56) in which Lacan states that the Other is
symbolic by nature (Seminar III, p. 56). The Other is also linked to
the unconscious in that the 'unconscious is the discourse of the
Other' (*Écrits*, p. 193). It is also in this period that the famous dictum
of 'the unconscious is structured like a language' is elaborated. From
all this, it can be inferred that the unconscious, the subject and the
law are closely interrelated in Lacan's early view on the symbolic.
Still at this stage, language is also defined as an autonomous order
of symbols. Here again, the work of Lévi-Strauss is involved, though
Lacan also uses a Freudian reference in speaking of the symbol. It
concerns a child's play described by Freud in *Beyond the Pleasure
Principle*; the child in question masters the presence and the absence
of a loved object (the mother) by means of a little spool tied to a
string which he throws away and pulls back, uttering something
that resembles the German, *fort!* (gone) and *da!* (here).

According to Lacan, the experience of the *fort! da!* illustrates 'the
appearance of a simple pair of symbols when confronted with the
contrasted phenomenon of presence and absence, that is to say the
introduction of the symbol reverses the positions. Absence is
evoked in presence and presence in absence' (Seminar I, p. 174). It
is within this context that the statement of the symbol as original,
'murder of the thing', should be placed (Seminar I, p. 173).

The elaboration of the symbol, as presence made of absence, can be seen as the first step in Lacan's articulation of the signifier. His notion of the signifier is developed in reference to Jakobson and de Saussure. In 'The agency of the letter in the unconscious or reason since Freud' (1977), Lacan writes that 'the structure of the signifier is ... that it should be articulated'.

'This means that ... these units are subjected to the double condition of being reducible to ultimate differential elements [the phonemes] and of combining them according to the laws of a closed order' (*Écrits*, p. 152). The notion of the signifying chain gives a tentative idea of what Lacan means by combining the elements according to the law of a closed order: 'rings of a necklace that is a ring in another necklace made of rings' (*Écrits*, p. 153).

Signifiers relate to one another along the lines of the two fundamental axes of language (Jakobson), namely the axis of combination or metonymy – based in the word-to-word connection – and the axis of selection or metaphor – one word for another. In contrast to de Saussure, Lacan further claims that the signifier, which as such has no meaning, only refers to another signifier of the signifying chain or to the whole ensemble of signifiers constituting language. This implies that Lacan rejects the idea of there being some kind of correspondence between signifier and signified. The sign in a fixed correlation to reality organizes the animal world, whereas the signifier, which only acquires value and meaning in its relation to other signifiers, organizes the human world. The notion of the signifier, which is also developed in a close reference to cybernetics, will preserve its role of being the foundation of the dimension of the symbolic throughout Lacan's works.

Thus, by the mid-1950s, Lacan conceives the symbolic order as something superimposed which 'provides a form into which the subject is inserted at the level of his being'. It is on the basis of the signifier that the subject recognizes himself as being 'this or that' (Seminar III, p. 179). Another element of importance is the link of the symbolic order with the death drive. In the symbolic, the subject constitutes himself 'as subject to death' (*Écrits*, p. 196). At the same time, the symbolic places the subject beyond death, because the signifier already considers the subject dead and immortalizes him by nature (Seminar III, p. 180).

By the 1960s, Lacan shifts his focus from the relations between speech and language in the subject, to language as a structure dividing the subject. Now the subject is subjected to the signifier. 'I symbolize the subject by the barred S [$], in so far as it is constituted as secondary in relation to the signifier' (Seminar XI, p. 141).

> Everything emerges from the structure of the signifier. This structure is based on what I first called the function of the cut ... The signifier, producing itself in the field of the Other, makes manifest the subject of its signification. But it functions as a signifier only to reduce the subject in question to being no more than a signifier, to petrify the subject in the same movement in which it calls the subject to function, to speak, as subject. (Seminar XI, pp. 206–7)

The signifier is here essentially understood as that which represents – not in the sense of representation, but in the sense of representative – the subject for another signifier, $S_1 \rightarrow \text{\$} \rightarrow S_2$. The subject emerges, that is, manifests itself in a movement of disappearance, in the interval between two signifiers. Lacan links this to the operation of alienation, one of the two operations – the other being the operation of separation – he articulates in the relation between the subject and the Other. This alienation is to be distinguished from the alienation which is at the core of the imaginary relation. All this implies that the symbolic is now no longer the order that realizes the subject, but is rather the structure that divides and hence, in a certain sense, abolishes the subject. Lacan speaks in terms of the fading of the subject.

In the meantime, two signifiers are positioned as central to the symbolic order and as special in nature since they don't conform to the definition of the signifier. They concern the Name-of-the-Father, as the signifier that links desire to law, and the Phallus as the signifier of desire. The Phallus also introduces the dimension of semblance. In this sense, semblance (*semblant*) is a result of the symbolic.

From the 1960s, Lacan explicitly speaks of a lack in the Other inherent in its very function as the treasure of the signifier, although the idea of the symbolic register showing some lack in the sense of falling short, is already present from the mid-1950s. Indeed, in his seminar on the psychoses, Lacan stated that the symbolic has no answer to the question of (sexual pro)creation and death on the level of the subject's singular existence (Seminar III, pp. 179–80).

When Lacan speaks of this lack in the symbolic as locus of the signifier, he refers to another statement of his, namely that there is no Other of the Other, that there is no such thing as a metalanguage. He explains this as follows: 'Any statement of authority has no other guarantee than its very enunciation, and it is pointless for it to seek it in another signifier, which could not appear outside this locus [of the signifier] in any way' (*Écrits*, p. 310). This is exactly what the *sigla* S(Ø) – read as signifier of a lack in the Other – refers to; it is a signifier which as such is inexpressible. 'It can be symbolized by the inherence of a (–) in the whole set of signifiers' (*Écrits*, p. 316).

In *Le Séminaire R.S.I.* (1974–75), Lacan reaffirms that the three dimensions of the real, the symbolic and the imaginary should always be considered in relation to one another. Lacan further links the dimension of the symbolic, as founded by the signifier, to the hole, *trou*. He identifies this hole, that is, the lack in the symbolic, as there being no sexual relation (*le non-rapport sexuel*), which he already developed at length in his seminar, *Encore* (1972–73). In *R.S.I.* Lacan also drew together what the three registers have in common, that is, their mutual dependence. He illustrated this through the model of the Borromean knot, three interlocking loops, all of which come apart if one is cut. In *Le Séminaire S* (S for symptom), (1976–77), he adds another loop to the Borromean knot. This fourth loop is the symptom; it holds the other three together. The symptom according to this schema, is one's ultimate identity.

See also: **alienation and separation, Borromean knot, discourse, mirror stage, Name-of-the-Father, phallus, real, signifier**
Other terms: ego, lack, language, law, other, symptom, unconscious

References

Freud, S. (1986) [1920] *Beyond the Pleasure Principle*, (vol.18). *Standard Edition, Complete Psychological Works*. London: Hogarth Press and Institute of Psychoanalysis.

Lacan, J. (1975) [1972–73]. *Le Séminaire de Jacques Lacan, Livre XX: Encore*. Paris: Seuil.

Lacan, J. (1975–76) [1974–75] 'Le Séminaire XXII: Réel symbolique, imaginaire' (Real, symbolic, imaginary), *Ornicar?* 2, 3, 4.

Lacan, J. (1976–77) [1973–74] 'Le Séminaire XXIII: S' (Le Sinthome), *Ornicar?* 6, 7, 8, 9, 10, 11.

Lacan, J. (1977) [1953] 'The function and field of speech and language in psychoanalysis', *Écrits: A Selection* (trans. A. Sheridan). London: Tavistock.

Lacan, J. (1977) [1957] 'The agency of the letter in the unconscious or reason since Freud', *Écrits: A Selection* (trans. A. Sheridan). London: Tavistock.

Lacan, J. (1977) [1960] 'The subversion of the subject in the dialectic of desire in the Freudian unconscious', *Écrits: A Selection* (trans. A. Sheridan). London: Tavistock.

Lacan, J. (1981) [1973] *Seminar XI: The Four Fundamental Concepts of Psycho-Analysis* (ed. J.-A. Miller; trans. A. Sheridan). New York:W. W. Norton.

Lacan, J. (1988) [1953–54] *Seminar I: Freud's Papers on Technique*, (trans. J. Forrester). Cambridge: Cambridge University Press.

Lacan, J. (1988) [1954–55] *Seminar II: The Ego in Freud's Theory and in the Technique of Psychoanalysis* (trans. S. Tomaselli). Cambridge: Cambridge University Press.

Lacan, J. (1993) [1955–56] *Seminar III: The Psychoses* (trans. R. Grigg). New York: W.W. Norton.

Katrien Libbrecht

Topology: The Möbius Strip between Torus and Cross-cap

Topology of Surfaces

A short history

Leibniz (1646–1716) first introduced the term *analysis situs* later developed by Euler, notably in his work on the classification of polyhedrons. Gauss (1777–1855) became interested in this new geometry of position and encouraged his disciple Listing (1808–82) to work on it. Listing coined the term 'topology' to designate this 'quasi mathematical discipline' which did not yet properly exist: 'Since the term "geometry" cannot appropriately characterize a science from which notions of measure and extension are excluded, since the expression "geometry of position" has already been allocated to another discipline, and since our science does not yet exist, I shall use the term "topology" which I deem suitable' (Pont, 1974, p. 110). Listing provided the following definition: 'Study of the qualitative laws of relations of place', and continued by saying 'I am convinced that this science will require an exact research method.'

In 1858, Listing discovered one-sided surfaces, the same year as Möbius (1790–1868). The ensuing question of priority was swept aside by the fact that this synchronicity was not a fluke of fate but rather the result of indications Gauss passed on to both of his students. However, posterity chose the name 'Möbius' for the famous strip, as J.C. Pont explains: 'For Listing it was only a secondary shape, an exception to those he was studying, juxtaposed to, rather than integrated in, his work. Conversely, for Möbius, the strip that boasts his name, is "a necessary and indispensable element"' (Pont, 1974).

The Möbius strip (MS) has an unusual property: it is a one-sided surface. It can be generated by twisting one end of a rectangular strip of paper through 180 degrees and joining it to the other end of the strip. One can physically check this property by tracing a finger in a continuous line from one point on the strip to the point directly underneath the latter without ever crossing an edge (Figure 18).

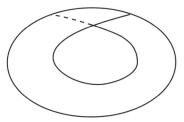

Figure 18

Now imagine this surface doubled (made up of two paper sheets sharing one edge), and then air being blown between the two sheets: the surface becomes a volume that resembles an air chamber, that is, a torus (Figure 19). The reverse procedure is also possible by pinching the torus to reproduce the fold that forms the edge of the Möbius strip; by flattening the torus along this line one produces the two-sheeted Möbius strip again (Figure 20). As we shall see, Lacan makes good use of this transformation of the torus into the Möbius strip in 'L'Étourdit' (Lacan, 1973).

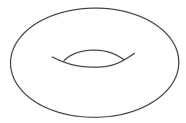

Figure 19

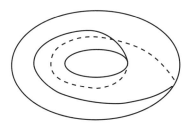

Figure 20

The torus

It has been said that a topologist is a mathematician who cannot tell the difference between a life buoy and a coffee cup. Indeed, topology deals with those transformations of figures that take place without tearing or re-covering and that serve to identify figures that are 'homeomorphic' or topologically equivalent; one can be deduced from the other by means of such a transformation. It doesn't take a huge leap of imagination to realize that this applies to the two objects mentioned above.

To be precise, a topological transformation is an application that is bijective and continuous in both directions (bicontinuous). Topology is the branch of mathematics dealing with properties that are unchanged by topological transformations, such as, for instance, a closed line. In contrast, the length of a line that involves use of measure, may be changed by such a transformation, hence properties of measure are excluded from topology.

The torus can thus be defined as a compact surface with no end and one hole in it. According to the classification of surfaces, compact surfaces without ends in usual three-dimensional (3D) space can be generated by sticking a finite number of loops to a punctured sphere. The torus is such a surface, with the genre 'one' since it can be identified as a sphere with **one** loop (Figure 21).

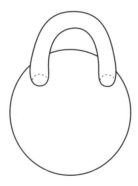

Figure 21

On the other hand, the torus is generated in a geometrical manner by the revolution of a circle (C1) about an axis outside itself but lying in its plane (Figure 22). Lacan uses the property of being generated by two circles (C1, the circle, and C2, the trajectory of its rotation) in 'L'Étourdit' to distinguish within repetition the twists of Demand from those of Desire (Lacan, 1973, pp. 42–3). Note that Lacan also uses the torus in the form of the result of the 'inflation' of the Möbius strip: torus = MS + inflation. We will come back to this.

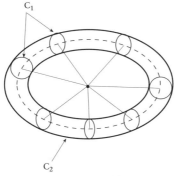

Figure 22

The Möbius strip

The Möbius strip is a unilateral surface – it only has one side – and it only has one edge. It cannot be orientated; that is, if one orientated a couple of vectors (V1, V2) in a trigonometric manner and they slid around the Möbius strip, after one turn around they would be facing in the opposite direction; in other words, the original orientation would be reversed.

The surfaces mentioned above (see the torus) that can be found in 3D **can** be orientated: adding a loop to a sphere does not cause the latter to lose its orientation. On the other hand, the Möbius strip has the particular property of divesting a sphere of its orientation if the following 'cosmetic surgery' is performed: make a hole in the sphere by removing a tiny disc and then identify, point by point, the edge of the hole with the single edge of a Möbius strip. The result is a compact surface with no edge that can neither be encountered in 3D nor orientated. Depending on the point of view it can be represented as a projective plane, a cross-cap (cc) or Boys surface. As we shall see, Lacan used, above all, the cross-cap representation: it allows one to either play on joining a disc to a Möbius strip (the punctured sphere of the operation above is homeomorphic to a disc), or divide the cross-cap into a Möbius strip and a disc: cc = MS + disc.

The Topology of the Subject

The subject is not a sphere

From the very beginning of his teaching, Lacan drew attention to the inadequacy of the representation of the subject of the unconscious as having an inside and an outside like a bag or sphere. What characterizes the subject for Lacan is rather that what appears to be its most intimate or radically interior part, is at the same time that which is most radically foreign or exterior to it. Note that the first Lacanian description of the unconscious was 'the discourse of the other'. The representation of the sphere is not even adequate at the level of the imaginary of the body: the body is traversed by a digestive tube for which a torus is a more fitting image – many of the subject's symptoms cannot be explained without reference to this representation.

As displayed above, there are few reference points in the topology of surfaces. At the level of the imaginary – remaining within bordered 3D space (compact) – there is only one compact surface at our disposition: the sphere with loops, the first of which is the torus (one loop). The latter is Lacan's point of departure in 'L'Étourdit': it is the structure of the neurotic subject. By pinching the torus in a particular way the torus flattens out and a two-sheeted Möbius strip is produced – Lacan terms it a 'fake' Möbius strip. If one cuts along the fold of these two sheets, separates the two, slides them together to arrange them side by side and then sews them together, a Möbius strip is formed that has a median seam. The seam-cut characterizes the 'true' Möbius strip. Lacan writes: 'At this point it is revealed that the Möbius strip is nothing other than the cut itself, the cut by which it disappears from its own surface' (Lacan, 1973, p. 27). By means of this median cut the Möbius strip does indeed unfold into a strip twice as long and with two twists: it has two edges and two sides. Due to these two twists it also has three 'reels' as Lacan puts it, borrowing Desargues' terminology (the seventeenth-century French mathematician who discovered the projective plane). The inverse procedure can then be performed again: on the basis of this double strip one can reconstitute the Möbius strip with the median seam, and then one can slide the two sheets on top of each other and reinflate the torus.

Starting with the torus one can only get a Möbius strip by means of the cut which becomes the latter's median cut: this prompted Lacan to write; '*Ergo* the cut = the Möbius strip' (Lacan, 1973, p. 27).

The asphere *or projective plane*

For Lacan, the structure of the subject of the unconscious as subject of the signifier is, in fact, the Möbius strip; a surface of inscription where front and back are but one continuous side. It is this structure that offers a solution to the problem of double inscription that so vexed Freud.

As mentioned above, there is another way of supplementing the Möbius strip: its edge can be sewn to a punctured sphere or disc. Of course, one can also sew the edges of two Möbius strips together and produce the Klein bottle. By doing this one obtains Desargues' projective plane, more recently termed the 'cross-cap'. As we know this edgeless surface whose inside and outside are continuous can neither be represented nor orientated in 3D: one has to move to four-dimensional space. Despite this, various figures *have* been proposed to represent this surface whose interior is continuous with its exterior, without there being an edge to it. Lacan calls it the *asphere*: 'what is remarkable about this composite object is that the *asphere*, being first a torus – the easiest way to visualize its genesis – only acquires the properties of asphericity when it is supplemented with a spherical cut' (Lacan, 1973, p. 28).

Lacan insists that this reference has nothing metaphorical about it and that it is the very matter of the analytic discourse to which it contributes (Lacan, 1973, p. 28). Indeed, once the representation of the subject as a sphere is discarded, the only surfaces at hand are the torus and the projective plane – generated respectively by sticking a loop or a Möbius strip onto a sphere. The latter causes the sphere to lose its orientation and involves a traversal of the Möbius strip that is impossible in 3D.

From the point of view of psychoanalysis, the Möbius strip thus appears to be an unstable figure, forever liable to inflate into a torus – the imaginary ego in which the symptom becomes implanted – or conversely, liable to supplement itself with a disc (object a). Object a thus becomes the cross-cap of fantasy – with the disc also liable to inflate with air (the imaginary). Thus these figures that are brought together by necessity in the topology of surfaces seem to correspond to the two ways in which the subject counters the absence of the sexual relation.

Lacan writes: 'Freud leads us to this point where ab-sense designates sex: this inflation of the absex-sense is where a topology is defined in which it is the word which cuts' (Lacan, 1973, p. 8). Indeed, certain comments or utterances act as circular cuts, leading to a cut, seam, or separation (Lacan, 1973, p. 29).

Working sketch (*Epure*)

It only takes one good look at how the two-sided strip turns into a Möbius strip, allowing the Möbius strip to become identified with the median cut, to realize that the cut as such is a cut 'without points' – any point would be as much on one side as the other, in other words, nowhere: it is a 'line without points' (Lacan, 1973, p. 27). Lacan imagines this cut parallel to other cuts closer to the edge (involving other properties beyond the scope of this article) allowing him to define the structure of the Möbius strip as a series of lines without points. Just as a disc can be topologically equivalent to a point, Lacan suggests that this series of lines is equivalent to one line without points. The cross-cap could thus be compared to a disc reduced to an out-of-line point (since the point is outside the lines of the Möbius strip) added to a line without points: 'An out-of-line point, once it supplements the line without points, produces what is referred to in topology as the "cross-cap"' (Lacan, 1973, p. 27).

The structure of the subject can thus be reduced to this working sketch: a line (without points) supplemented by a point (out-of-line) – the *asphere*.

See also: **the cut**, **subject**

References

Lacan, J. (1973) 'L'Étourdit', *Scilicet 4*, Paris: Le Seuil.
Pont, J.C. (1974) *La Topologie algabrique des origines Poincar*. Paris: Presses Universitaires de France.

Nathalie Charraud (trans. Dominique Hecq and Oliver Feltham)

Treatment

Contrary to what his abstract writings seem to indicate, Lacan developed his theory in a constant reference to psychoanalytic experience. This becomes clear from two different perspectives. First, Lacan created a large part of his theory against the backdrop of a critique of mainstream psychoanalytic technique and theory. Second, he explicitly stated that the theory that is used directs the psychoanalytic praxis and technique. This implies that 'Lacanian treatment' should be brought in line with the evolution and elaboration of all of Lacan's major concepts.

This entry elaborates these two approaches, the first focusing on Lacan's critical dialogue with mainstream (psychoanalytic) thinking, the second examining the consequences of the evolution of Lacan's theorizations for the direction of the psychoanalytic process. However, some preliminary remarks are necessary. The first concerns the notion of psychoanalytic treatment (*cure analytique*) itself. Lacan, and to some extent also Freud, stated that one is not cured through analysis, if curing means that a kind of healing (in the medical sense of the word) takes place.

In this respect, the English translation of the French term *cure* should be read as 'treatment' rather than cure. The second remark concerns the stereotype of Lacan's use of short sessions and sessions of variable length. This was one of the major difficulties Lacan encountered with the Institute of Psycho-Analysis (IPA) from the 1950s onwards, and which finally led to his exclusion from the IPA in 1964. However, the use of the variable length session is misleading as far as Lacan's contributions to psychoanalytic treatment are concerned. First, it reduces them to a mere technicality with regard to the handling of (logical) time in the treatment, and second, Lacan rarely insisted on the use of sessions of variable length in his later work (1960s–70s).

What Lacanian treatment is not

Throughout his writings and teachings, Lacan delineated psychoanalysis as a praxis that is radically different from what is presented within the discourse of mental life (e.g., psychology), including what is standard within IPA circles. 'It gives me no pleasure to point out these deviations; my aim is rather that these reefs should serve as beacons on our route' (*Écrits*, 1977, p. 229).

With respect to the question of how psychoanalysis and psychotherapy, or treatment and therapy, are related to one another Lacan stated (for instance in 'Variantes de la cure type'), that the therapeutic effects of analysis are of a supplementary nature, are *bénéfice de surcroît* (*Écrits*, 1977, p. 324). In this sense, analytic treatment can be considered as 'not a therapy like the others' (*pas une thérapeutique comme les autres*; *Écrits*, 1977, p. 324).

Lacan also explicitly referred to Freud's warning against the danger of the *furor sanandi*. This means that the therapeutic effects of analysis are not essential in so far as they do not realize what analysis aims at. This further implies that the analyst is not the one who wants the best for the analysand; the analyst does not provide the analysand a (Sovereign) Good (*un bien*). Psychoanalysis is also not concerned with re-education or adaptation to some kind of norm or standard and hence does not address the patient's ego. What differentiates analysis from therapy is a question of ethics, which involves both the position and the desire of the analyst. The way the analyst listens determines who speaks, the subject of the ego.

In an article in *Écrits*, Lacan also addressed the question of psychoanalytic treatment and its so-called variations. According to Lacan, the question of the standard treatment and its variations can only be read as a concern for purity in means and ends, an ethical rigour that requires a theoretical formalization, in the absence of which there is only one (ironical) answer, namely that analysis is that which, or can be, expected from an analyst. The same line of reasoning, which eliminates both standard and variation, applies to the alleged difference between the so-called therapeutic analysis and the didactic analysis. For Lacan, there is only one kind of analytic treatment, the (possible) didactic character of which can only be established afterwards. To this end, Lacan introduced the practice of the pass in 1967, as a means to formalize the passage from analysand to analyst. Basic to the procedure of the pass is that the analysand testifies to the end of his or her analysis.

What Lacanian treatment is

After delineating Lacan's position in terms of what treatment is not, the question is posed: what is treatment? A crucial issue in investigating Lacan's conceptualization of psychoanalysis concerns the direction of the treatment.

In his early article 'Intervention on Transference' (1951) Lacan speaks of the treatment as a dialectical experience, comprising a series of reversals, 'a scansion of structures in which truth is transmuted for the subject' (p. 64).

This conception of the treatment is embedded in what Lacan, at that stage, considered essential in the relation of the subject to speech as revealed in the intersubjective dialogue. In analysis, the subject is 'constituted' through a discourse to which the mere presence of the analyst brings the dimension of dialogue (p. 62). What is at stake at the end of analysis is a decline of the imaginary world. 'That is when the continent falls away – the accidental, the trauma, the hitches of history – And it is being which then comes to be constituted' (Seminar I, 1953–54, p. 232). In this sense, Lacan speaks of analysis in terms of the symbolic 'realization' of the subject, which implies the subject's realization of its history as a symbolic creation.

> The analysis must aim at the passage of true speech, joining the subject to another subject, on the other side of the wall of language [S-A]. That is the final relation of the subject to a genuine Other, to the Other who gives the answer one doesn't expect, which defines the terminal point of the analysis. (Seminar II, 1954–55, p. 246)

In other words, the end of analysis as contained in Freud's phrase 'Wo es war, soll Ich werden', is read by Lacan as: the subject takes the place of the ego in that it is the subject that must be called on to speak (full speech), instead of the ego (empty speech) (Seminar II, p. 246). In contrast to this, where the subject ends up believing in the ego, treatment has pushed the subject to a form of alienation, akin to paranoia. Here the treatment is *paranoia dirigée*.

The analytic relation can be characterized as the relation between free association (of the analysand) and interpretation (of the analysis), in which transference, perceived as function of the 'subject supposed to know', plays a pivotal role.

In the article 'The Direction of the Treatment and the Principles of Its Power' (1958), Lacan confirms the power of speech and states that the direction of the treatment implies that the analyst by means of the use of free association, does not 'direct' the subject towards a free speech that is painful but leaves the subject free to try it. The direction of the treatment is ordered to a process that begins with the [dialectical] notification of the subject's relation with the real and proceeds first to the development of transference, then to interpretation (p. 237).

Of the crucial moments of the treatment, two are of special importance, namely the beginning of the treatment (and thus of transference) and the end of treatment. This accords with Freud's comparison (in 'On Beginning the Treatment', 1958 [1913]) of the analytic process to a game of chess. What the treatment is directed towards (the end of treatment), is the subject's avoidance of his/her desire.

The preponderant role of desire – the reality of the human condition – in the treatment is rendered explicit in the seminar on the 'Ethics of Psychoanalysis' (1959–60), in which Lacan formulizes that 'the only thing of which one can be guilty is of having given ground relative to one's desire [*cédé sur son désir*]' (Seminar VII, p. 319). He also speaks of this in terms of moral weakness (*lâcheté morale*). Hence the treatment is conceived as the place where desire can be elaborated, can be worked through, in terms of the ethical question 'Have you acted in conformity with your desire?' (Seminar VII, p. 311). 'To have carried an analysis through to its end is no more nor less than to have encountered that limit in which the problematic of desire is raised. That this problematic is central for access to any realization of oneself whatsoever constitutes the novelty of analysis' (Seminar VII, p. 300).

In the seminar 'Ethics', Lacan also introduces the notion of the desire of the analyst as an experienced desire; it is the only thing the analyst has to offer. This desire of the analyst, which is linked to the position he or she takes in the analytic process, is pivotal in the direction of the treatment. The role of this desire is further elaborated in the seminar on *The Four Fundamental Concepts of Psycho-Analysis* (1978), where Lacan introduces the object a (cause of desire) in the movement of transference. Whereas the transference operates in the direction of identification, the desire of the analyst tends in a direction that is its exact opposite, namely the direction of absolute difference:

> the operation and manipulation of the transference are to be regulated in a way that maintains a distance between the point at which the subject sees himself as lovable [Identification] – and that other point where the subject sees himself caused by a lack of *a*, and where a fills the gap constituted by the inaugural division of the subject [S]. The petit a never crosses this gap. [...] It is at this point of lack that the subject has to recognize himself. (Seminar XI, 1981, p. 270)

In this sense, the analytic process does not tend to a restitution of the subject (completing the subject), but to a destitution of the subject (acceptance of the fundamental lack).

Here, the essence of analytic treatment as a process becomes the mapping of the subject in relation to *a*, that is, the construction of the fundamental fantasy, both as 'the support of desire' (Seminar XI, 1981, p. 185) and 'that by which the subject sustains himself at the level of his vanishing desire' (*Écrits*, 1977, p. 272). The fundamental fantasy also expresses the subject's particular mode of *jouissance*. It should be stressed that the fantasy always has two sides: on the one hand, the side of the subject, which is the side of speech and of desire; on the other hand, the side of the object, as *a*, which is also the side of *jouissance*.

The construction of the fantasy is conceptualized by Lacan by means of the operations of alienation and separation (destitution of the subject), the latter being a function of the analyst's direction of the treatment, thus of his/her act (interpretation, handling of transference, position of the analyst). Furthermore, the loop of the subject to *a* should be run several times (*durcharbeiten*): the subject traverses the fundamental fantasy. Here, 'the experience of the fundamental fantasy becomes the drive' (Seminar XI, 1981, p. 273).

In 1969, Lacan introduced the discourse of the analyst – one of four social bonds founded in language – as a further formalization of the analytic process, stressing that the discourse of the analyst is not to be confused with the analysing discourse (Séminaire XVII, 1969–70, p. 35). The position of the analyst, as place of semblance, is that of a, object cause of desire of the analysand; this implies the structural introduction, by means of artificial conditions, of the discourse of the hysteric (in which S functions as semblance). This enables the analysand to construct the fundamental fantasy ('Proposition of 9 October 1967'). Adding to Lacan's earlier elaboration of the place of desire in analytic treatment, the analytic process coined here in terms of the place of truth and knowledge (*savoir*), in the discourse of the analyst, knowledge functions in the place of truth. This does not mean that the analyst uses his/her knowledge as truth, but it means knowledge functions in the same way as truth, namely as half-saying (*mit-dire*). In this sense, the analyst can only intervene by means of an enigma or a citation (Séminaire XVII, 1969–70, pp. 39–40).

See also: **desire**, **discourse**, *jouissance*, **object a**, **pass**, **separation**
Other terms: act, analysis, cure, ethics, drive, transference

References

Freud, S. (1958) [1913] 'On Beginning the Treatment' (*Further Recommendations on the Technique of Psychoanalysis 1*), *Standard Edition, Complete Psychological Works of S. Freud*. Volume 12. London: Hogarth Press.

Lacan, J. (1982) [1951] 'Intervention on Transference' in *Feminine Sexuality; Jacques Lacan and the école freudienne* (pp. 61–73) (eds. J. Mitchell and J. Rose, trans. J. Rose). New York: W.W. Norton.

Lacan, J. (1965) 'Variantes de la cure type'. In *Écrits* (pp. 323–67). Paris: Seuil.

Lacan, J. (1992) [1959–60] Seminar VII: *The ethics of psychoanalysis* (ed. J.-A. Miller; trans. D. Porter). New York: W.W. Norton.

Lacan, J. (1977) [1966] 'The direction of the treatment and the principles of its power', *Écrits: A Selection* (trans. A. Sheridan). London: Tavistock.

Lacan, J. (1978) *The Four Fundamental Concepts of Psycho-Analysis* (trans. A. Sheridan). New York: W.W. Norton.

Lacan, J. (1978) 'Proposition du 9 October 1967'. Premier version. *Analytica*. Supplément d'*Ornicar?* 8.

Lacan, J. (1991) [1969/70] Le Séminaire XVII: *L'envers de la Psychanalyse* (ed. J.-A. Miller). Paris: Seuil.

Katrien Libbrecht

Index

Compiled by Sue Carlton